THE CAMBRIDGE BIBLE COMMENTARY

NEW ENGLISH BIBLE

GENERAL EDITORS
P. R. ACKROYD, A. R. C. LEANEY
J. W. PACKER

THE SHORTER BOOKS OF THE APOCRYPHA

THE SHORTER BOOKS OF THE
APOCRYPHA

TOBIT, JUDITH, REST OF ESTHER
BARUCH, LETTER OF JEREMIAH
ADDITIONS TO DANIEL
AND PRAYER OF MANASSEH

COMMENTARY BY

J. C. DANCY
Principal, St Luke's College, Exeter

WITH CONTRIBUTIONS BY

W. J. FUERST AND R. J. HAMMER

CAMBRIDGE

AT THE UNIVERSITY PRESS

1972

Published by the Syndics of the Cambridge University Press
Bentley House, 200 Euston Road, London NW1 2DB
American Branch: 32 East 57th Street, New York, N.Y.10022

© Cambridge University Press 1972

Library of Congress Catalogue Card Number: 72-76358

ISBNS:
0 521 08614 0 hard cover
0 521 09729 0 paperback

Printed in Great Britain
at the University Printing House, Cambridge
(Brooke Crutchley, University Printer)

GENERAL EDITORS' PREFACE

The aim of this series is to provide the text of the New English Bible closely linked to a commentary in which the results of modern scholarship are made available to the general reader. Teachers and young people have been especially kept in mind. The commentators have been asked to assume no specialized theological knowledge, and no knowledge of Greek and Hebrew. Bare references to other literature and multiple references to other parts of the Bible have been avoided. Actual quotations have been given as often as possible.

The completion of the New Testament part of the series in 1967 provides a basis upon which the production of the much larger Old Testament and Apocrypha series can be undertaken. The welcome accorded to the series has been an encouragement to the editors to follow the same general pattern, and an attempt has been made to take account of criticisms which have been offered. One necessary change is the inclusion of the translators' footnotes since in the Old Testament these are more extensive, and essential for the understanding of the text.

Within the severe limits imposed by the size and scope of the series, each commentator will attempt to set out the main findings of recent biblical scholarship and to describe the historical background to the text. The main theological issues will also be critically discussed.

Much attention has been given to the form of the volumes. The aim is to produce books each of which will be read consecutively from first to last page. The introductory material leads naturally into the text, which itself leads into the alternating sections of the commentary.

The series is accompanied by three volumes of a more general character. *Understanding the Old Testament* sets out to provide the larger historical and archaeological background, to say something about the life and thought of the people of the Old Testament, and to answer the question 'Why should we study the Old Testament?'. *The Making of the Old Testament* is concerned with the formation of the books of the Old Testament and Apocrypha in the context of the ancient near eastern world, and with the ways in which these books have come down to us in the life of the Jewish and Christian communities. *Old Testament Illustrations* contains maps, diagrams and photographs with an explanatory text. These three volumes are designed to provide material helpful to the understanding of the individual books and their commentaries, but they are also prepared so as to be of use quite independently.

P.R.A.
A.R.C.L.
J.W.P.

CONTENTS

THE FOOTNOTES TO THE
N.E.B. TEXT

The footnotes to the N.E.B. text are designed to help the reader either
to understand particular points of detail – the meaning of a name, the
presence of a play upon words – or to give information about the actual
text. Where the Hebrew text appears to be erroneous, or there is
doubt about its precise meaning, it may be necessary to turn to manuscripts which offer a different wording, or to ancient translations of the
text which may suggest a better reading, or to offer a new explanation
based upon conjecture. In such cases, the footnotes supply very briefly
an indication of the evidence, and whether the solution proposed is
one that is regarded as possible or as probable. Various abbreviations
are used in the footnotes:

(1) Some abbreviations are simply of terms used in explaining a
point: *ch(s).*, chapter(s); *cp.*, compare; *lit.*, literally; *mng.*, meaning;
MS(S)., manuscript(s), i.e. Hebrew manuscript(s), unless otherwise
stated; *om.*, omit(s); *or*, indicating an alternative interpretation; *poss.*,
possible; *prob.*, probable; *rdg.*, reading; *Vs(s).*, version(s).

(2) Other abbreviations indicate sources of information from which
better interpretations or readings may be obtained.

Aq. Aquila, a Greek translator of the Old Testament (perhaps about
A.D. 130) characterized by great literalness.

Aram. Aramaic – may refer to the text in this language (used in parts
of Ezra and Daniel), or to the meaning of an Aramaic word.
Aramaic belongs to the same language family as Hebrew, and is
known from about 1000 B.C. over a wide area of the Middle East,
including Palestine.

Heb. Hebrew – may refer to the Hebrew text or may indicate the
literal meaning of the Hebrew word.

Josephus Flavius Josephus (A.D. 37/8–about 100), author of the *Jewish
Antiquities*, a survey of the whole history of his people, directed
partly at least to a non-Jewish audience, and of various other works,
notably one on the *Jewish War* (that of A.D. 66–73) and a defence of
Judaism (*Against Apion*).

Luc. Sept. Lucian's recension of the Septuagint, an important
edition made in Antioch in Syria about the end of the third
century A.D.

Pesh. Peshitta or Peshitto, the Syriac version of the Old Testament.
Syriac is the name given chiefly to a form of Eastern Aramaic used

by the Christian community. The translation varies in quality, and is at many points influenced by the Septuagint or the Targums.

Sam. Samaritan Pentateuch – the form of the first five books of the Old Testament as used by the Samaritan community. It is written in Hebrew in a special form of the Old Hebrew script, and preserves an important form of the text, somewhat influenced by Samaritan ideas.

Scroll(s) Scroll(s), commonly called the Dead Sea Scrolls, found at or near Qumran from 1947 onwards. These important manuscripts shed light on the state of the Hebrew text as it was developing in the last centuries B.C. and the first century A.D.

Sept. Septuagint (meaning 'seventy'; often abbreviated as the Roman numeral LXX), the name given to the main Greek version of the Old Testament. According to tradition, the Pentateuch was translated in Egypt in the third century B.C. by 70 (or 72) translators, six from each tribe, but the precise nature of its origin and development is not fully known. It was intended to provide Greek-speaking Jews with a convenient translation. Subsequently it came to be much revered by the Christian community.

Symm. Symmachus, another Greek translator of the Old Testament (beginning of the third century A.D.), who tried to combine literalness with good style. Both Lucian and Jerome viewed his version with favour.

Targ. Targum, a name given to various Aramaic versions of the Old Testament, produced over a long period and eventually standardized, for the use of Aramaic-speaking Jews.

Theod. Theodotion, the author of a revision of the Septuagint (probably second century A.D.), very dependent on the Hebrew text.

Vulg. Vulgate, the most important Latin version of the Old Testament, produced by Jerome about A.D. 400, and the text most used throughout the Middle Ages in western Christianity.

[...] In the text itself square brackets are used to indicate probably late additions to the Hebrew text.

(Fuller discussion of a number of these points may be found in *The Making of the Old Testament* in this series)

TOBIT

WHAT TOBIT IS ABOUT AND WHY IT IS
WORTH READING

Tobit is a short but well-known folk-tale carrying a firm religious message. In Luther's words, it 'offers a delicate, lovable, pious comedy, with a God-fearing peasant or bourgeois suffering greatly in his married life, but God always standing by to help and in the end bringing him joy'.

It is actually about the fortunes of *two* related Jewish families living in exile in what are now Iraq and Iran. Each family falls, through no fault of its own, into misfortune. Tobit, head of one family, loses his job and goes blind. Sarah, daughter of the other family, is possessed by a demon who prevents her successive attempts at marriage. Both call upon God, who intervenes through his angel Raphael. Raphael guides Tobit's son Tobias on various adventures which lead to his marriage with his kinswoman Sarah. In the end the fortunes of both families are restored.

The book is interesting from many points of view. Theologically, it has important things to say about marriage and family life, and also about angels; and underlying all is a stress on God's constant care for his suffering people. Historically, we should be wrong to take it as a record of actual events, but we can rely upon its description of the simple piety of Jewish family life, such as has preserved the Jews in all the misfortunes of their history. From the literary point of view, we can enjoy the author's mixture of art and artlessness in telling his story.

As well as that, Tobit offers two other chances to the critical student of the Bible. First, we have available for Tobit, more than for any other biblical book, the raw material, mostly non-Jewish, out of which the author composed his tale, and we can study the way he used it for his own moral and religious purposes. Secondly, the manuscript tradition is unusually complex. The N.E.B. follows different manuscripts from those followed by the Authorized Version and the Revised Version and its translation therefore sometimes diverges widely from them.

To these points we now turn.

THE AUTHOR'S SOURCES

*The folk-tale of 'The Grateful Dead' and
'The Unlucky Bride'*

The basic story of the book of Tobit comes from a combination of two well-known folk-tales, known to scholars as 'The Grateful Dead' and 'The Unlucky Bride'. The combination itself is found in twenty-four different versions, which come from most parts of Europe and also from Armenia. The last, which is most relevant to Tobit, runs briefly as follows.

A rich merchant, on his travels, saw some foreigners maltreating the corpse of a man who had died owing them money. Being a pious man, he paid the debt and gave the corpse honourable burial. Later, having fallen into poverty and other misfortunes, he followed the advice of a mysterious slave and married a rich man's daughter. She had had five previous husbands, but on each occasion they had been killed on their wedding night by a serpent coming out of her mouth. This time, however, as the serpent came out in search of its victim, it was killed by the slave, who thereupon revealed that he was the spirit of the dead man.

The other versions contain various further details relevant to Tobit. For example, the 'helper' often demands as his reward half the first-born child – or even half the wife: the hero eventually, to save his beloved, says 'take all', whereupon the helper renounces all.

It so happens that we have, in addition to Tobit, a second

Jewish story based upon the tale of 'The Unlucky Bride'. It comes from a late Jewish work, the Midrash Tanhuma, which seems to go back to about the fifth century A.D. In it the daughter of a rich man is married to three successive husbands, each of whom is found dead the morning after the wedding. She decides to remain a widow until God has mercy upon her. But there comes to woo her a cousin, one of ten sons of a poor man living far away. During their wedding feast a mysterious stranger arrives, sent by God to fetch the soul of the hero. He asks first for a year with his wife, then for a month, then for a week, finally for a day: each request is refused in turn. He then quotes to the stranger the regulation of Deut. 24: 5: 'When a man is newly married, he shall...remain at home exempt from (military) service for one year and enjoy the wife he has taken.' The stranger then withdraws, after revealing himself as an angel, and the couple live happily ever afterwards.

There is no reason to suppose that Tobit drew on the story in the Midrash Tanhuma (though there are some details in common; see note on 8: 9) but the latter throws light on Tobit because it shows how Jewish authors could use the same basic story to illustrate two quite different morals.

'The Story of Ahikar the Wise', or 'The Wisdom of Ahikar'

Into this double folk-tale, modified in various ways (see below), the author of Tobit wove some material of a different kind, from the story of Ahikar. Ahikar may well in origin have been an historical person. Certainly his story was well known in the ancient world. Greek authors ranked him with the Seven Wise Men and imitated his maxims; he is also mentioned in the Koran and the *Arabian Nights. The Story* or *Wisdom of Ahikar* has survived in various versions, European and Semitic, but for our purposes the version that matters is one written on papyrus in the fifth century B.C., and found in

1906 in the excavation of a Jewish colony at Elephantine on the Upper Nile. The story runs as follows.

Ahikar the Wise became chancellor to Sennacherib king of Assyria (705–681 B.C.) and then to his son Esarhaddon III (681–669 B.C.). Having no children of their own, he and his wife adopted his nephew Nadab. Hoping that Nadab might succeed him at court, he gave him some wise advice in the form of maxims. But Nadab repaid him ungratefully: he accused him falsely to Esarhaddon, who had him arrested and condemned to death. But when the captain of the guard came to kill him, he realized that once before Ahikar had saved him in a similar situation, and so he helped him to escape and go into hiding underground.

One day Pharaoh challenges Esarhaddon to produce a wise man who can solve certain problems. All the wise men of the Assyrian court, from Nadab downwards, fail, and Esarhaddon is heard to say how much he regrets the death of Ahikar. The captain of the guard owns up, Ahikar is released and sent to Egypt where he solves Pharaoh's problems. On his return to Nineveh he is restored to office and Nadab is handed over to his mercy. He imprisons Nadab and takes the opportunity to read him a second series of maxims. Finally Nadab dies in prison, and the story ends.

Ahikar is an Assyrian name, and the story must have come originally from that part of the world. The version found at Elephantine is written in Aramaic, which was used as the diplomatic language in much of the Near East at this time, and was therefore understood by the Jews as well as by the Assyrians. As far as we can tell, the story was not altered to suit Jewish readers except in one respect: where other versions refer to various heathen Gods, the Jewish version always refers to the God of Israel.

THE AUTHOR'S HANDLING OF HIS SOURCES

To put it briefly, the author of Tobit drew on *Ahikar* for the background setting of his story (chapter 1 and the second half of chapter 14) and for the two sets of maxims which he puts into Tobit's mouth (chapter 4 and, to a lesser extent, chapter 14). But the story itself derives from the double folk-tale, influenced by biblical works (especially Gen. 24, Job and Isa. 60) and radically reworked to suit the author's purposes.

To take the folk-tale first, there were certain changes that *had* to be made to bring it into line with basic Jewish thinking. The Jews could never have a dead man coming back to life and showing gratitude. Their prophets were constantly forbidding them to 'seek guidance of ghosts' (Isa. 8: 19), and there was a Rabbinic saying that 'the kindness a man shows the dead is kindness indeed, for the doer has no hope of a reward'. It follows that the slave-companion of the folk-tale can no longer be identical with the dead man. It was a master-stroke – though one natural to a Jew – to make him into an angel. This means that God can guide the action without dominating it. But the presence of the angel in the foreground and God in the background leaves a much humbler role for the hero: the only 'heroic' deeds in Tobit are done by the angel. In fact the character who was the hero in the folk-tale is here split into two, father and son; but their original identity may account for their having the same name (see note on 1: 1). Tobias, being only a boy, does not need to be a hero yet; Tobit, being old and blind, need no longer be. But being each of them weak in different ways, they are more realistic representatives of the Jewish people; for the true heroism of the book of Tobit is the heroism not of action (as in Judith) but of suffering.

Other changes tally. The motif of the unpaid debt was inappropriate in a Jewish setting and was dropped. An angel could not be a party to anything as crude as the demand for half of a person; instead Raphael is given half the money recovered (12: 2). Indeed the whole story of the money on deposit with Gabael, which is rather half-heartedly worked into the book (see note on chapter 9), probably came in to replace the debt-motif.

The interweaving of the Ahikar story was much less successful. The author used it in a variety of ways. First he boldly made Ahikar a nephew of Tobit; Ahikar helps Tobit in 1: 22 and 2: 10, and Tobit explicitly quotes the story of Ahikar to Tobias in 14: 10f. Secondly, the story of Tobit is modelled on that of Ahikar in so far as he holds high office under Shalmaneser and later falls from favour (1: 13 and 19); also in that he gives two separate sets of maxims. Thirdly, Tobit quotes in various places without acknowledgement from the *Wisdom of Ahikar*: see notes on 4: 2, 15, 17, 19 and 14: 10.

It seems that what the author of Tobit chiefly derived from his use of *Ahikar* is that he associated his own story and hero with another story and hero which (even though not in the Bible) were widely known, respected and regarded as historical. Perhaps also the story of Ahikar contributed one feature which was absent from the story of Tobit as he had revised it, namely an illustration of the belief that, if a man does a good turn to another, he will be rewarded. But if that is the case, the author of Tobit does not make the most of it, and indeed the overall impression remains that the story of Ahikar is never properly worked into Tobit.

In addition to these two main sources from outside the Bible, the author drew heavily on biblical literature. Perhaps in a way, it is wrong to speak at all of his 'drawing upon it'. Rather, like all pious Jews of the last centuries B.C., he was living in a community where the events and sayings recorded in the scriptures were in a sense more *real* than what he saw and heard about him every day. It was not that he quoted from the Bible; rather he thought and felt naturally in biblical terms.

So when he was writing of undeserved suffering, his mind

went to the book of Job (see notes on 2: 11 and 3: 6). When he was writing of Tobias' journey to Media, where he found Sarah, his thoughts kept recurring to the story of Abraham sending away for a wife for Isaac (Gen. 24) and other similar tales of the patriarchs. When looking ahead to the New Jerusalem, his mind is filled with phrases from relevant passages in the prophets, especially Isa. 60.

All these sources (except perhaps *Ahikar*) the author used with considerable skill to make a story which is coherent and well-rounded. It has its prologue and epilogue like Job; moving inwards towards the centre, one next finds two sections (chapters 3 and 10–11) where the fortunes of the two families are interwoven; finally there is the core (chapters 4–9), entitled in N.E.B. 'The adventures of Tobias', where the interest follows Tobias as he moves from one family to the other and back again.

The narrative proceeds fairly rapidly, though it is apt to be over-full, for our taste, with emotional descriptions of greetings and partings – even when one makes allowances for the importance of such moments in a widely scattered community. The numerous exchanges of conversation suffer from the same weakness at times (see note at the end of chapter 5), but at other times, particularly between Tobit and Anna, they reveal the psychology of married life with economy and humour (2: 11–14; 10: 1). The narrative is varied like all biblical narratives by many prayers and by a formal song of praise (chapter 13); also by one large and one short collection of maxims.

Some of these literary points are taken further in a note on pp. 127 ff. where there is a discussion on the place of the books of Tobit and Judith within the body of Western literature. But the author would never have wanted us to judge his book by these criteria: far more important to him was the message it was written to convey.

7

THE RELIGIOUS IDEAS IN TOBIT

From our point of view the basic religious idea in Tobit is one which the author would never have thought of as such; that is the idea of God's presence everywhere and of his loving concern for every aspect of his people's lives. The author would never have argued for this idea, if only because he would have found nobody among his own people to argue against it. He just takes it for granted.

Similarly, although he was particularly concerned about suffering of all kinds (physical, mental and material), he was not interested in the so-called problem of suffering: 12: 13 is the only reference to a matter which takes up a whole chapter in Judith. His interest centred on the way in which God moves to help his people's suffering – provided, of course, that they remain loyal to him and to his laws.

The laws are, certainly, of very great importance, and this goes both for what we should call religious and for what we should call social duties (the Jews made no such sharp distinction). On the religious side, the references to the Temple (1: 4; 13: 10–18; 14: 5) and to the payment of tithes (1: 6–8) all come from the prologue or epilogue. There are no other references to worship, nor any to the keeping of the Sabbath. The emphasis is all on private religious duties, especially prayers and almsgiving; the latter is of special importance in a poor community.

In certain respects, however, the author goes beyond or outside the law – at least, the Law as contained in the first five books of the Bible. If there is one specific message which he wants to get across, it is the duty to marry within one's tribe and, if possible, within the extended family. This motif is not present in the original folk-tale, and is not necessary even to the story of Tobit; but it is constantly stressed (3: 15; 4: 12; 6: 12; 7: 10). The stress is reinforced by appeal to Moses, and it is even suggested that Moses laid down the death penalty for anyone who disobeyed it. In fact Moses did no

8

such thing, and it seems that the custom itself more or less died out after the exile; it is therefore a puzzle why the author made so much of it.

In the matter of religious beliefs, Tobit has quite an important part to play among biblical books. This is especially true of the belief in angels and demons. The angel Raphael has an essential role in the story, and in the course of telling it the author takes Old Testament ideas about angels further than ever before – indeed in some respects further than the New Testament (see notes on 3: 17 and 12: 12–19). But the belief is never, in Tobit, a purely intellectual speculation: it derives from and keeps closely to the firm belief in God's constant care for his people. The author of Tobit also develops, less helpfully, the doctrine of demons (see note on 3: 8).

The author's interest in angels and demons, coupled with his concern for the details of the Law – to which one might add his delight in written documents (5: 3 and 7: 14) – are all typical of the Pharisees. But we miss any clear reference to the specific Pharisaic belief in resurrection. The New Jerusalem in chapter 13 is firmly located in this world, and the rewards and punishments for the deeds of individuals all come in this life (see 3: 6; at first sight 4: 10 and 14: 10 seem to refer to an after life, but see notes).

Perhaps more important than all these points is the teaching of Tobit on marriage. It is not so much the explicit advice of 4: 12f., still less the un-biblical expansion offered by Jerome's Vulgate text of 6: 17 (where see note). It is the implicit assumptions: that sex is good but married love is better; and that youth is good but married old age is also among God's blessings (8: 17). The family fulfils the needs of the parents and provides the true framework for the growth and happiness of the children. Nor is the family just the 'nuclear' family of the modern West: it is the 'extended' family, involving all the cousins and aunts and stretching out even to the whole tribe.

In its teaching about the family, as in its teaching about

God, the book of Tobit is most valuable where it is least explicit. We might be inclined to add that it is also most valuable where it is least 'supernatural'; but fortunately the author's simple piety somehow 'carries' both demons and angels so that they do not jar.

WHEN AND WHERE THE BOOK WAS WRITTEN

The religious ideas of the book of Tobit are clearly 'late', i.e. after the exile. At the other extreme, the latest possible date is given by the existence of manuscripts of Tobit in the Qumran community (see below), i.e. not later than the first century A.D. Can we narrow it down further?

At one end, the name Tobias would probably not have been used for a hero until long after the time of Tobias the enemy of Nehemiah about 450 B.C. At the other end, the book of Tobit contains no reference whatever to the most traumatic event in late Jewish history, the persecution by Antiochus Epiphanes (about 165 B.C.), which seems to rule out any date much after 200 B.C. On the whole a date between 250 and 200 B.C. seems likely.

It is even harder to tell *where* the book was written. The author makes out that he was writing in the exile (see especially 13: 6), but his ignorance of the geography of Babylonia and Media rules out that region. In fact any location outside Judaea is made unlikely by the probability that our Greek manuscripts were translated from a Hebrew rather than an Aramaic original. The conclusion is that our version of Tobit was written in Judaea, though directed particularly towards Jews of the Dispersion.

THE MANUSCRIPTS OF TOBIT

The manuscripts of Tobit are particularly interesting. If we leave aside for the moment the Qumran fragments, they fall into two main groups. These groups offer two texts which differ chiefly in length: one is about half as long again as the other. The Authorized Version and Revised Version translated the shorter: the N.E.B. and most modern translations have preferred the longer. The choice between the two was to some extent a matter of personal preference until the Qumran fragments were discovered.

Unfortunately these fragments have not yet been published. But we know that there are parts of one Hebrew and four Aramaic manuscripts, which between them cover nearly half the book. The two types of text (Hebrew and Aramaic) are not identical, but both of them correspond roughly to the longer text in the Greek manuscripts.

This longer text is preserved for us in a family of manuscripts of which the most important are the Greek Codex Sinaiticus (S) and the manuscripts of the translation of that Greek into Latin (the so-called Old Latin translation). In such a case, scholars need to consider the whole 'family' of manuscripts – called a family because they must all descend from a single ancestor – since in any given place one single manuscript may well contain mistakes. That is how the book of Tobit has been produced in the Jerusalem Bible (the latest Roman Catholic version) and in almost all other modern texts and translations. But the N.E.B. translators chose, as they tell us in their introduction to the Apocrypha, 'to translate the Codex Sinaiticus text of Tobit', thus depriving themselves in many places of the help which the other members of S's family could give. True, in some twenty places they have nevertheless tacitly dropped S in favour of its family. But in a further twenty or so places – mostly in the last few chapters, where S itself loses accuracy – they have almost alone of modern translators stuck to S. These latter include some most important passages; see notes on 4: 17–18; 5: 3; 11: 1; 11: 18; 13: 6–10. On the other hand, there is at least an equal number of places where S alone of its family is right.

Of the manuscripts that preserve the shorter text the most important is Vaticanus (B), which has its own 'family' like S. It is not certain what is the relation between the shorter and the longer texts. On the whole it looks as if the shorter was an abbreviation of the longer, made in the interests of style. But passages from the shorter are quoted in the notes on 5: 21 and 8: 19–21, so that the reader may judge for himself.

If these manuscripts (including the Qumran fragments) contain two different texts, nevertheless almost all our surviving texts belong to one single version of the story. The only exceptions are two medieval manuscripts, one Hebrew and one Aramaic, which give different versions of the end of the story. If we could rely more certainly on Jerome as a translator, we might suppose that the Aramaic manuscript which he says he had before him preserved another such variant version. But it seems more likely that, where he departs furthest from the S tradition, he is not so much translating as commenting (see note on 6: 17). Since he tells us that he translated the whole of Tobit in a single day, and that it was his custom to translate the sense rather than the words, we can hardly put much *critical* weight upon the translation that he provided – though it is still the translation officially used by the Roman Catholic Church in worship.

THE PLACE OF TOBIT AMONG THE JEWS AND IN THE CHURCH

We have direct evidence that the book of Tobit was popular with the Qumran community (say between 100 B.C. and A.D. 100). The existence of the shorter text shows that at least one other Jewish community had its own version. And internal evidence strongly suggests that it was also familiar to various sections of the early Christian Church (see notes on 12: 16–22). But, though popular, it was written too late to be included in the canon of the Old Testament when it was set up about A.D. 100.

In later times it has been much drawn upon for the services

of the Church. Roman Catholics have used passages for holy days in honour of angels and for various wedding ceremonies. In the Church of England the 1662 Prayer Book quoted 3: 3 in the Litany and 4: 7–9 in the offertory sentences of the Communion; see also note on 6: 17, the idea of which has influenced the preface to the marriage service.

✻   ✻   ✻   ✻   ✻   ✻   ✻   ✻   ✻   ✻   ✻   ✻   ✻

The troubles of Tobit

TOBIT'S EARLY LIFE IN ISRAEL

THIS IS THE STORY of Tobit, son of Tobiel, son of **1** Hananiel, son of Aduel, son of Gabael, son of Raphael, son of Raguel, of the family of Asiel, of the tribe of Naphtali. He was taken captive in the time of Shalmaneser*a* king **2** of Assyria, from Thisbe which is south of Kedesh Naphtali in Upper Galilee above Hazor, behind the road to the west, north of Peor.

I, Tobit, made truth and righteousness my lifelong guide; **3** I did many acts of charity for my kinsmen, those of my nation who had gone into captivity with me at Nineveh in Assyria. When I was quite young in my own country, **4** Israel, the whole tribe of Naphtali my ancestor broke away from the dynasty of David,*b* and from Jerusalem, the city chosen out of all the tribes of Israel as the one place of sacrifice. It was there that God's dwelling-place, the temple,

[*a*] *Gk.* Enemessaros.   [*b*] *Gk. adds* my ancestor.

5 had been consecrated, built to last for all generations. All
my kinsmen, the whole house of Naphtali my ancestor,
sacrificed on the mountains of Galilee to the calf which
6 Jeroboam, king of Israel, had made in Dan; at the festivals
I was the only one to make the frequent journey to
Jerusalem prescribed for all Israel as an eternal commandment. I used to hurry off to Jerusalem with the firstfruits of
crops and herds, the tithes of the cattle, and the first shearings of the sheep; and I gave them to the priests of Aaron's
7 line for the altar, and the tithe of wine, corn, olive oil,
pomegranates and other fruits to the Levites ministering in
Jerusalem. The second tithe for the six years I converted
into money, and I went and distributed it in Jerusalem
8 year by year among the orphans and widows, and the
converts who had attached themselves to Israel. Every
third year when I brought it and gave it to them, we held
a feast according to the rule laid down in the law of Moses
and the instructions given by Deborah the mother of
Hananiel our grandfather; for my father had died leaving
me an orphan.

* I. The name *Tobit* is a rarer contracted form of Tobias,
the name which Tobit gave his son. Its meaning is 'The Lord
is my good'. As a name Tobias is found only once in the Bible
before the exile (2 Chron. 17: 8) but became common during
and after it.

the tribe of Naphtali occupied territory in northern Galilee,
and formed part of the northern kingdom, called Israel
(verse 4), whose capital was Samaria.

2. *Shalmaneser king of Assyria* reigned 727–722 B.C. Like his
predecessor and his successor, he conducted campaigns
against Israel and carried off captives. The exact details of
these campaigns are uncertain – the Jewish account in 2 Kings

does not always tally with the official Assyrian records – but since Tobit is not a historical work the difficulties can be omitted here. The name Enemessaros (see N.E.B. footnote), which is given by the two main Greek manuscripts, S and B, is unknown; fortunately the manuscripts of the 'family' of S (see introduction) give what is obviously the right text.

The place names likewise are confused in the manuscripts. *Kedesh* (Greek *Kudios*) and *Hazor* (Greek *Asser*) are well-known places and can be taken as fairly certain. But *Thisbe* and *Peor* (Greek *Phogor*) are unknown.

3. *I, Tobit* – the story is told in the first person from here to 3: 17, but then reverts to the third. To us this seems odd, but the same variation is found in the books of Ezra and Daniel, and also in the *Story of Ahikar* (see p. 3). *truth* is a favourite word of the author's: it usually means loyalty, here loyalty to God. *righteousness* means good works, and it includes *acts of charity*, especially those mentioned in verse 17.

4. *the whole tribe of Naphtali* actually *broke away* about 200 years earlier, after Solomon's death in 931 B.C. (1 Kings 12: 25–33). The repetition of the words *my ancestor* (see N.E.B. footnote) is a plain mistake in S.

5. *the calf which Jeroboam...made*: see 1 Kings 12: 28.

6. *I was the only one*: Tobit himself later (5: 13) lets it be known that this is not strictly true. The author is clearly much concerned about the supremacy of the Temple in *Jerusalem*. The *festivals* of the Passover, the Feast of Weeks and the Feast of Tabernacles were so *prescribed* in Exod. 23: 17.

6–8. The correct payment of *firstfruits*, *tithes*, etc., is something else which means a great deal to the author: he is stressing the fact that Tobit complied with all the requirements of the Law. Those requirements, as set out in Num. 18, were that the firstfruits (which would include the *first shearings*) should go to the *priests of Aaron's line*, but that the tithes should go to the *Levites*. (From this it appears that *the tithes of the cattle* are out of place in verse 6.)

Deuteronomy went into much greater detail about the

tithes and the Levites. Deuteronomy 14: 22–7 said that, whereas it was best for the tithes to be given to *the Levites ministering in Jerusalem*, if the journey was too far and the produce too heavy, the produce might be *converted into money* and spent elsewhere; but in that case the local Levites must be invited to share it. Deuteronomy 14: 28f. and 26: 12 also laid down that *every third year* the tithes must be used for the benefit not only of the local Levites but also of the local *orphans and widows* and foreign *converts* to Judaism.

The mention of *the six years* in verse 7 is a reference to the fact that every seventh year the land had to be left untilled so there were no tithes (Exod. 23: 10). The phrase *every third year* in verse 8 suggests that the six years were divided into two groups of three. In that case *the second tithe* in verse 7 would mean the tithes in years two and four; alternatively two tithes were given every year to different recipients. *

TOBIT IN CAPTIVITY AT NINEVEH

9 When I came of age I took a wife from our kindred, and
10 had a son by her whom I called Tobias. After the deportation to Assyria when I was taken captive and came to Nineveh, everyone of my kindred and nation ate gentile
11,12 food; but I myself scrupulously avoided doing so. Since
13 I was whole-heartedly mindful of my God, the Most High endowed me with a presence which won me the favour of
14 Shalmaneser, and I became his buyer of supplies. As long as he lived I used to travel to Media and buy for him there. I deposited bags of money to the value of ten talents of silver with my kinsman Gabael son of Gabri in Media.
15 When Shalmaneser died and was succeeded by his son Sennacherib, the roads to Media passed out of Assyrian control and I could no longer make the journey.

In the time of Shalmaneser, I did many acts of charity for 16
my fellow-countrymen: I shared my food with the hungry
and provided clothes for the naked. If I saw the dead body 17
of any man of my race lying outside the wall of Nineveh,
I buried it. I buried all those who fell victim to Sennacherib 18
after his flight from Judaea, when the King of heaven
executed judgement on him for all his blasphemies, and in
his rage he killed many of the Israelites. I stole their bodies
away and buried them, and Sennacherib looked for them
but could not find them. One of the Ninevites informed 19
the king that I was giving burial to his victims; so I went
into hiding. When I learnt that the king knew about me
and that I was wanted for execution, I took fright and ran
away. All my property was seized and put into the royal 20
treasury; I was left with nothing but Anna my wife and my
son Tobias. However, less than forty days afterwards, the 21
king was murdered by two of his sons. They took refuge in
the mountains of Ararat, and his son Esarhaddon succeeded
him. He appointed Ahikar son of my brother Anael to
supervise all the finances of his kingdom; he had control of
the entire administration. Then Ahikar interceded on my 22
behalf and I came back to Nineveh. For he had been chief
cupbearer, keeper of the privy seal, comptroller, and
treasurer when Sennacherib was king of Assyria; and
Esarhaddon renewed the appointments. Ahikar was my
nephew and so one of my kinsmen.

✻ 9. *wife from our kindred*: one of the main themes of Tobit
is the importance of marrying not merely within the tribe
but within the extended family: see note on 4: 12.

Tobias: see note on verse 1. It has been suggested that the
author purposely gave the same name to father and son

because he was taking what in the folk-tale was a single character and splitting him into two.

10. Daniel likewise in captivity was very careful to avoid *gentile food* (1: 5–8, etc.).

13. *won me the favour of Shalmaneser*: it was part of the Jewish dream that, even though a Jew would be unlikely to achieve a position of direct power in the gentile world, he might still become the adviser of the powerful. So Joseph with Pharaoh, Nehemiah with Artaxerxes, Daniel with Nebuchadnezzar, and Mordecai with Ahasuerus in the book of Esther.

14. *Media* was one of the parts of the Assyrian Empire to which captive Jews were deported (2 Kings 17: 6).

ten talents of silver was a very large sum, running into thousands of pounds.

Gabael had the name of one of Tobit's ancestors (see verse 1).

15. *Sennacherib* reigned from 705 to 681 B.C. On his accession there were revolts in many parts of the Assyrian Empire (2 Kings 18: 13ff.), and it is quite likely that communications were cut by the hill tribesmen between the Median plateau and the plain of Nineveh. Sennacherib was in fact the son and successor not of *Shalmaneser* but of Sargon; but Sargon seems to have been the victim of a conspiracy of silence on the part of the Jews. He is never mentioned in the Bible, and his capture of Samaria in 721 B.C. is attributed by the Jews to Shalmaneser. The Assyrian records on the other hand say much of Sargon and next to nothing of Shalmaneser.

16. Tobit's *acts of charity* were restricted, as in verse 3, to his *fellow-countrymen*. This attitude that 'charity begins at home' is understandable among the Jews of the Dispersion, but it gave them a bad name with the Gentiles. The Roman poet Juvenal (*Satires*, 14: 103) says that, if you ask a Jew the way, he won't show it you unless you are a fellow-Jew. We need, however, to appreciate the problems of a religious group trying to be faithful among an alien, and often hostile, population.

17. *hungry...naked*: cp. the parable of the sheep and the

goats: 'when I was hungry, you gave me food...when naked you clothed me' (Matt. 25: 35).

The burial of the dead was a sacred duty imposed by all religions, not only Jewish but Assyrian and Greek (cp. the Greek story of Antigone). That is one reason why the folktale of *The Grateful Dead* (see p. 2) has been found in so many countries.

lying: Greek 'thrown'. *outside the wall*: i.e. on the town rubbish dump, where e.g. the dead dogs would be thrown, and so would the bodies of those who had been put to death by royal command.

18. *Sennacherib* was besieging Jerusalem in 701 B.C. when a mysterious happening caused him to withdraw his army hastily (2 Kings 19: 35). It was natural that *after his flight from Judaea* he should take it out of the Jews in exile in Nineveh.

21. *the king was murdered*: the details given here of the succession of his younger *son Esarhaddon* (681–668 B.C.) agree with those given in the Assyrian records, as well as with 2 Kings 19: 37.

Ahikar, chancellor to Sennacherib and Esarhaddon, was the hero of a well-known tale, one of the tales drawn upon by the author of Tobit (see p. 3). *

TOBIT'S OWN MISFORTUNES

During the reign of Esarhaddon, I returned to my house, **2** and my wife Anna and my son Tobias were restored to me. At our festival of Pentecost, that is the Feast of Weeks, a good dinner was prepared for me and I sat down to eat. The table was laid and a lavish meal was put before me. I said **2** to my son Tobias: 'Go, my boy, and if you can find any poor man of our captive people in Nineveh who is wholeheartedly mindful of God, bring him and he shall share my dinner. I will wait for you until you return.' Tobias **3**

went to look for a poor man of our people, but he came back and said, 'Father!' 'Yes, my son?' I replied. He answered, 'Father, one of our nation has been murdered and his body is lying in the market-place. He was strangled
4 only a moment ago.' I jumped up and left my dinner untasted. I took the body from the square and put it in one of
5 the outbuildings until sunset when I could bury it; then I went home, duly bathed myself, and ate my food in
6 sorrow. I recalled the saying of the prophet Amos in the passage about Bethel:

> 'Your feasts shall be turned into mourning,
> and all your songs[a] into lamentation',

7 and I wept. After sunset I went and dug a grave and buried
8 the body. The neighbours jeered at me and said: 'Is he no longer afraid? He ran away last time, when they were hunting for him to put him to death for this very offence;
9 and here he is burying the dead again!' That night I bathed myself and went into my courtyard. I lay down to sleep by the courtyard wall, leaving my face uncovered because
10 of the heat. I did not know that there were sparrows in the wall above me; and their droppings fell, still warm, right into my eyes and produced white patches. I went to the doctors to be cured, but the more they treated me with their ointments, the more my eyes were blinded by the white patches, until I lost my sight. For four years I was blind. All my kinsmen grieved for me, and Ahikar looked after me for two years until he moved to Elymais.

11 During that time my wife Anna used to earn money by
12 women's work. When she took what she had done to her

[a] *So one Vs. (compare Amos 8: 10); Gk.* ways.

employers they would pay her wages. One day, the seventh of Dystrus, when she had cut off the piece she had woven and delivered it, the owners not only paid her in full, but also gave her a kid from their herd of goats to take home. When my wife came in to me the kid began to bleat. 13 I called out to her: 'Where does that kid come from? I hope it was not stolen? Give it back to its owners; we have no right to eat anything stolen.' She assured me: 'It was given 14 me as a present, over and above my wages.' I did not believe her and insisted that she should give it back to its owners, and I blushed with shame for what she had done. She retorted: 'So much for all your good works and acts of charity! Now we can see what you are!'

In deep distress I groaned and wept, and as I groaned I **3** prayed: 'Thou art just, O Lord, and all thy acts are just; 2 in all thy ways thou art merciful and true; thou art judge of the world. Remember me now, Lord, and look upon 3 me. Do not punish me for the sins and errors which I and my fathers have committed. We have sinned against thee 4 and disobeyed thy commandments, and thou hast given us up to plunder, captivity, and death, until we have become a byword, a proverb, and a taunt to all the nations among whom thou hast scattered us. I acknowledge the justice 5 of thy many judgements, the due penalty for my sins, for we have not obeyed thy commandments and have not lived in loyal obedience before thee. And now deal with 6 me at thy pleasure, and command that my life be taken away, so that I may be removed from the face of the earth and turned to earth. I should be better dead than alive, for I have had to hear undeserved reproaches and am in deep grief. Lord, command that I may be released from this misery; let me go to my long home; do not turn thy face from me, O Lord. It is better for me to die than to live in such misery and to hear such reproaches.'

☆ 1. *the Feast of Weeks* took place seven weeks after the Passover and celebrated the harvesting of the corn. It was laid down (Deut. 16: 11) that 'aliens, orphans, and widows' should be invited to the feast. Being in exile, Tobit reasonably looks for a poor Jew to invite in place of an alien. *Pentecost*, being Greek for 'the fiftieth day', is obviously the later name for the festival. 2 Maccabees 12: 31–2 talks of 'the Feast of Weeks...Pentecost, as it is called'. Pentecost is also the original name for the festival of Whitsun, which fell on that same day (Acts 2: 1ff.).

3. Strangling was one of the official methods of execution.

4–5. Tobit waited *until sunset*, for concealment rather than for ritual reasons; but he bathed himself because he was impure. Numbers 19: 11 says: 'Whoever touches a corpse shall be ritually unclean for seven days.'

6. The quotation from Amos 8: 10 is not actually from a *passage about* Bethel, though Amos did write a good deal about Bethel. The correct text *songs* is preserved only in two Old Latin manuscripts.

9. Why did Tobit *sleep* outside? B adds a note saying it was because he was still unclean.

10. *white patches*: Greek *leucoma*, which is the medical name for a certain form of blindness. There is no reason to suppose that it can be caused in this way, but the point is that Tobit's blindness was a natural calamity, for which he was in no way responsible. It is in fact his third major misfortune, all of them undeserved: the first was captivity, the second loss of his job.

In other versions of his story Ahikar moved to Egypt at this juncture. The change to *Elymais* keeps the story of Tobit within closer limits: Elymais, the biblical Elam, was the province south of Media.

12. *the seventh of Dystrus*: it is odd that the author should use the Greek name for the month which Jews and Assyrians both called Adar (February–March). The 'whole month of Adar' was 'a time of...sending...gifts to the poor' (Esther 9: 22), as part of the celebrations of the Feast of Purim, which fell on the fourteenth.

14. *we can see what you are*: Anna's parting shot, literally 'these things with you are known', probably means: 'we can see how much good these things i.e. your acts of charity have done you.'

This sad little scene, in verses 11–14, is psychologically all too convincing. The sufferings of Tobit make him suspicious and, like those of Job (2: 9), set up friction between him and his wife. By our standards Tobit is more open to criticism than Anna, but the author meant rather to contrast Anna's impatience with Tobit's patience and scrupulousness. The parallel with Job's wife led to an addition in Jerome's text in which other relations of Tobit came and echoed Anna's taunts, just as Job's friends did.

3: 1–5. Tobit's prayer falls into two parts. The first part (verses 2–5) is a recognition of man's disobedience and the justice of God's punishment. In it Tobit is thinking rather of the Jewish nation than of himself personally (though to a Jew there was a natural link between the two); the text shifts from 'I' to 'we', and the manuscripts vary considerably among themselves as to which they choose. There are many such prayers in the Old Testament, especially Dan. 9: 4ff., much imitated in Baruch 2: 11 – 3: 8. Most of them go on to say that we now repent and ask for God's forgiveness and his support in the future.

6. Tobit, however, in the second part of his prayer asks rather to be put out of his personal misery by death. In this he is following prayers made by e.g. Job (7: 15) and Jonah (4: 3) in moments of despair. The idea that one is better dead than alive is of course a commonplace one, but its tone depends upon what the speaker believes will happen after death: con-

trast the similar wish of Antigone in Sophocles' play (461–4 'anyone who lives in misfortune, as I do, is bound to be better off in death') with St Paul's words in Phil. 1: 23 'what I should like is to depart and be with Christ'. In Tobit's mind there seems to be no thought of any life after death (in spite of 4: 10 and 12: 9), but just of rest and escape from present torture. The phrase *long home* is an intentional echo of Eccles. 12: 5, Authorized Version (N.E.B. 'everlasting home'), and makes clear that there is nothing beyond death. Tobit's thought is just like Job's and Jonah's, and it is worth reading Job 3: 1–19 to see how the same thought is handled by a writer of genius. ✳

SARAH'S TROUBLES

7 On that same day it happened that Sarah, the daughter of Raguel who lived at Ecbatana in Media, also had to listen to reproaches from one of her father's maidservants,
8 because she had been given in marriage to seven husbands, and before the marriage could be regularly consummated they had all been killed by the wicked demon Asmodaeus. The maidservant said to her: 'It is you who kill your husbands! You have already been given in marriage to seven,
9 and you have not borne the name of any one of them. Why punish us because they are dead? Go and join your husbands! I hope we never see son or daughter of yours!'
10 She was sad at heart that day, and went in tears up to the attic in her father's house meaning to hang herself. But she had second thoughts and said to herself: 'Perhaps they will reproach my father and say to him, "You had one dear daughter and she hanged herself because of her troubles", and so I shall bring my aged father in sorrow to the grave. No, I will not hang myself; it would be better to beg the Lord to let me die and not live on to hear such reproaches.'

Then at once she spread out her hands towards the window 11
in prayer and said: 'Praise to thee, merciful God, praise to
thy name for ever; let all thy works praise thee for evermore. Now I lift up my eyes and look to thee. Command 12, 13
me to be removed from this earth so that I may no longer
hear such reproaches. Thou knowest, Lord, that I am a 14
virgin, guiltless of intercourse with any man; I have not 15
disgraced my name nor my father's name in the land of my
exile. I am my father's only child; he has no other to be his
heir, nor has he any near kinsman or relative who might
marry me, and for whom I should stay alive. Already
seven husbands of mine have died. What have I to live for
any longer? If it is not thy will, O Lord, to let me die,
listen now to my complaint.'

At that very time the prayers of both of them were heard 16
in the glorious presence of God. His angel Raphael was 17
sent to cure them both of their troubles: Tobit, by remov-
ing the white patches from his eyes so that he might see
God's light again, and Sarah daughter of Raguel by giving
her in marriage to Tobias son of Tobit and by setting her
free from the wicked demon Asmodaeus; for it was the
destiny of Tobias and not of any other suitor to possess her.
At the moment when Tobit went back from the courtyard
into his house, Sarah daughter of Raguel came down from
the attic.

* 7. Tobit's troubles are complemented by those of his
second cousin, Sarah. The parallel is symbolized by *that same
day*. *Sarah* and *Raguel* are both good biblical names. Raguel
was a kinsman of Tobit (6: 10).

Ecbatana was the capital of *Media*. But it is possible that the
author's choice of Ecbatana here springs rather from a folk-

tale associated with it. This tale, which is known to us in an Egyptian version of the fifth century B.C., concerns a princess who lived there and was possessed by an evil spirit. Her father went to consult the god Khonsu at Thebes in Egypt. Khonsu freed the princess, and the spirit went off 'in peace to the place where he would be'.

maidservants: clearly Raguel was much better off than Tobit.

8. The tale of the *demon* who *killed* her seven husbands *before the marriage could be...consummated* is a version of the old folk-tale of 'The Unlucky Bride' (see p. 2). In another version, from Serbia, the poor girl had ninety-nine previous husbands! The Tobit version is found here and in 3: 17, 6: 14ff. and 8: 3. Other manuscripts of Tobit add further information. B notes at 6: 14 that the demon did not harm her 'because he loved her', but that is probably a contamination from another folk-tale, that of 'The Bride and The Monster' (familiar to us as *Beauty and the Beast*). A late Aramaic manuscript implies that the demon was supposed to inhabit her body.

The *demon Asmodaeus* appears here for the first time in Jewish literature. Later he became an important and sinister figure. In the *Testament of Solomon*, a work of about A.D. 300, he introduces himself as follows: 'My role is to conspire against the newly-wed and prevent them from making love.' The origin of the name is much disputed. The simplest explanation is that it comes from a Hebrew root 'to destroy'. The idea of a destroying angel is found in 2 Sam. 24: 16, and 'the destroyer' fits nicely here against Raphael the healer.

10. *one dear daughter*: like Tobias she was an only child, and both of them were worried about causing grief to their parents (6: 14). The phrase *bring...in sorrow to the grave* is one of the refrains in the story of Joseph (Gen. 42: 38; 44: 29, 31).

11-15. Sarah's prayer is dramatically parallel to Tobit's in 3: 1-6. It is, however, much more personal and concrete, less concerned with the general state of the nation. It is noticeable that her prayer is nearly as long as 'her' narrative (verses 7-10).

11. In the corresponding passage in Daniel 6: 10 *the window* faces towards Jerusalem, and that is surely the implication here.

15. Sarah's sweeping statement that her father has no *near kinsman* is surprising. In fact her parents knew a good deal about Tobit (7: 2–7), just as Tobias did about Sarah (6: 13).

listen now to my complaint: in place of these words in S, all other manuscripts give 'let me no longer hear such reproaches', which provides a most satisfactory echo to the end of Tobit's prayer, as well as picking up Sarah's own words at the end of verse 10.

17. This announcement by the author of God's intention *to cure them both of their troubles* removes the suspense from the story. Our interest from now on lies not in what happens but how – as when we go to see a famous or familiar play. In modern books suspense matters a great deal to us, because we read them only once. But in earlier times, when books were scarce and therefore read many times, it mattered less. In any case, by sacrificing suspense a biblical author gains a major advantage: it is much easier for him to convey the idea that God's providence orders every detail in the lives of his faithful servants. He also gains a minor, literary, advantage in the use of dramatic irony (see notes on 5: 13 and 16).

The word *angel* is not in the manuscripts at this point, but it comes at 5: 4. The belief in angels as intermediaries between God and men developed gradually during the period of the Old Testament. As early as Gen. 24: 7 Abraham says to his servant, who is going out to look for a wife for Isaac, that God 'will send his angel before you'. But the belief was much advanced during the exile, especially under Persian influence, and we gradually find angels multiplied, named, and given special functions for good or ill.

The name *Raphael* is found in the Old Testament only as that of a man (1 Chron. 26: 7). He is here first mentioned as an angel, but he is much in evidence later, specially as 'the healer'. In traditional Christian belief, he is one of three archangels, together with Michael and Gabriel.

The narrative has now moved imperceptibly to the point where Tobit is being referred to in the third person – necessarily so because we, as readers, are now in the know, whereas Tobit is not. ✳

The adventures of Tobias

TOBIT'S PARTING ADVICE

4 That same day Tobit remembered the silver that he had
2 deposited with Gabael at Rages in Media, and he said to himself, 'I have asked for death; before I die ought I not to send for my son Tobias and explain to him about this
3 money?' So he sent for Tobias, and when he came he said to him: 'Give me decent burial. Show proper respect to your mother, and do not leave her in the lurch as long as she lives; do what will please her, and never grieve her
4 heart in any way. Remember, my son, all the dangers she faced for your sake while you were in her womb. When
5 she dies, bury her beside me in the same grave. And remember the Lord every day of your life. Never deliberately do what is wrong or break his commandments. As long
6 as you live do what is right. Do not fall into evil ways; for an honest life leads to prosperity. To all who keep the law,
19 the Lord gives good guidance, and as he chooses he humbles men to the grave below.[a] Now, my son, remember

[a] To all...below: *in place of these words some witnesses have* To all who keep the law (7) give alms from what you possess and never give with a grudging eye. Do not turn your face away from any poor man, and God will not turn away his face from you. (8) Let your almsgiving match your means. If you have little, do not be ashamed to give the little you can afford; (9) you will be laying up a sound insurance against the day of adversity. (10) Almsgiving saves the giver from death and

these commands; let them never be effaced from your mind.

'Well now, my boy, let me tell you that I have ten talents 20 of silver on deposit with Gabael son of Gabri, at Rages in Media. Do not be anxious because we have become poor; 21 there is great wealth waiting for you, if only you fear God and avoid all wickedness and do what is good in the sight of the Lord your God.'

* 1. It is surprising that Tobit did not remember *the silver that he had deposited* (1: 14) long before now, when his wife first had to go out to work (2: 11). The recovery of the money is now supposed to be the reason for Tobias' journey

keeps him from going down into darkness. (11) All who give alms are making an offering acceptable to the Most High.

(12) 'Beware, my son, of fornication; above all choose your wife from the race of your ancestors. Do not take a foreign wife who is not of your father's tribe, because we are descendants of the prophets. Remember, my son, that Noah, Abraham, Isaac, and Jacob, our ancestors, back to the earliest days, all chose wives from their kindred. They were blessed in their children, and their descendants shall possess the earth. (13) And you like them, my son, must love your kindred. Do not be too proud to take a wife from among the women of your own nation. Pride breeds ruin and anarchy, and the waster declines into poverty; waste is the mother of starvation.

(14) 'Pay your workmen their wages the same day; do not make any man wait for his money. If you serve God you will be repaid. Be circumspect, my son, in all that you do, and show yourself well-bred in all your behaviour. (15) Do not do to anyone what you yourself would hate. Do not drink to excess and so let drunkenness become a habit. (16) Give food to the hungry and clothes to the naked. Whatever you have beyond your own needs, give away to the poor, and do not give grudgingly. (17) Pour out your wine and offer your bread on the tombs of the righteous; but give nothing to sinners. (18) Ask any sensible man for his advice; do not despise any advice that may help you. (19) Praise the Lord God at all times and ask him to guide your course. Then all you do and all you plan will turn out well. The heathen all lack such guidance; it is the Lord himself who gives all good things, or humbles men at will, as he chooses.

(neither he nor Tobit so much as mentions Sarah at this stage). Yet Tobit's parting advice, whether we take the longer or the shorter form of it, does not get round to the money until the very end, and then contains no explicit instructions to Tobias to go and get it. Indeed the motif of the money never seems properly worked into the book of Tobit (see note on 9: 1). Perhaps the author was not very interested in it – for the alleged Jewish concern for money was not typical of the Jews in the ancient world.

3. Jews certainly *were* interested in family life and love, and it is typical that Tobit's advice should begin with that. Before the words *Give me decent burial* all other manuscripts add the clause 'When I die', which avoids the abrupt opening.

5ff. Tobit now gives Tobias some general advice on the conduct of his life. Such death-bed advice, known as a testament, is common in later Jewish literature: indeed a whole late book was written entitled the *Testaments of the Twelve Patriarchs*.

7–18. These verses are omitted by S, but they are found in all other manuscripts of any consequence, both those of the longer and those of the shorter version of the book, also in the Hebrew fragment from Qumran, and they are printed as part of the text by all other modern editors. The only arguments against regarding them as genuine are these: (i) They are not an integral part of the book: they can apparently come out without harming things. *But* verses 12 and 13 expound an idea about marriage which was very important to the author and which, without them, is stressed only from Anna's and not from Tobias' side. (ii) The link between verses 6 and 7 looks weak in the N.E.B. translation. *But* that translation is hardly fair; better to group the words differently and translate 'an honest life leads to prosperity for all who keep the law'. (iii) Tobit is given a fair-sized testament in chapter 14, so he doesn't need a long one here. *But*, curiously, Ahikar is given two testaments in his story.

Against these arguments the weight of the manuscripts

must tell, and we must treat these verses with as much respect as any others in the book. The fact that S has omitted a second long passage which certainly *is* integral, in chapter 13, shows that, though it is an excellent manuscript, it is far from infallible.

7–11. The section on almsgiving is very like that in Ecclus. 29: 8–13.

10. The saying here and at 12: 9 that *Almsgiving saves the giver from death* is not a hint of any after-life, but refers rather to the actual history of Ahikar (see 14: 10f.).

12–13. The section on marriage is an amplification of the rule in Exod. 34: 16 that Jews should not let their sons marry the daughters of Gentiles, or 'when their daughters go wantonly after their gods, they may lead your sons astray too'. Tobit goes further in urging marriage within one's *father's tribe* as a greater safeguard still. The term *prophets* could be applied to the patriarchs (Ps. 105: 15). *Abraham* married Sarah his half-sister (Gen. 20: 12); *Isaac* shared great-grandparents with his wife Rebecca (Gen. 24: 4); Leah and Rachel were *Jacob*'s cousins (Gen. 28: 2). The Old Testament tells us nothing of *Noah*'s wife, but the book of *Jubilees*, roughly of the same time as Tobit, says that he too married his cousin.

14. The command to *Pay your workmen their wages the same day* is in Lev. 19: 13. Deuteronomy 24: 15 goes further and says that if a workman is poor he must be paid before sunset.

well-bred: this sort of worldly advice is common enough in Jewish proverbial writing.

15. This so-called Golden Rule of morality is not found elsewhere in the Old Testament or Apocrypha, but is in *Ahikar* (2: 88 in the Armenian version). There is also a story about Rabbi Hillel who was asked by a man to teach him the whole Law while he stood on one foot: Hillel replied: 'What you yourself would hate, you must not do to anyone else. That is the whole Law, and the rest is commentary.' Jesus' version, 'Treat others as you would like them to

treat you' (Luke 6: 31), characteristically makes the saying positive.

17. The recommendation to *offer your bread on the tombs of the righteous* seems to run counter to an implied command in Deut. 26: 14. But it is found in *Ahikar* (2: 7 Arm.) and perhaps the author of Tobit took it from here without proper consideration. Ecclesiasticus, somewhat later than Tobit, was in two minds about it (contrast 7: 33 with 30: 18).

19. The slighting reference to the *guidance* of *the heathen* is surprising after verse 18 – and also after quotations from *Ahikar*! But the Jews were always in this dilemma in their attitude to gentile wisdom (see Baruch 3: 9–4: 4, where the question is treated at length), and the Christian Church has also from time to time fallen into the same narrow attitude to secular knowledge.

20. *Rages* near Teheran dominates the pass from the plain up to the Median plateau, and has therefore always been an important place. ✳

TOBIAS SETS OUT

5 Then Tobias said: 'I will do all that you have told me,
2 father. But how shall I be able to get this money from him, since he does not know me and I do not know him? What proof of identity shall I give him to make him believe me and give me this money? Also I do not know the roads to
3 Media or how to get there.' To this Tobit replied: 'He gave me his note of hand, and I gave him mine, which I divided in two. We took one part each, and I put mine with the money. It is twenty years since I made this deposit. And now, my boy, find someone reliable to go with you, and we will pay him up to the time of your return; then go and recover the money from Gabael.'

4   Tobias went out to find a man who knew the way and

would accompany him to Media, and found himself face
to face with the angel Raphael. Not knowing he was an 5
angel of God, he questioned him: 'Where do you come
from, young man?' 'I am an Israelite,' he replied, 'one of
your fellow-countrymen, and I have come here to find
work.' Tobias asked, 'Do you know the road to Media?'
'Yes,' he said, 'I have often been there; I am familiar with 6
all the routes and know them well. I have often travelled
into Media and used to lodge with Gabael our fellow-
countryman who lives there in Rages.[a] It is two full days'
journey from Ecbatana to Rages; for Rages is in the hills,
and Ecbatana is in the middle of the plain.' Tobias said: 7
'Wait for me, young man, while I go in and tell my
father. I need you to go with me and will pay you your
wages.' 'All right, I will wait,' he said; 'only do not be too 8
long.'

Tobias went in and told his father. 'I have found a fellow-
Israelite to accompany me', he said. His father replied,
'Call the man in, my son. I want to find out his family and
tribe and make sure that he will be a trustworthy com-
panion for you.'

Tobias went out and called him: 'Young man, my father 9
is asking for you.' He went in, and Tobit greeted him first.
To Raphael's reply, 'May all be well with you!', Tobit
retorted: 'How can anything be well with me now? I am a
blind man; I cannot see the light of heaven, but lie in darkness like the dead who cannot see the light. Though still
alive, I am as good as dead. I hear men's voices, but the
men I do not see.' Raphael answered: 'Take heart; in
God's design your cure is at hand. Take heart.' Tobit went

[a] *Probable reading (compare 4: 1); Gk.* Ecbatana.

on: 'My son Tobias wishes to travel to Media. Can you go with him as his guide? I will pay you, my friend.' 'Yes,' he said, 'I can go with him; I know all the roads. I have often been to Media; I have travelled over all the plains and
10 mountains there, and am familiar with all its roads.' Tobit said to him, 'Tell me, my friend, what family and tribe
11 you belong to.' He asked, 'Why need you know my tribe?' Tobit said, 'I do indeed wish to know whose son
12 you are, my friend, and what your name is.' 'I am Azarias,' he replied, 'son of the older Ananias, one of your kinsmen.'
13   Tobit said to him: 'Good luck and a safe journey to you! Do not be angry with me, my friend, because I wished to know the facts of your descent. It turns out that you are a kinsman, and a man of good family. I knew Ananias and Nathan the two sons of the older Semelias. They used to go with me to Jerusalem and worship with me there; they never went astray. Your kinsmen are worthy men; you
14 come of a sound stock. Good luck go with you.' Tobit added: 'I will pay you a drachma a day and allow you the
15 same expenses as my son. Keep him company on his
16 travels, and I will add something to your wages.' Raphael answered: 'I will go with him. Never fear; we shall travel there and back without mishap, because the road is safe.' Tobit replied, 'God bless you, my friend.' He called his son and said to him: 'My boy, get ready what you need for the journey, and set off with your kinsman. May God in heaven keep both of you safe on your journey there and restore you to me unharmed. May his angel safely escort you both.' Before setting out Tobias kissed his father and mother, and Tobit said to him, 'Goodbye, and a safe journey!'

Then his mother burst into tears. 'Why have you sent 17
my boy away?' she said to Tobit. 'Is he not our prop and
stay? Has he not always been at home with us? Why send 18
money after money? Write it off for the sake of our boy!
Let us be content to live the life the Lord has appointed for 19
us.' Tobit said to her: 'Do not worry; our son will go 20
safely and come back safely, and you will see him with
your own eyes on the day of his safe return. Do not worry
or be anxious about them, my dear. A good angel will go 21
with him, and his journey will prosper, and he will come
back safe and sound.' At that she stopped crying.   22

✻ 3. The N.E.B. translation is very difficult to follow, partly
because it is trying to keep to S. A better and clearer text and
translation would run as follows: 'He gave me his signature
and I gave him mine (i.e. on a clay tablet). I then divided it in
two and we took one part each: [one half I kept myself, the
other] half I put with the money.' The words in square
brackets, which are necessary for the sense, are found in the
Old Latin manuscripts.

4. *angel Raphael*: see note on 3: 17.

6. *Rages*: S has made a straight mistake here, and the N.E.B.
has rightly followed the Old Latin. The mention of *Ecbatana*
is odd, in that Tobias had no thought of going there; but
Raphael knew better! The author of Tobit is very weak in
geography: Ecbatana is 200 miles from Rages, and it lies on
the plateau 2,500 feet higher up.

9. Even if Tobias' suspicions were not aroused by the
reference to Ecbatana, one would have expected Tobit, on
hearing the words *your cure is at hand*, to wonder if this was
just ordinary politeness.

12. *Ananias* and *Azarias* are favourite names in later
Judaism: cp. Daniel's three friends (Dan. 1: 6).

13. *you are...a man of good family*: to readers who are

aware that he is addressing an angel, the dramatic irony is enjoyable. Knowing that all is under the providence of God, we can laugh at Tobit's fussiness, just as we can laugh at Anna's fearfulness in 10: 7; but, because neither of them is portrayed as a heroic character, our laughter is still sympathetic.

14. *a drachma* was a normal wage for *a day*. Note the author's love of a formal agreement: cp. 5: 3 and 7: 13.

16. *May his angel safely escort you both*: another enjoyable touch of dramatic irony; see note on 3: 17.

17. Anna's lack of faith is contrasted with Tobit's faith: cp. 2: 14 *b*.

18. *Write it off*: the exact translation of the Greek is difficult, but the general sense is certain, that the boy is far more important than the money. The maternal psychology of these verses is good.

20. *with your own eyes* is a good touch from the blind Tobit.

21. *A good angel*: another pleasant touch. On the whole, however, S's longer narrative of chapter 5 is less effective than the shorter version of B. B omits the whole of verse 9, but sharpens up Raphael's question in verse 11: 'Is it a tribe and family you want, or a hired man to go with your son?' B also halves verse 16, cutting out both the exchange between Tobit and Raphael ending *God bless you my friend* and the final sentence ending *Goodbye, and a safe journey*, as well as the *Good luck go with you* at the end of verse 13. ✳

THE JOURNEY TO MEDIA

6 The boy and the angel left the house together, and the dog came out with him and accompanied them. They travelled until night overtook them, and then camped by the river
2 Tigris. Tobias went down to bathe his feet in the river, and a huge fish leapt out of the water and tried to swallow
3 the boy's foot. He cried out, and the angel said to him, 'Seize the fish and hold it fast.' So Tobias seized it and

hauled it on to the bank. The angel said to him: 'Split the 4
fish open and take out its gall, heart, and liver; keep them
by you, but throw the guts away; the gall, heart, and
liver can be used as medicine.' Tobias split the fish open, 5
and put together its gall, heart, and liver. He cooked and
ate part of the fish; the rest he salted and kept.

They continued the journey together until they came
near Media. Then the boy asked the angel: 'Azarias, my 6
friend, what medicine is there in the fish's heart, liver, and
gall?' He said: 'You can use the heart and liver as a fumiga- 7
tion for any man or woman attacked by a demon or evil
spirit; the attack will cease, and it will give no further
trouble. The gall is for anointing a man's eyes when white 8
patches have spread over them, or for blowing on the
white patches in the eyes; the eyes will then recover.'

When he had entered Media and was now approaching 9
Ecbatana, Raphael said to the boy, 'Tobias, my friend.' 10
'Yes?' he replied. Raphael said: 'We must stay the night
with Raguel. He is your kinsman and he has a daughter
named Sarah. Apart from Sarah he has neither son nor
daughter. You are her next of kin and have the right to 11
marry her and inherit her father's property. The girl is 12
sensible, brave, and very beautiful, and her father is an
honourable man.' He went on: 'It is right that you should
marry her. Be guided by me, my friend; I will speak to
her father about the girl this very night and ask for her
hand as your bride, and on our return from Rages we will
celebrate her marriage. I know that Raguel cannot with-
hold her from you or betroth her to another man without
incurring the death penalty according to the ordinance
in the book of Moses; and he is aware that his daughter

belongs by right to you rather than to any other man. Now be guided by me, my friend; we will talk about the girl tonight and will betroth her to you, and when we return from Rages we shall take her back with us to your home.'

13 Then Tobias answered Raphael: 'Azarias, my friend, I have heard that she has already been given to seven hus-bands and they died the very night they went into the
14 bridal chamber to her. I have been told that it is a demon who kills them. And now it is my turn to be afraid; he does her no harm, but kills any man who tries to come near her. I am my father's only child; I am afraid that if I die I shall bring my father and mother to the grave with grief for me. They have no other son to bury them.'
15 Raphael said to him: 'Have you forgotten the orders your father gave you? He told you to take a wife from your father's kindred. Now be guided by me, my friend: do not worry about the demon, but marry her. I am sure that
16 this night she shall be given you as your wife. When you enter the bridal chamber, take some of the fish's liver and
17 its heart, and put them on the smoking incense. The smell will spread, and when the demon smells it he will make off and never be seen near her any more. When you are about to go to bed with her, both of you must first stand up and pray, beseeching the Lord of heaven to grant you mercy and deliverance. Have no fear; she was destined for you before the world was made. You shall rescue her and she shall go with you. No doubt you will have children by her and they will be very dear to you.*a* So do not worry!' When Tobias heard what Raphael said, and learnt that

[a] *Literally* be like brothers to you.

she was his kinswoman and of his father's house, he was filled with love for her and set his heart on her.

✶ 1. *the dog*, i.e. the family dog, is another surprise. In the Old Testament dogs feature as scavengers or at best watch-dogs (Isa. 56: 10) rather than companions. We do not yet know how the Aramaic fragment from Qumran treats it, but the medieval Hebrew and Aramaic manuscripts of Tobit omit all reference to the dog, and even S may have had qualms about it (see note on 11: 4). But in Mesopotamia, as in Greece and Rome, the dog was a familiar household animal; and in the *Story of Ahikar* (2: 38 in the Syrian version) we read that 'the dog's tail brings him food, his mouth brings him blows'.

2. The *fish* which *tried to swallow the boy's foot* was perhaps a crocodile in the earliest version of this adventure.

7. *fumigation* was regularly recommended in ancient magi-cal texts for driving away demons.

8. The use of fishes' *gall* was likewise regularly recom-mended in ancient medical texts as a cure for leucoma. To us the mixture of magic and medicine is disconcerting; but much magic is nothing but primitive medicine. The anticipa-tion here of Tobit's cure is quite skilful.

9. They would not in fact have gone near *Ecbatana* on the way to Rages, but the author has his geography muddled (see note on 5: 6).

12. *It is right* for Tobias to *marry her*, because of his general duty to marry within the tribe, reinforced by Tobit's personal advice (4: 12). It was right for her to marry him because of the same general duty, reinforced by the fact that, having no brothers, she was an heiress (Num. 36: 8f.). But there is no mention in the Old Testament of any *death penalty*, which must be another example of the way in which later Jews tried to tighten up the original law.

13. *I have heard*: we have to suppose that it was not until Raphael mentioned Sarah that Tobias remembered what he

had heard about her marital misfortunes. For the demon's activity see note on 3: 8.

16. It is uncertain whether the *smoking incense* has a religious or a secular purpose.

17. Within the overall providence of God, it is simply the magic which drives off the demon. Tobit had no family advantage over her seven previous husbands, who were also kinsmen (7: 11). Nor has his prayer anything to do, in S, with the demon's departure, as is clear also from the narrative in chapter 8. Jerome's translation suggests otherwise. His version of the end of Raphael's speech runs as follows: 'Those who on entering marriage forget God and give themselves up to physical desire "like horse and mule which have no understanding" – they are in the power of the demon. But you, when you have married her, spend three days in chastity and prayer. On the first night, the demon will be driven out by the smoking gall... When the third night is over, you may take your virgin wife in the fear of the Lord.'

That advice was certainly not followed by Tobias and Sarah (though conceivably Jerome thought it was – see note on 8: 8), nor is it in line with normal Jewish attitudes to marriage. Presumably it comes out of Jerome's head rather than out of any manuscript. But some bishops in the Church after Jerome did from time to time try to enforce three days' continence after marriage. There is an echo of Jerome also in our own 1662 Book of Common Prayer, where the introduction to the Marriage Service says that 'Matrimony... is not to be taken in hand... wantonly to satisfy men's carnal lusts and appetites, like brute beasts that have no understanding'.

he was filled with love for her: to us, who are not used to arranged marriages, it seems odd that he could say that he loved her before meeting her, but actually it is in order, because this is a story not about romantic love but about marriage. *

TOBIAS MEETS SARAH

When they reached Ecbatana, Tobias said, 'Azarias, my 7
friend, take me straight to our kinsman Raguel.' So Azarias
brought him to Raguel's house, and they found him sitting
by the courtyard door. They greeted him first, and he
replied, 'A hearty welcome to you, friends. I am glad to
see you well after your journey.' He took them into his
house and said to Edna his wife, 'Is not this young man like 2
my kinsman Tobit?' Edna asked them, 'Where do you 3
come from, friends?' 'We belong to the tribe of Naphtali,'
they answered, 'now in captivity at Nineveh.' 'Do you 4
know our kinsman Tobit?' she asked, and they replied,
'Yes, we do.' 'Is he well?' she said. 'He is alive and well', 5
they answered, and Tobias added, 'He is my father.'
Raguel jumped up and, with tears in his eyes, he kissed 6
him and said, 'God bless you, my boy, son of a good and 7
noble father. But what grievous news that so good and
charitable a man has gone blind!' He embraced Tobias
his kinsman and wept; and Edna his wife and their daughter 8
Sarah also wept for Tobit. Then Raguel slaughtered a ram
from the flock and made them warmly welcome.

After they had taken a bath and washed their hands, and
had sat down to dinner, Tobias said to Raphael, 'Azarias,
my friend, ask Raguel to give me Sarah my kinswoman.'
Raguel overheard and said to the young man: 'Eat, drink, 9
and be happy tonight. There is no one but yourself who 10
should have my daughter Sarah; indeed I have no right to
give her to anyone else, since you are my nearest kinsman.
But I must tell you the truth, my son: I have given her in 11
marriage to seven of our kinsmen, and they all died on

their wedding night. My son, eat now and drink, and may the Lord deal kindly with you both.' Tobias answered, 'I will not eat or drink anything here until you have
12 disposed of this business of mine.' Raguel said to him, 'I will do so: I give her to you as the ordinance in the book of Moses prescribes. Heaven has ordained that she shall be yours. Take your kinswoman. From now on, you belong to her and she to you; she is yours for ever from this day. The Lord of heaven prosper you both this night, my son, and grant you mercy and peace.'

13 Raguel sent for his daughter Sarah, and when she came he took her hand and gave her to Tobias, saying: 'Take her to be your wedded wife in accordance with the law and the ordinance written in the book of Moses. Keep her and take her home to your father; and may the God of heaven keep you safe and give you peace and prosperity.'
14 Then he sent for her mother and told her to bring paper, and he wrote out a marriage contract granting Sarah to
15 Tobias as his wife, as the law of Moses ordains. After that they began to eat and drink.

16 Raguel called his wife and said, 'My dear, get the spare
17 room ready and take her in there.' Edna went and prepared the room as he had told her, and took Sarah into it. Edna
18 cried over her, then dried her tears and said: 'Courage, dear daughter; the Lord of heaven give you joy instead of sorrow. Courage, daughter!' Then she went out.

* 1. *I am glad to see you well after your journey*: the N.E.B. translation reads as if he expected them, but the Greek just means 'welcome and good health to you'; the formula is still used in parts of Greece.
2. *Edna* is not elsewhere found as a name in the Bible.

3–5. Edna's questions are closely modelled on those of
Jacob to the shepherds of Laban when he was looking for a
wife (Gen. 29: 4–6). This accounts for the otherwise strange
statement that Tobit *is well*.

6–8. The weeping seems to us somewhat overdone, but in
fact it is common at peasant family reunions the world over.
See also Gen. 45: 14f., the reunion of Joseph and Benjamin.

10. *Eat, drink, and be happy tonight*: is there a gruesome
reference here to the well-known saying 'let us eat, drink
and be merry, for tomorrow we die'?

11. *I will not eat...until...*: so Abraham's servant said to
Laban when he was on the way to fetch Rebecca as a wife for
Isaac (Gen. 24: 33).

14. *a marriage contract* was common all over the Assyrian
empire from the time of the Code of Hammurabi (about
1700 B.C.). There is no reference to it in the Old Testament, but
Jews living in Egypt used marriage contracts, and so doubtless did those in Assyria, etc. In Egypt it was written on
papyrus or *paper*, in Assyria on a clay tablet. Its clauses would
have included Raguel's promises in 8: 21 (where see note)
and 10: 10. It would also have been sealed by the signet
ring of Raguel and Tobias, as most manuscripts here say it was.

as the law of Moses ordains: these words refer not to the
writing of a marriage contract (of which there is no mention
in the Law of Moses) but to *granting Sarah to Tobias as his wife*.
So an Egyptian Jewish papyrus of 218 B.C. contains the
formula 'be you my wife according to the Law of Moses'.

16. *Raguel called his wife*: because women, according to
Eastern custom, were not present at the meal; similarly he
sent for Sarah in verse 13 and Edna in verse 14. *

TOBIAS AND SARAH HAPPILY MARRIED

When they had finished eating and drinking and were **8**
ready for bed, they escorted the young man to the bridal
chamber. Tobias recalled what Raphael had told him; he ²

took the fish's liver and heart out of the bag in which he

3 kept them, and put them on the smoking incense. The smell from the fish held the demon off, and he took flight into Upper Egypt; and Raphael instantly followed him there and bound him hand and foot.

4 When they were left alone and the door was shut, Tobias rose from the bed and said to Sarah, 'Get up, my love; let us pray and beseech our Lord to show us mercy and keep

5 us safe.' She got up and they began to pray that they might be kept safe. Tobias said: 'We praise thee, O God of our fathers, we praise thy name for ever and ever. Let the

6 heavens and all thy creation praise thee for ever. Thou madest Adam, and Eve his wife to be his helper and support; and those two were the parents of the human race. This was thy word: "It is not good for the man to be

7 alone; let us make him a helper like him." I now take this my beloved to wife, not out of lust but in true marriage. Grant that she and I may find mercy and grow old to-

8,9 gether.' They both said 'Amen', and slept through the night.

Raguel got up and summoned his servants, and they

10 went out and dug a grave. For he said, 'He may have been killed, and then we shall have to face scorn and disgrace.'

11 When they had finished digging the grave, Raguel went

12 into the house and called his wife: 'Send one of the maidservants', he said, 'to go in and see if he is alive. If he is

13 dead, let us bury him so that no one may know.' They lit a lamp, opened the door, and sent a maidservant in; and

14 she found them sound asleep together. She came out and told them: 'He is alive and has come to no harm.'

15 Then they praised the God of heaven: 'We praise thee,

O God, we praise thee with all our heart. Let men praise thee throughout all ages. Praise to thee for the joy thou 16 hast given me; the thing I feared has not happened, but thou hast shown us thy great mercy. Praise to thee for 17 the mercy thou hast shown to these two, these only children. Lord, show them mercy, keep them safe, and grant them a long life of happiness and affection.' Then he ord- 18 ered his servants to fill in the grave before dawn came.

He told his wife to bake a great batch of bread; he went 19 to the herd and brought two oxen and four rams and told his servants to get them ready; so they set about the preparations. He then called Tobias and said: 'You shall 20 not stir from here for two weeks. Stay with us; let us eat and drink together and cheer my daughter's heart after all her suffering. Here and now take half of all I have, and 21 go home to your father safe and sound; and the other half will come to you both when my wife and I die. Be reassured, my son, I am your father and Edna is your mother; we are as close to you as to your wife, now and always. You have nothing to fear, my son.'

* 3. *Upper Egypt* was about as far away as one could get. Demons were thought to inhabit waterless places (Matt. 12: 43). *bound him* throws some light on the reference in Matt. 12: 29 to tying 'the strong man up before ransacking the house'.

4. *Tobias rose* because prayer was made standing. His prayer followed the usual form. It began with praise (cp. verse 15 and Anna's prayer 3: 11). It then referred to past benefits of God, and concluded with a request for present help.

6. The *word* comes from Gen. 2: 18.

7. *true marriage*: the phrase does not mean 'marriage in the true sense of the word' but 'marriage with a true heart',

i.e. undertaken with intention of lifelong fidelity (see note on 1: 3).

grow old together is a happy turn of phrase, which means more than a prayer for long life for each separately.

8. *slept* does not imply that the marriage was not consummated. In fact it certainly *was*, or the wedding celebrations would not have been held.

9. *dug a grave*: this somewhat macabre incident is found also in the Midrash Tanhuma (see p. 3): 'when midnight came, the man and woman arose to prepare a grave for their son-in-law before daybreak.'

20. *two weeks* was twice the usual period for a wedding celebration (Gen. 29: 27).

21. *take half of all I have*: the parallels from the stories of the patriarchs in Genesis, upon which the author of Tobit draws so heavily for his narrative, differ in this one respect, that there the suitor brought a bride-price to his future father-in-law (Gen. 34: 12), as well as presents for the bride and other members of her family (Gen. 24: 53). Tobias and Raguel however follow the custom which was common elsewhere, of which this Babylonian marriage-contract of 546 B.C. is an example: 'I and my husband took Bin-addu-amara to sonship, and wrote a tablet of his sonship, and made known that the dowry of my daughter was 2 minas 10 shekels and the furniture of a house.' But the idea that the suitor got *half* his father-in-law's property belongs to the earliest strata of the folk-tale, familiar to us from numerous fairy-tales where the king promises the hero, if he kills the dragon, the hand of his daughter and half his kingdom.

19–21. To illustrate the difference between the S and the B texts, here is the equivalent in B of 8: 19–21: 'He made a wedding-feast for them for a fortnight. Before the period was up, he forbade Tobias on oath to leave until the fortnight's celebrations were completed: then he should take half his property and go home with his blessing: the rest when I and my wife die.' *

46

THE DEPOSIT WITH GABAEL IS RECOVERED

Tobias called Raphael and said to him: 'Azarias, my **9**1,2 friend, take four servants with you, and two camels, and make your way to Rages. Go to Gabael's house, give him the bond and collect the money, and bring him with you to the wedding-feast. You know that my father will 4 be counting the days and, if I am even one day late, it will distress him. You see what Raguel has sworn, and I cannot 3 go against his oath.' Raphael went with the four servants 5 and the two camels to Rages in Media and lodged there with Gabael. He gave him his bond and informed him that Tobit's son Tobias had taken a wife and was inviting him to the wedding-feast. At once Gabael counted out the bags to him with their seals intact, and they put them together. They all made an early start and came to the 6 wedding. When they entered Raguel's house and found Tobias at the feast, he jumped up and greeted Gabael. With tears in his eyes Gabael blessed him and said: 'Good sir, worthy son of a worthy father, that upright and charitable man, may the Lord give Heaven's blessing to you and your wife, your father and your mother-in-law. Praise be to God that I have seen my cousin Tobias, so like his father.'

---

* This part of the story is very briefly told. Moreover, Tobias does not go himself to get the money but sends Raphael instead, on the excuse that he cannot afford the time. In fact the motif of the deposit serves only to complicate the whole story. The deposit was not necessary as the reason for Tobias' setting out: he could have gone, straightforwardly, to win Sarah as his wife (see notes on 4: 1 and 6: 13). Nor was it necessary for the relief of Tobit's poverty, once Tobias had married an heiress. Since the motif was not present in the original folk-tale, it is a puzzle why the author first decided to include it and then did it so half-heartedly.

1. *Tobias called Raphael*: for the first time in the story Tobias, newly-wed, shows initiative!

2. *the bond* is what was called a 'note of hand' in 5: 3, where see note.

3. Raguel had not *sworn* in the S text, but he did so in the Old Latin, as also in B, so we can be sure that the reference to it in 8: 20 was left out by mistake in S. The numbering of verses 3 and 4 looks odd in N.E.B. This is due to the fact that in B (and therefore in the Authorized Version) the verses come the other way round, and the N.E.B. translators wanted to keep the verse-numbering of the Authorized Version for cross-reference.

5. The *seals* were not mentioned before, but they were standard practice in Assyria, etc.

6. *When they entered*: in place of the somewhat unnecessary fullness of the rest of this verse, B has just the cryptic words 'and Tobias blessed his wife' (perhaps a mistake for 'and they blessed Tobias and his wife'). Here again it looks very much as if the shorter text of B is later than the longer of S.

your father and your mother-in-law is hardly credible: the Old Latin preserves the obvious reading 'your father-in-law and your mother-in-law'. ✳

Tobias' homecoming

THE RETURN JOURNEY

10 Now day by day Tobit was keeping count of the time Tobias would take for his journey there and back. When
2 the days had passed and his son had not returned, Tobit

said: 'Perhaps he has been detained there. Or perhaps Gabael is dead and there is no one to give him the money.' And he grew anxious. Anna his wife said: 'My child has 3, 4 perished. He is no longer in the land of the living.' She began to weep and lament for her son: 'O my child, the 5 light of my eyes, why did I let you go?' Tobit said to her: 6 'Hush, do not worry, my dear; he is all right. Something has happened there to distract them. The man who went with him is one of our kinsmen and can be trusted. Do not grieve for him, my dear; he will soon be back.' But she 7 answered: 'Be quiet! Leave me alone! Do not try to deceive me. My boy is dead.' Each day she would rush out and look down the road her son had taken, and would listen to no one; and when she came indoors at sunset she could never sleep, but wept and lamented the whole night long.

The two weeks of wedding celebrations which Raguel had sworn to hold for his daughter came to an end, and Tobias went up to him and said: 'Let me be off on my journey; for I am sure that my parents are thinking they will never see me again. I beg you, father, let me go home now to my father Tobit. I have already told you how I left him.' Raguel said to Tobias: 'Stay, my son. Stay with me, 8 and I will send news of you to your father.' But Tobias 9 answered: 'No; please let me go home to my father.' Then without further delay Raguel handed over to Tobias 10 Sarah his bride and half of all that he possessed, male and female slaves, sheep and cattle, donkeys and camels, clothes, money, and furniture. He saw them safely off and 11 embraced Tobias, saying: 'Goodbye, my son; a safe journey to you! May the Lord of heaven give prosperity

to you and Sarah your wife; and may I live to see your
12 children.' To his daughter Sarah he said: 'Go to your father-
in-law's house; they are now your parents as much as if
you were their own daughter. Go in peace, my child;
I hope to hear good news of you as long as I live.' He bade
them both goodbye and sent them on their way. Edna
said to Tobias: 'Child and beloved cousin, may the Lord
bring you safely home, you and my daughter Sarah, and
may I live long enough to see your children. In the sight
of the Lord I entrust my daughter to you; do nothing to
hurt her as long as you live. Go in peace, my son. From
now on I am your mother and Sarah is your beloved wife.
May we all be blessed with prosperity to the end of our
days!' She kissed them both and saw them safely off.
11 Tobias parted from Raguel in good health and spirits,
thankful to the Lord of heaven and earth, the king of all,
for the success of his journey. Raguel's last words to him
were: 'May the Lord give you the means to honour your
parents all their lives.'

* 1–7*a*. The events in this section could well have come
later, after 11: 4. But both sequences 'happened' at the same
time, so the author can do what he likes. And what he likes
is, as in chapters 1–3, a rapid change from joy to sorrow and
vice versa.

Again the contrast between Tobit and Anna is well conceived: he worried about the arrangements and the money,
she simply about the danger to her son. Typically feminine,
she both supposed him dead and went out to *look down the road*
for his return, like the father of the Prodigal Son (Luke 15: 20).
He, typically masculine, is first of all worried himself but then,
when she worries, turns round to reassure her.

4. *My child has perished*: Anna's first speech begins with the

50

identical words with which she ends her second speech in verse 7. It is a pity that N.E.B. has chosen to vary the translation, because the trick of style is typically Jewish.

6. Something similar has happened to the exchange between Tobit and Anna. His first words *Hush, do not worry* are picked up by hers which mean 'Hush yourself, do not deceive me'.

10: 7*b* – 11: 1. Another somewhat long-winded section. B is shorter but still rather long for our taste.

10: 12. Instead of *Go to your father-in-law's house*, all important manuscripts except S have the words 'honour your parents-in-law', which gives a preferable sense (see also 14: 13).

11: 1. *Raguel's last words*: this final section of the episode is so found only in S. All other important manuscripts agree that it closed with a blessing by Tobias of his parents-in-law, and the Jerusalem Bible gives a probable text as follows: 'He gave this blessing to Raguel and his wife Edna: "May it be my happiness to honour you all the days of my life."' This makes a more suitable close to the episode, and also fits better with the reference in the preferable text of the previous verse. ✲

TOBIT'S BLINDNESS CURED

When they reached Caserin close to Nineveh, Raphael 2 said: 'You know how your father was when we left him; let us hurry on ahead of your wife and see that the 3 house is ready before the others arrive.' As the two of them 4 went on together Raphael said: 'Take the fish-gall in your hand.' The dog went with the angel and Tobias, following at their heels.

Anna sat watching the road by which her son would 5 return. She saw him coming and exclaimed to his father, 6 'Here he comes, your son and the man who went with him!' Before Tobias reached his father's house Raphael 7

said: 'I know for certain that his eyes will be opened.
8 Spread the fish-gall on his eyes, and the medicine will make the white patches shrink and peel off. Your father
9 will get his sight back and see the light of day.' Anna ran forward and flung her arms round her son. 'Here you are, my boy; now I can die happy!' she cried out with tears in her eyes.
10 Tobit rose to his feet and came stumbling out through
11 the courtyard door. Tobias went up to him with the fish-gall in his hand and blew it into his father's eyes, and took
12 him by the arm and said: 'It will be all right, father.' Then
13 when he had put the medicine on and applied it, using both hands he peeled off the patches from the corners of
14 Tobit's eyes. Tobit flung his arms round him and burst into tears. 'I can see you, my son, the light of my eyes!' he cried. 'Praise be to God, and praise to his great name, and to all his holy angels. May his great name rest upon us.
15 Praised be all the angels for ever. He laid his scourge on me, and now, look, I see my son Tobias!'

Tobias went in, rejoicing and praising God with all his strength. He told his father about the success of his journey, how he had brought the money with him and had married Sarah daughter of Raguel. 'She is on her
16 way,' he said, 'quite close to the city gate.' Tobit went out joyfully to meet his daughter-in-law at the gate, praising God as he went. At the sight of him passing through the city in full vigour and walking without a guide, the
17 people of Nineveh were astonished; and Tobit gave thanks to God before them all for his mercy in opening his eyes. When he met Sarah, the wife of his son Tobias, he blessed her and said to her: 'Come in, my daughter, and

welcome. Praise be to your God who has brought you to us, my daughter. Blessings on your father, and on my son Tobias, and blessings on you, my daughter. Come into your home, and may health, blessings, and joy be yours; come in, my daughter.' It was a day of joy for all the Jews in Nineveh; and Ahikar and Nadab, Tobit's cousins, 18 came to share his happiness.

✻ 2. *Caserin* is unknown.

3. *hurry on ahead*: so Judah was sent ahead when Israel was coming to Joseph in Gen. 46: 28.

4. *The dog*: S actually reads 'The Lord' here, a plain mistake. In a few manuscripts (followed by the Vulgate) the dog goes ahead, and is the first thing to be seen by the *watching* Anna in verse 5. But in most manuscripts the dog plays no part in the story, and seems to be a part of the folk-tale that has survived precariously (see note on 6: 1).

9. This verse is modelled on Gen. 46: 29f.

13. *peeled off the patches*: cp. the description in Acts 9: 18 of Paul's cure from blindness: 'it seemed that scales fell from his eyes.' It is the same Greek word which is translated 'scales' and 'patches'.

14. The author, conscious of the presence of Raphael, has Tobit include a reference to *angels*.

17. *your God* is odd: all manuscripts except S omit 'your'.

18. All good manuscripts except S add the following words to round off the episode: 'and the wedding celebrations went on with great joy for a week.' As well as these two mistakes, S makes six others in the second half of chapter 11, and indeed it is generally less reliable from now on. ✻

12 When the marriage-feast was over, Tobit called Tobias
and said, 'My son, see that you pay the man who went
with you, and give him something extra, over and above
2 his wages.' Tobias said: 'Father, how much shall I pay him?
It would not hurt me to give him half the money he and
3 I brought back. He has kept me safe, cured my wife, helped
me bring the money, and healed you. How much extra
4 shall I pay him?' Tobit replied, 'It is right, my son, for
him to be given half of all that he has brought with him.'
5 So Tobias sent for him and said, 'Half of all that you have
brought with you is yours for your wages; take it, and
fare you well.'

6   Then Raphael called them both aside and said to them:
'Praise God and thank him before all men living for the
good he has done you, so that they may sing hymns of
praise to his name. Proclaim to all the world what God has
done, and pay him honour; do not be slow to give him
7 thanks. A king's secret ought to be kept, but the works
of God should be acknowledged publicly. Acknowledge
them, therefore, and pay him honour. Do good, and evil
8 shall not touch you. Better prayer with sincerity, and
almsgiving with righteousness, than wealth with wicked-
9 ness. Better give alms than hoard up gold. Almsgiving
preserves a man from death and wipes out all sin. Givers of
10 alms will enjoy long life; but sinners and wrong-doers are
their own worst enemies.

11   'I will tell you the whole truth; I will hide nothing from
you. Indeed I told you just now when I said, "A king's
secret ought to be kept, but the works of God should be

publicly honoured." When you and Sarah prayed, it was 12
I who brought your prayers into the glorious presence of
the Lord; and so too whenever you buried the dead. That 13
day when you got up from your dinner without hesitation
to go and bury the corpse, I was sent to test you; and again 14
God sent me to cure both you and Sarah your daughter-
in-law at the same time. I am Raphael, one of the seven 15
angels who stand in attendance on the Lord and enter his
glorious presence.'

The two men were shaken, and prostrated themselves 16
in awe. But he said to them: 'Do not be afraid, all is well; 17
praise God for ever. It is no thanks to me that I have been 18
with you; it was the will of God. Worship him all your
life long, sing his praise. Take note that I ate no food; what 19
appeared to you was a vision. And now praise the Lord, 20
give thanks to God here on earth; I am ascending to him
who sent me. Write down all these things that have happened to you.' He then ascended, and when they rose to 21
their feet, he was no longer to be seen. They sang hymns of 22
praise to God, giving him thanks for these great deeds he
had done when his angel appeared to them.

* 1. The *something extra* was promised in 5: 15 just for keeping Tobias company, but of course Raphael had done far
more than that.

2. *half the money*: in the Armenian version of 'The Grateful
Dead' the unknown man offers to become the servant of the
hero for half his future wealth. The author of Tobit removed
the idea from 5: 15, but it slips out here.

6–20. Raphael's speech is a curious mixture of styles and
subjects. It begins with very general remarks: Tobit must
praise God in public (6–7a); God always rewards almsgiving

(7*b*–10). Then, after an unconvincing link-verse (11), he explains the part he himself has played in their story (12–15). Finally he generalizes again, about the role of angels in carrying out the will of God (16–19), and ends with a further command to praise God (20).

6. *aside*, Greek 'secretly', is odd. It contradicts the idea in *before all men living*, which is repeated in Raphael's speech many times, culminating in the command in verse 20 to write a book.

7. Keeping the *king's secret* does not refer to anything particular; it merely makes the contrast with *publicly* acknowledging the *works of God*. The idea is in *Ahikar* (2: 1 Arm.).

8. *with sincerity* S; other manuscripts have 'with fasting', which however is not a theme of Tobit (unlike Judith).

9. The idea that *Almsgiving preserves a man from death* is found also at 4: 10, where see note. The idea that it *wipes out all sin* is found in Dan. 4: 27 and Ecclus. 3: 30; the same chapter of Ecclus. (verse 3) says, interestingly, that 'Respect for a father atones for sins'.

11. *I told you just now*: this echo of his own words was a characteristic of Jesus in speaking, at least in St John's gospel (e.g. 14: 11, 28).

12. This idea of an angel as a mediator or intercessor between man and God is found first in Job 33: 23: 'an angel... a mediator between him and God, to expound what he has done right'. Similarly in Acts 10: 4 the angel says to Cornelius: 'Your prayers and acts of charity have gone up to heaven to speak for you before God.'

13. *to test you*: the idea that God tests men's faith by sending misfortunes (cp. our phrase 'trials and tribulations') is common enough in the Bible. Usually it is God himself who does the testing (Deut. 13: 3; Judith 8: 25); sometimes it is Satan with God's permission (Job 1 and 2); nowhere else does an angel do it.

15. *one of the seven angels*: this is the first mention of the number seven, which was later accepted as the number of

the 'angels that stand in the presence of God' (Rev. 8: 2).
Seven is a conventional number; cp. 3: 15.

19. *I ate no food; what appeared...was a vision*: angels did
not eat (Judg. 13: 16) and in that sense they were visions.
Contrast the passage in Luke 24: 39–42, where the risen Jesus
eats precisely in order to show that he is *not* a vision.

16–22. In fact this whole section seems to have had considerable influence upon the story of Jesus' transfiguration,
resurrection and ascension in the Gospels and Acts, an influence which is sometimes obscured by the N.E.B. translation.

16. Cp. Matt. 17: 6: 'at the sound of the voice the disciples
fell on their faces in terror'.

17. *Do not be afraid*: cp. Matt. 28: 5, 10.

all is well, literally, 'peace be unto you', cp. Luke 24: 36;
John 20: 19, 21, 26.

19. Cp. Luke 24: 39–42 (see above).

20. Cp. John 16: 5: 'I am going away to him who sent me'
and John 20: 17: 'I am now ascending to my Father'.

Write down: cp. John 21: 25.

21. Cp. Acts 1: 9: 'he was lifted up, and a cloud removed
him from their sight.'

The cumulative effect of these parallels shows that at least this
chapter of Tobit was well known in early Christian circles. ✳

TOBIT'S PSALM OF THANKSGIVING

Tobit said: **13**

'Praise to the ever-living God and to his kingdom.

He punishes and he shows mercy;   2

he brings men down to the grave below,

and up from the great destruction.

Nothing can escape his power.

Give him thanks, men of Israel, in the presence of the   3
    nations,

for he has scattered you among them;

4   there he has shown you his greatness.
Exalt him in the sight of every living creature,
for he is our Lord and God;
he is our Father and our God for ever.

5   He will punish you for your wickedness,
and he will show mercy to you all,
gathering you from among all the nations
wherever you have been scattered.

6   When you turn to him with all your heart and soul
and act in loyal obedience to him,
then he will turn to you
and hide his face from you no longer.
Consider now the deeds he has done for you,
and give him thanks with full voice;
praise the righteous Lord
and exalt the King of ages.
In the land of my exile I give thanks to him
and declare his might and greatness to a sinful nation.
Turn, you sinners, and do what is right in his eyes;
who knows whether he may not welcome you and show
    you mercy?

7   I will exalt my God
and rejoice in the King of heaven.

8   Let all men tell of his majesty
and give him thanks in Jerusalem.

9   O Jerusalem, the holy city,
he will punish you for what your sons have done,
but he will again show mercy on the righteous.

10   Thank the good Lord and praise the King of ages.
Your sanctuary[a] shall be rebuilt for you with rejoicing.

[a] *Or* home.

May he give happiness to all your exiles
and cherish all who mourn and your descendants for
    ever.

Your light shall shine brightly to all the ends of the earth. 11
Many nations shall come to you from afar,
from all the corners of the earth to your holy name;
they shall bring gifts in their hands for the King of
    heaven.

In you endless generations shall utter their joy;
the name of the chosen city shall endure for ever and
    ever.

There shall be a curse upon all who speak harshly to you, 12
upon all who destroy you and pull down your walls,
upon all who demolish your towers and burn your
    houses;
but blessings shall be for evermore upon those who hold
    you in reverence.

Come then, be joyful for the righteous,   13
for they shall all be gathered together
and shall praise the eternal Lord.

How happy shall they be who love you and rejoice in 14
    your prosperity,
happy all who grieve for you in your afflictions;
they shall rejoice over you and for ever be witness of
    your joy.

My soul, praise the Lord, the great king,   15
for Jerusalem shall be built as a city for him to dwell in 16
    for ever.

How happy I shall be when the remnant of my descen-
    dants shall see your splendour
and give thanks to the King of heaven.

The gates of Jerusalem shall be built of sapphire and
   emerald,
and all your walls of precious stones.
The towers of Jerusalem shall be built of gold,
their battlements of the finest gold.

17   The streets of Jerusalem shall be paved with garnets and
   jewels of Ophir.

18   The gates of Jerusalem shall sing hymns of joy
and all her houses shall say Alleluia,
praise to the God of Israel!
Blessed by him, they shall bless his holy name for ever
   and ever.'

✻ Tobit's psalm is a fine composition. It is superior to all the
other prayers in the book in content, style and movement.
It plays the same part in the book of Tobit as Judith's song
(chapter 16) in the book of Judith, but it is less derivative and
it also contains less that is specific to Tobit's own case. Its
main theme is that what God has done for Tobit and other
Jews, he can and will also do for Jerusalem the holy city;
the key phrase 'he will punish and he will show mercy' is
echoed from verse 5 to verse 9. The break between the two
halves comes at verse 9, with verse 8 as a link-verse. Some
scholars have attempted to break it down further and
organize it into stanzas; but until we have a Hebrew text
published, the attempt is rash. As to style, though it suffers in
places from the excessive fullness of other parts of the book,
its language is both more vigorous and more poetical than
anything the author produces elsewhere. In fact, its second
half is the literary and theological climax of the book.

Before looking at the text in detail, it may be well to settle
the status of the verses missing from S, namely 6b–10a. They
are present in all other manuscripts except one (also in an
Aramaic fragment from Qumran) and are printed in all

modern editions. Their presence is essential to the understanding of verses 10–12: without them there is nothing for
the 'you' and 'your' (both of them singular) in those verses
to refer to. Moreover it is easy to see how they came to be
lost from S: a scribe's eye jumped from the words 'the King
of ages' in 6*a* to the same words in 10*a*.

2. *up from the great destruction*: cp. Hannah's song in 1 Sam.
2: 6:

> The LORD kills and he gives life,
>
> he sends down to Sheol, he can bring the dead up again.

There is no reference here to resurrection.

3. The semi-colon at the end of the verse is strange. The
sequence of thought seems to be: thank God because, having
scattered you, he has (now) *shown you his greatness.*

6. *When you turn…then he will turn*: the idea is found in
Deut. 30: 2f., but the repetition of the word *turn* seems to be
the author's own.

a sinful nation here clearly means unfaithful Jews; contrast
the righteous in verse 13.

7. *the King of heaven* is a late title of God, found in the Old
Testament only in Dan. 4: 37.

10. *sanctuary* is obviously the right translation, as against
home of the footnote. The rebuilding of the temple forms a
most important part of the author's picture of Jewish restoration after the exile (see 14: 5).

11. *Your light shall shine*: this is how Isaiah 60 begins, a
chapter which has greatly influenced the second half of Tobit's
psalm, as it has also influenced Baruch 4.

14. The text of S is fuller here than N.E.B.'s translation:

> How happy shall they be who love you and *happy*
>   *who* rejoice in your prosperity,
>
> Happy all *men* who grieve for you in *all* your afflictions,
>   they shall rejoice over you and ever be witness of *all*
>   your joy.

16. The *precious stones* of various kinds come from Isa.
54: 11f.

17. *Ophir* in the Old Testament is a regular source of gold and *jewels*. It has not been certainly located but is probably India.

18. *Blessed by him* is a strange translation of a word which only S has, probably wrongly.

for ever is a refrain of this psalm which comes eleven times in the Greek, nine of them at the end of a verse. ✳

POSTSCRIPT AT NINEVEH

14 So ended Tobit's thanksgiving. He died peacefully at the age of a hundred and twelve, and was given honourable 2 burial in Nineveh. He was sixty-two years old when his eyes were injured, and after he recovered his sight he lived in prosperity, doing his acts of charity and never ceasing to praise God and proclaim his majesty.

3 When he was dying he sent for his son Tobias, and gave him these instructions: 'My son, you must take your 4 children and make your escape to Media, for I believe God's word against Nineveh spoken by Nahum. It will all come true; everything will happen to Asshur and Nineveh that was spoken by the prophets of Israel whom God sent. Not a word of it will fall short; everything will be fulfilled when the time comes. It will be safer in Media than in Assyria and Babylon; I know, I am convinced, that all God's words will be fulfilled. It will be so; not one of them will fail. Our countrymen who live in Israel will all be scattered and carried off into captivity out of that good land, and the whole territory of Israel laid waste. Samaria and Jerusalem will lie waste, and for a time the house of God will be in mourning; it will be burnt to the ground.

5 'Then God will have mercy on them again and will

bring them back to the land of Israel. They will rebuild
the house of God, but not as it was before, not until the
time of fulfilment comes. Then they will all return from
their captivity and rebuild Jerusalem gloriously; then
indeed the house will be built in her as the prophets of
Israel foretold. All the nations of the world will be con- 6
verted to the true worship of God; they will abandon their
idols which led them astray into falsehood, and praise the 7
eternal God according to his law. All the Israelites who
survive at that time and are firm in their loyalty to God
will be brought together; they will come to Jerusalem to
take possession of the land of Abraham, and live there
for ever in safety. Those who love God in truth will
rejoice; and sinners and wrong-doers will disappear from
the earth. Now, my children, I give you this command: 8
serve God in truth and do what pleases him. Train your 9
children to do what is right and give alms, to keep God in
mind at all times and praise his name in sincerity with all
their strength.

'And now, my son, you must leave Nineveh. Do not 10
stay here; once you have laid your mother in the grave
with me, do not spend another night within the city
boundaries. For I see that the place is full of wickedness
and shameless dishonesty. My son, think what Nadab did
to Ahikar who brought him up: he forced him to hide in
a living grave. Ahikar survived to see God requite the
dishonour done to him; he came out into the light of day,
but Nadab passed into eternal darkness for his attempt to
kill Ahikar. Because I gave alms, Ahikar escaped from the
fatal trap Nadab set for him, and Nadab fell into the trap
himself and was destroyed. So, my children, see what 11

comes of almsgiving, and see what comes of wickedness
– death. But now my strength is failing.'

Then they laid him on his bed, and he died; and they
12 gave him honourable burial. When his mother died,
Tobias buried her beside his father. He and his wife went
away to Media and settled at Ecbatana with his father-in-
13 law Raguel. He honoured and cared for his wife's parents
in their old age. He buried them at Ecbatana in Media,
and he inherited the estate of Raguel as well as that of his
14 father Tobit. He died greatly respected at the age of one
15 hundred and seventeen. He lived long enough to hear of
the destruction of Nineveh by Ahasuerus king of Media
and to see his prisoners of war brought from there into
Media. So he praised God for all that he had done to the
people of Nineveh and Asshur; and before he died he
rejoiced over the fate of Nineveh and praised the Lord
God who lives for ever and ever.

Amen.

* 1, 2. These first two verses mark the real conclusion of the
story (cp. the end of Judith); the rest of the chapter is a post-
script with some rather strange features.

3. *When he was dying*: what follows is the second 'testament' of Tobit; see note on 4: 5. Although some of its content is the same as the first (verses 8 and 9), most of it is
a prose version of the second part of his psalm.

4. In place of *Nahum*, B gives Jonah, who also foretold the
destruction of Nineveh (3: 4).

Asshur (i.e. Assyria) *and Nineveh* is a curious phrase found
only in Tobit (see verse 15 also) and in *Ahikar*.

when the time comes is a typical phrase of late prophecy,
implying not merely that God will cause certain things to

happen but that he has already fixed the time for them: cp. *for a time* at the end of verse 4 and *the time of fulfilment* in verse 5. Of course all these things had already happened by the time the book of Tobit was written, but the author is doing the same as the author of Daniel, i.e. offering pseudo-prophecy (verse 4) as a guarantee of the true prophecy that follows (verses 6 and 7).

Israel originally meant the northern kingdom (1: 4) with its capital at Samaria, but came later to be used of the whole land. Presumably it is being used in the latter sense here.

scattered: S itself here has an untranslatable text, and N.E.B. rightly follows the other manuscripts of its family.

Jerusalem actually fell to the Babylonians about 125 years after Samaria had fallen to the Assyrians. Many Jews of the southern kingdom were *carried off into captivity* in Babylon. For the temple being *burnt to the ground* see Isa. 64: 11.

5–7. These verses recapitulate in prose the splendid vision of 13: 10–18.

5. After another half-century Babylon was overthrown and some of the Jews allowed to return to Judaea. The *house of God* was rebuilt but it was regarded as much inferior to the old temple. Ezra 3: 12 tells how 'many of the priests...who were old enough to have seen the former house, wept...when they saw the foundation of this house laid'. Consequently it was a lasting hope of the Jews that one day they would *rebuild Jerusalem gloriously*, and *the house* likewise, as *foretold* especially by Ezek. 40–2.

6. The idea that *the nations...will be converted*, which recalls the great prophecy of Isa. 2: 3, is more explicit here than in 13: 11. It contrasts with the general destruction foretold for Gentiles in Judith 16: 17. But in either case it is a characteristic Jewish interpretation of history: that Jewish national sufferings (the exile) and successes (the return) are part of God's grand plan, and so have meaning for the whole of the rest of the world.

7. cp. Isa. 60: 21:

> Your people shall all be righteous
> and shall for ever possess the land.

9. *Train your children to . . . give alms*: we are now back with two of the main concerns of the book of Tobit: family life and almsgiving.

10. The allusive references here to *Ahikar* cannot be understood without knowledge of the full story; see p. 4. The author of the S text was clearly familiar with the story, but the author of the B text was not, because he has got most of the proper names wrong. Even in S, however, the sentence that introduces the Ahikar passage is unconvincing as a transition, which suggests that the passage has been dragged in.

Because I gave alms offers a most improbable sequence of events. The text of S could equally mean: because *he* gave alms (or showed kindness) to *me* (see 1: 22); but more likely the original reference was to the kindness that Ahikar showed to the captain of the guard.

15. *Ahasuerus king of Media* is a puzzle. Nineveh in fact fell about 612 B.C. to Nabopolassar of Babylon and Cyaxares of Media.

rejoiced over the fate of Nineveh: this is the very emotion which the book of Jonah was written to condemn. But fortunately it is not at all typical of Tobit either; see 14: 6 for a more constructive attitude.

✳   ✳   ✳   ✳   ✳   ✳   ✳   ✳   ✳   ✳   ✳   ✳   ✳

JUDITH

✼　✼　✼　✼　✼　✼　✼　✼　✼　✼　✼　✼　✼

GENERAL SUMMARY

The book of Judith is a short historical novel which carries a strong religious message. The exciting tale of a Jewish 'resistance' heroine illustrates the moral that, if the Jews are both faithful and brave, God will save them from their enemies.

The book falls into two parts. The second, and much the finer, part (chapters 8 to the end) tells of the heroic deed itself. Its narrative style is vivid and fast-moving and is lightened by humour and irony. The story itself keeps within the bounds of realism; the heroine has no magical or supernatural powers. The second part also contains (in chapter 8) some advanced thinking about man's relationship to God, which goes some way to make up for the rather bloodthirsty patriotism which Judith shows elsewhere.

The first part is duller in thought and flatter in style. Its aim is to give a historical setting for the heroic deed, but it does so without the economy or the accuracy that a modern reader looks for.

THE ORIGIN OF THE STORY

The story itself is of great dramatic power. Holophernes, an overweening tyrant, invades Judaea at the head of a huge Assyrian army. There goes out to meet him Judith, a young and beautiful widow, unarmed and (except for her maid) alone. Against all the odds she succeeds in killing him without loss of honour and escaping again with his head to her own village of Bethulia.

Heroines are universally popular, and Judith is in the best

Jewish tradition of Jael and Esther. Her nearest modern parallel is Joan of Arc, and in fact the French use many phrases from the book of Judith in their liturgical celebrations of Joan of Arc.

Among the Jews themselves the story of Judith was known in other versions and other settings. Most commonly the story is set in Maccabean times: Jerusalem then replaces the unknown Bethulia, Holophernes becomes a Greek general and (in one case – repudiated by the Rabbis) Judith is a sister of Judas Maccabaeus. All that is obviously later than our book. But another tradition that Judith actually *did* seduce Holophernes looks more likely to be early.

Of our book the earliest part was probably the song of Judith in chapter 16. In origin this song would have been *about* Judith, not 'by' her, and would have been sung in a village procession to celebrate the local heroine. Only secondly, as men's memory faded, would there have been any need to tell the story itself; and the historical introduction would have been added later still.

THE AUTHOR'S TREATMENT OF HIS SUBJECT

The first part of the book is so much weaker that one would like to reserve the title 'author' for the writer of chapters 8 to the end. But apart from anything else, the crucial character of Achior spans the two parts, so one must judge the book as a whole.

The historical setting has few merits. Dramatically it is spoiled by tedious descriptions (especially 1: 2–4, 4: 9–15) and confusions (e.g. 2: 21–7), stylistically by exaggerations (e.g. 1: 16) and empty rhetoric (e.g. 2: 5–13).

Nor does the author set his scene in one period of history, but in a mixture of at least three, covering a span of 400 years. If the references to Assyria are omitted, the 'periods' upon which the author draws are those of Babylonian rule in the sixth century B.C. (Nebuchadnezzar), of the Persians in the fourth (Holophernes) and of the Greek successors of Alexander in the second century, the time of the Maccabees. It is as if an English author writing to-day were to combine in a single work the political background of the Spanish Armada (with echoes even of the Norman Conquest), the military background of the Napoleonic Wars and the ideology of the war against Hitler – all in the language of the Authorized Version.

The contrasting merits of the second part of the book are such as to need little further introduction. But in a later place something more is said of the literary qualities of the books of Judith and Tobit and of their place within the tradition of Western literature (see pp. 127–31).

In style and language, the narrative parts of Judith remind one at every turn of books like Joshua and Judges; the prayers and songs embedded in the book are naturally modelled on the Psalms.

The author's general treatment of his theme is in fact typically Jewish. To him the events mattered less than their interpretation, historical accuracy less than eternal truth. The historical background was important because God is Lord of history; but the details were put in for dramatic rather than historical reasons. The story of Judith was a good story, which he enjoyed telling and knew his readers would enjoy reading. But the object of the book was to carry the same message as the rest of the Old Testament – that 'we are his people' and he is our God.

THEOLOGY

The special theological ideas of the book could be called late rather than advanced. The strong emphasis on the temple and its worship, on purifications, fastings and prayer (private and public), is just like that of the Pharisees as described in the Gospels. But there is no mention of the well-known Pharisaic beliefs in angels and in resurrection.

Typical Jewish notes are, on the one hand, concern for

the humble and poor (9: 11) and, on the other, unrestrained gloating over the fallen enemy (chapter 16) – for to ancient Jewish thought the enemies of God's people are understood as enemies of God himself (cp. the final line of the Song of Deborah, Judg. 5: 31). More interesting, because less typical, is the characterization of Achior, the believing Gentile who is contrasted with the faithless Jewish elder Ozias.

Theologically the finest part of the book is Judith's speech in chapter 8, which does not come short of the book of Job in its depth of faith and insight. True, the book of Judith cannot offer any better explanation of suffering than that of the Prologue of Job or the best that Job's friends can suggest (see note on 8: 18–27). But on the subject of man's general relationship to God, her remarks in verses 12–17 do develop the ideas implied by God's answer to Job.

DATE OF COMPOSITION

In dating the composition of any book, one looks first for the *latest* of its historical references. In the case of Judith, these belong to the age of Antiochus Epiphanes and the Maccabees, roughly mid-second century B.C. For no enemy king before Antiochus had ever 'planned to desecrate thy sanctuary, to pollute the dwelling-place of thy glorious name' (9: 8, cp. 8: 21). This dating fits also the political organization of the Jews as described in Judith, under a high priest and senate (4: 8 etc.). Numerous minor references (see notes on 3: 7, 15: 12f.) confirm that the book cannot have been written before the Maccabean period.

Certain ritual details suggest a date somewhat later than that. The specific mention of the eves of the Sabbath and the new moon (8: 6) and the prohibition upon touching the first-fruits (11: 13) strongly suggest a date after the rise to power of the Pharisees, i.e. early in the first century B.C. At the other end the book must have been written in time to be mentioned about A.D. 90 by Clement of Rome.

There are good general grounds for supposing that Judith was written in Hebrew, even though no Hebrew or Aramaic manuscript survives, even in fragmentary form. The Greek in which our oldest surviving manuscripts are written, though correct and even elegant, has a strong Hebraic colouring. It is Hebraic not just in phrasing but in certain points of grammar which stick out like a sore thumb in Greek; it is scarcely conceivable that they could have been used by anyone writing *original* Greek.

There is in fact no reason to doubt – though it is impossible to prove – that the book was written by an orthodox Pharisee early in the first century B.C.; and if so it would certainly have been written in Hebrew.

THE PLACE OF JUDITH IN THE
BIBLE AND IN THE CHURCH

Nevertheless the Jews did not admit the book of Judith to the strict canon of the Bible when they came to set it up about A.D. 100. It is uncertain why. In theology Judith is much superior to Esther; but Esther was included because it explained the origin of the popular Feast of Purim. Historically Judith is less wild than Daniel. Possibly the authorities resented the suggestion in 11: 14 that Jerusalem was less faithful to the Law than little Bethulia. Alternatively, its obvious association with Maccabean times may have cost it its place: no book which glorified the Maccabees and their successors the Hasmonaean kings was admitted to the canon by their enemies the Pharisees.

The book fared better at the hands of the early Church, chiefly because Judith was taken as a 'type' of the Virgin Mary, and sometimes of the Church itself. Roman Catholics have continued to favour it for the same reasons: along with the rest of the Apocrypha they treat it as canonical, and they use parts of it (especially 13: 18–20 and 15: 9f.) regularly on feasts of the Virgin. Protestants however have given less weight to that possible symbolism, and serious-minded Protestant scholars have also been put off by Judith's lack of truthfulness (see note on 11: 5).

The text of Judith poses few problems. No Hebrew or Aramaic manuscripts have been found, in part or in whole, either among the Dead Sea Scrolls or among later manuscripts, though Jerome had an Aramaic version of Judith as of Tobit (see note on 14: 1 and also p. 12). Our text therefore rests upon the Greek manuscripts of the Septuagint, supported and sometimes corrected by other Greek manuscripts and by the Old Latin and the Syriac translations. All these manuscripts, whose wide variety shows the popularity of the tale, descend from a common Greek ancestor, now lost. Between them we can reconstruct a text which (except in the matter of proper names) is reliable and clear. There are only about five places in the whole book where we are in real doubt as to what was in the author's mind, and none of them is of great importance.

✻   ✻   ✻   ✻   ✻   ✻   ✻   ✻   ✻   ✻   ✻   ✻   ✻

The Assyrian invasion

NEBUCHADNEZZAR'S EASTERN CAMPAIGN

1   IN THE TWELFTH YEAR of the reign of Nebuchadnezzar, who reigned over the Assyrians from his capital, Nineveh, Arphaxad was ruling the Medes from Ecbatana.
2   He it was who encircled Ecbatana with a wall built of hewn stones which were four and a half feet thick and nine feet long.[a] He made the wall a hundred and five feet high and

[a] *In verses 2–4 the measurements are given in cubits in the Greek.*

seventy-five feet thick, and at the city gates he set up 3
towers a hundred and fifty feet high with foundations
ninety feet thick; and he made the gates a hundred and 4
five feet high and sixty feet wide to allow his army to
march out in full force with his infantry in formation.
It was in those days, then, that King Nebuchadnezzar 5
waged war against King Arphaxad in the great plain on
the borders of Ragau. Nebuchadnezzar was opposed by 6
all the inhabitants of the hill-country, by all those who
lived along the Euphrates, the Tigris, and the Hydaspes;
and, on the plain, by Arioch king of Elam; and many tribes
of the Chelodites joined forces with them.

Then Nebuchadnezzar king of Assyria sent a summons 7
to all the inhabitants of Persia, and to all who lived in the
west: the inhabitants of Cilicia and Damascus, Lebanon
and Antilebanon, all who lived near the coast, the peoples 8
in Carmel and Gilead, Upper Galilee, and the great plain
of Esdraelon, all who were in Samaria and its towns, 9
and on the west of Jordan as far as Jerusalem, Betane,
Chelus, Cadesh, and the frontier*a* of Egypt, those who lived
in Tahpanhes, Rameses, and the whole land of Goshen
as far as Tanis and Memphis, and all the inhabitants of 10
Egypt as far as the borders of Ethiopia. But the entire region 11
disregarded the summons of Nebuchadnezzar king of
Assyria and did not join him in the war. They were not
afraid of him, for he seemed to them to stand alone*b* and
unsupported; and they treated his envoys with contempt
and sent them back empty-handed.

This roused Nebuchadnezzar to fury against the whole 12

[*a*] *Literally* river.
[*b*] *One witness reads* to be no more than their equal...

region, and he swore by his throne and his kingdom that he would have his revenge on all the territories of Cilicia, Damascus, and Syria, and put their inhabitants to the sword, along with the Moabites, the Ammonites, and the people in all Judaea and in Egypt as far as the shores of the two seas.

13 In the seventeenth year of his reign he marshalled his forces against King Arphaxad and defeated him in battle,
14 routing his entire army, cavalry, chariots, and all. He occupied his towns; and when he reached Ecbatana he captured its towers, looted its bazaars, and turned its
15 splendour to abject ruin. He caught Arphaxad in the mountains of Ragau, speared him through, and so made an end
16 of him. Then he returned with his spoils to Nineveh, he and his combined forces, an immense host of warriors. There he rested and feasted with his army for four months.

✻ The Jews of the Old Testament, being convinced that their own nation had a special destiny in world history, tended also to believe that incidents in Jewish history had world-wide repercussions. So here, typically, Nebuchadnezzar's invasion of Palestine is represented as part of a grand campaign against the people of the Near and Middle East; and, again typically, the Jews are the only people to offer effective resistance.

But the author is more concerned to paint a convincing picture than to be what we should call accurate. Modern scholars can point to many historical inaccuracies in the first three chapters, of which only the most obvious are worth mentioning. To start with the first verse of the book, Nineveh was indeed capital of the Assyrian Empire, but it had been destroyed in 612 B.C. by the father of Nebuchadnezzar. Nebuchadnezzar himself (605–562 B.C.) ruled a Babylonian Empire from his capital Babylon, to which he carried off the

Jews into exile – yet in Judith (4: 3) the Jews have already *returned* from exile. Ecbatana was indeed the capital of the Medes, but it was captured, not by Nebuchadnezzar (1: 14), but in 550 B.C. by Cyrus king of Persia. Arphaxad is not mentioned in any other source.

For these and many other reasons almost all modern scholars are agreed that the book of Judith cannot be taken seriously as a work of history. They see it rather as a historical novel with a moral and religious message. Instead therefore of pointing out e.g. that the walls of Ecbatana are given dimensions in verses 2–4 which are both excessive and disproportionate, they observe that the author is drawing a contrast between the capital city of Ecbatana which fell to Nebuchadnezzar and the Jewish village of Bethulia which resisted him successfully.

The author's geography is no more accurate than his history: for example the Hydaspes of verse 6 is in fact a famous Indian river. But again the details need not concern us: the point being made is that the whole of what we call the Near and Middle East was involved in the war.

7–12. Nebuchadnezzar then decided to strengthen his forces by summoning contingents from his vassals and allies in the west and south. The author gives two lists of these, of which that in verse 12 is simpler to follow than that in verses 7–10. Each list moves from north to south: in modern terms, the extreme south of Turkey (Cilicia), then Syria (*Damascus ...the coast* of verse 7), then Israel and Jordan (*Upper Galilee...the frontier of Egypt* of verses 8 and 9, *the Moabites* and *the Ammonites* of verse 12), and finally Egypt itself (*Tahpanhes...Goshen* of verse 10) down to its southern border of Ethiopia (verse 10; *the two seas* of verse 12 is obscure).

11. The words *alone and unsupported* translate the Greek 'as one man'. That phrase is found only here and in 6: 3 where N.E.B. translates more literally. The two passages reinforce one another, and the reading in the footnote here need not be considered.

13. It took Nebuchadnezzar five years, without his western vassals, to defeat Arphaxad. After an unusually long victory celebration, he was ready to turn his attention west. *

HOLOPHERNES PREPARES TO MOVE WEST

2 In the eighteenth year, on the twenty-second day of the first month, a proposal was made in the palace of Nebuchadnezzar king of Assyria to carry out his threat of

2 vengeance on the whole region. Assembling all his officers and nobles, the king laid before them his personal decision about the region and declared his intention of putting an

3 end to its disaffection. They resolved that everyone who had not obeyed his summons should be put to death.

4 When his plans were completed,[a] Nebuchadnezzar king of Assyria summoned Holophernes, his commander-in-chief, who was second only to himself, and said to him,

5 'This is the decree of the Great King, lord of all the earth: Directly you leave my presence, you are to take under your command an army of seasoned troops, a hundred and twenty thousand infantry with a force of twelve thousand

6 cavalry, and march out against all the peoples of the west

7 who have dared to disobey my command. Tell them to have ready their offering of earth and water, for I am coming to vent my wrath on them. Their whole land will be smothered by my army, and I will give them up to be

8 plundered by my troops. Their dead will fill the valleys, and every stream and river will be choked with corpses;

9 and I will send them into captivity to the ends of the

10 whole earth. Now go and occupy all their territory for me. If they surrender to you, hold them for me until the time

[a] *Or* When he had finished stating his purpose...

comes to punish them. But show no mercy to those who 11
resist; let them be slaughtered and plundered throughout
the whole region. By my life and my royal power I swear: 12
I have spoken and I will be as good as my word. As for 13
you, do not disobey a single one of my orders, but see that
you carry them out exactly as I your sovereign have commanded you. Do this without delay.'

After leaving his sovereign's presence, Holophernes 14
assembled all the marshals, generals, and officers of the
Assyrian army, and mustered picked men, as the king had 15
commanded, a hundred and twenty thousand infantry
and twelve thousand mounted archers, drawing them up 16
in battle order. He took an immense number of camels, 17
asses, and mules for their baggage, innumerable sheep,
oxen, and goats for provisions, and ample rations for every 18
man, as well as a great quantity of gold and silver from the
royal palace. Then he set out with all his army to go ahead 19
of King Nebuchadnezzar and to overrun the entire region
to the west with chariots, cavalry, and picked infantry.
Along with them went a motley host like a swarm of 20
locusts, countless as the dust of the earth.

* 1. Again the air of historicity given by the dating is
deceptive.

4. The name of Holophernes is obviously Persian and thus
belongs to the centuries after the fall of the Babylonian
Empire. There is in fact a whole layer of references to the
Persian period (about 550–330 B.C.) in Judith, culminating
in the specific mention of the Medes and Persians as enemies
of the Jews in 16: 10. Holophernes demands earth and water
(2: 7), the Persian token of submission, he appoints satraps
(5: 2, N.E.B. 'governors') and he carries a Persian sword

(Revised Version, 'scimitar') in 16: 9. Moreover Bagoas, the name of the 'eunuch in charge of all his affairs' (12: 11), is the Persian word for a eunuch. Indeed in the rest of the book, for all the continued references to Nebuchadnezzar, the colour of the invading army is mainly Persian.

Specifically, we know from Greek historians of two men named Holophernes. One of them was a Cappadocian prince who took part in the campaign against Egypt by the Persian king Artaxerxes III in 341 B.C. Likewise, of those known to have borne the name of Bagoas the obvious candidate is one who took part in that same campaign as a member of the royal household.

5. The cheap rhetoric with which Nebuchadnezzar instructs Holophernes (especially in verses 7–11) is part of the stock portrait of the heathen tyrant. ✻

HOLOPHERNES APPROACHES JUDAEA

21 From Nineveh they marched for three days towards the plain of Bectileth, and encamped beside Bectileth near
22 the mountain north of Upper Cilicia. From there, Holophernes advanced into the hill-country with his whole
23 army, infantry, cavalry, and chariots. He devastated Put and Lud, and plundered all the people of Rassis, and the Ishmaelites on the edge of the desert south of the land of
24 the Cheleans. Then he followed[a] the Euphrates and traversed Mesopotamia, destroying all the fortified towns
25 along the river Abron as far as the sea. He occupied the territory of Cilicia and cut down all who resisted him. Then he came south to the borders of Japheth fronting
26 Arabia. He surrounded the Midianites, burnt their en-
27 campments, and plundered their sheepfolds. At the time of wheat harvest he went down to the plain of Damascus,

[a] *Or* crossed.

burnt their crops, exterminated their flocks and herds, sacked their towns, laid waste their fields, and put all their young men to the sword. Fear and dread of him fell on 28 all the inhabitants of the coast at Tyre and Sidon, of Sur and Okina, and of Jemnaan; the people of Azotus and Ascalon were terrified of him.

They sent envoys to sue for peace, who said: 'We are **3** 1,2 servants of the Great King Nebuchadnezzar, we lie prostrate before you; do with us as you please. Our buildings, 3 our territory, our wheat fields, our flocks and herds and every sheepfold in our encampments, all are yours to do with as you wish. Our towns and their inhabitants are 4 subject to you; come and deal with them as you think fit.'

When the envoys came to Holophernes with this 5 message, he went down to the coast with his army and 6 garrisoned all the fortified towns, taking from them picked men as auxiliaries. Both there and in all the surrounding 7 country he was welcomed with garlands, dancing, and tambourines. He demolished all their sanctuaries[a] and cut 8 down their sacred groves, for he had been commissioned to destroy all the gods of the land, so that Nebuchadnezzar alone should be worshipped by every nation and invoked as a god by men of every tribe and tongue.

Holophernes then advanced towards Esdraelon, near 9 Dothan, which faces the great ridge of Judaea, and en- 10 camped between Geba and Scythopolis, where he remained for a whole month to collect supplies for his army.

* 2: 21-6. The description of Holophernes' route is badly confused. The sequence *Cilicia* (verse 21)–*Mesopotamia*

[a] *So one Vs.; Gk.* borders.

(verse 24)–*Cilicia* (verse 25) cannot be right. We might seek to cure it by supposing the text to be disordered, but it is more likely that the author neither knew nor cared about geography. Most of the places and people mentioned are either unidentifiable (*Bectileth*, *Rassis*, *the Cheleans*, *Abron*) or imprecisely defined (*the Ishmaelites*, *Japheth*, *Arabia*, *the Midianites*) or, if identified, are too far off (*Put* and *Lud* = Pisidia and Lydia).

27 f. Eventually the author gets down to places with which he is more familiar: *Damascus* and the coastal towns of Phoenicia (*Tyre*, *Sidon* and *Okina*–Acco–Acre; *Sur* is probably an erroneous repetition of *Tyre*) and of Philistia, beginning with *Jemnaan*–Jamnia.

3: 7. The reaction of the Phoenician cities is characteristically different from that of the Jews. Of the three symbols of welcome, *dancing and tambourines* are familiar from the story of Jephthah in Judg. 11 whose daughter came to meet him with them. But the use of crowns in celebration (N.E.B. *garlands*) belongs to the hellenistic (Greek) period (Wisd. of Sol. 2: 8, cp. Judith 15: 13).

8. Holophernes' reaction is unexpected – not the garrisoning and recruitment but the religious measures. Here for the first time religion is mentioned in Judith, and the mention is historically strange. For neither Persian nor Babylonian nor Assyrian kings demanded to be worshipped as gods: the hellenistic kings were the first to do that. True, Nebuchadnezzar in Dan. 3 is said to have demanded divine honours; but the author of Daniel was certainly using the name of Nebuchadnezzar to stand for the Greek king Antiochus Epiphanes (175–163 B.C.), and we shall not go wrong if we see this verse in Judith and others like it (6: 2, 9: 8) as referring to the policy of Antiochus.

The N.E.B.'s *sanctuaries* is bold and correct. It is found only in the Syriac translation. The sanctuaries and *sacred groves* are in the Old Testament called hill-shrines and sacred poles.

9f. At last Holophernes approaches Judaea itself. The Plain

80

of *Esdraelon*, known elsewhere in the Bible as the Valley of Jezreel, was strategically vital. *Dothan* can scarcely be said to face *the great ridge of Judaea* so perhaps there is something wrong with the text. *Geba* is unidentified. *Scythopolis* is the Greek name for Bethshan, the town at the eastern end of Esdraelon. ✳

THE JEWS PREPARE TO RESIST

When the Israelites who lived in Judaea heard of all that **4** had been done to the nations by Holophernes, the com- mander-in-chief of Nebuchadnezzar king of Assyria, and how he had plundered and totally destroyed all their temples, they were terrified at his approach. They were in **2** great alarm for Jerusalem and for the temple of the Lord their God. For they had just returned from captivity, and **3** it was only recently that the people had been re-united in Judaea, and the sacred vessels, the temple, and the altar sanctified after their profanation. So they sent out a warn- **4** ing to the whole of Samaria, Cona, Beth-horon, Belmain and Jericho, Choba and Aesora and the valley of Salem, and occupied the tops of all the high hills. They fortified **5** the villages on them and laid up stores of food in prepara- tion for war; for their fields had just been harvested. Joa- **6** kim, who was high priest in Jerusalem at the time, wrote to the people of Bethulia and Bethomesthaim, which is opposite Esdraelon facing the plain near Dothan. He **7** ordered them to occupy the passes into the hill-country, because they controlled access to Judaea, and it was easy to hold up an advancing army, for the approach was only wide enough for two men. The Israelites obeyed the orders **8** of the high priest Joakim and the senate of all Israel in Jerusalem. Fervently they sent up a cry to God, every man **9**

of Israel, and fervently they humbled themselves before
10 him. They put on sackcloth – they themselves, their wives,
their children, their livestock, and every resident foreigner,
11 hired labourer, and slave – and all the inhabitants of
Jerusalem, men, women, and children, prostrated themselves in front of the sanctuary, and, with ashes on their
heads, spread out their sackcloth before the Lord. They
12 draped the altar in sackcloth, and with one voice they
earnestly implored the God of Israel not to allow their
children to be captured, their wives carried off, their
ancestral cities destroyed, and the temple profaned and
13 dishonoured, to the delight of the heathen. The Lord
heard their prayer and pitied their distress.

For many days the whole population of Judaea and
Jerusalem fasted before the sanctuary of the Lord Almighty.
14 Joakim the high priest and the priests who stood in the
presence of the Lord, and all who served in the temple,
wore sackcloth when they offered the regular burnt-
offering and the votive and freewill offerings of the people;
15 and with ashes on their turbans they cried aloud to the
Lord to look favourably on the whole house of Israel.

* The scene now shifts to the Jewish side, first to Jerusalem.
The author again tries to give us some historical background,
and again succeeds only in confusing us.

3. The return from the exile began about 538 B.C. It is
true that successive groups of Jews went on returning until
about 400 B.C., but even that is too far in the past to be recent
if Holophernes is to be put at 341 B.C. However, as we have
seen, it is a mistake to expect that kind of accuracy from the
author.

4. A second surprise is the mention of *Samaria*. When the

Jews did return from the exile, Samaria was much too hostile to be 'warned' in this sort of way, and remained hostile until it was captured by the Jews about 108 B.C. It is possible that here (as in 1 Macc. 11: 28) the mention of Samaria has been added by a later hand in order to give the impression that it was now under Jewish domination. *Beth-horon* is another of the villages that commands an ascent up to the 'great ridge': it was the scene of a famous victory of Judas Maccabaeus (1 Macc. 3: 16–24), but has not been precisely identified. *Cona* and *Belmain...Salem* are all unknown except *Jericho*, which is obviously out of place.

6. A third problem is presented by *Joakim*. There was a priest of that name in Persian times (1 Esdras 5: 5), but no priest or even high priest in those days wielded such authority as we see Joakim wield here. Indeed it was not till Maccabean times (152 B.C.) that a high priest was also a military leader (Jonathan in 1 Macc. 10: 20). Further evidence of Maccabean times is provided by mention in verse 8 of the *senate* as an official body supporting the high priest (cp. 2 Macc. 11: 27). Moreover the reference in verse 3 to *profanation* of the temple is much more appropriate to the second than to the sixth century B.C.

When these points are taken together, they leave no doubt that the book of Judith was written in or after the Maccabean period.

It is strange that *Bethulia*, the scene of the action of the rest of the book, also cannot be identified. The most likely interpretation is that the word means 'house of God' (cp. Bethel), and thus can stand for any place which is shown as faithful to God. *Bethomesthaim* is also unknown.

The Jews made not only military but also religious preparations to repel the enemy. Everything was done strictly in accordance with traditional rituals.

9. The repetition of *fervently* (Greek 'with great fervour') is erroneous; on the second occasion the word 'fervour' has probably ousted a word meaning 'fasting', which however

is correctly preserved in a number of Greek and Latin manuscripts.

10. For putting *sackcloth* on their *livestock* cp. the repentance of the Ninevites in Jonah 3: 7.

11. The only unusual feature in the description is the report that *they draped the altar in sackcloth*. This custom is not otherwise known, and the words used perhaps arise from a mistaken comment on the preceding phrase. *

ACHIOR WARNS HOLOPHERNES

5 When it was reported to Holophernes, the Assyrian commander-in-chief, that the Israelites had prepared for war, and that they had closed the passes in the hill-country,
2 fortified all the heights, and dug pitfalls in the plains, he was furious. He summoned all the rulers of Moab, the Ammonite commanders, and all the governors of the
3 coastal region, and said to them, 'Tell me, you Canaanites, what nation is this that lives in the hill-country? What towns do they inhabit? How big is their army? What gives them their power and strength? Who is the king that
4 commands their forces? Why are they the only people of the west who have refused to come and meet me?'
5   Then Achior, the leader of all the Ammonites, said to him, 'My lord, if you will allow your servant to speak, I will tell you the truth about this nation that lives in the
6 hill-country near here; and no lie shall pass my lips. They
7 are descended from the Chaldaeans; and at one time they settled in Mesopotamia, because they refused to worship
8 the gods their fathers had worshipped in Chaldaea. They abandoned the ways of their ancestors and worshipped the God of Heaven, the god whom they now acknowledged. When the Chaldaeans drove them out from the

presence of their gods, they fled to Mesopotamia, where
they lived for a long time. Then their god told them to 9
leave their new home and go on to Canaan. They settled
there and acquired great wealth in gold, silver, and
livestock.

'Because of a famine which spread over the whole of 10
Canaan, they went down to Egypt and lived there as long
as they were supplied with food. While in Egypt, they
multiplied so greatly that their numbers could not be
reckoned, and the king of Egypt turned against them. He 11
exploited them by setting them to hard labour making
bricks, and he reduced them to abject slavery. They cried 12
out to their god, and he inflicted incurable plagues on the
whole of Egypt. So the Egyptians turned them out; and 13
their god dried up the Red Sea for them and led them on to 14
Sinai and Cadesh-barnea. Then they drove out all the
inhabitants of the wilderness and settled in the land of 15
the Amorites, and they destroyed all the people of Heshbon
by force of arms. After that they crossed the Jordan and
occupied all the hill-country, driving out the Canaanites, 16
the Perizzites, the Jebusites, the Shechemites, and all the
Girgashites. There they settled for a long time.

'As long as they did not sin against their god, they 17
prospered; for theirs is a god who hates wickedness. But 18
when they left the path he had laid down for them, they
suffered heavy losses in many wars and were carried captive to a foreign country; the temple of their god was
razed to the ground, and their towns were occupied by
their enemies. But now that they have returned to their 19
god, they have come back from the places where they
had been dispersed, and have taken possession of Jerusa-

lem, where their sanctuary is, and have settled in the hill-country, because it was uninhabited.

20 'Now, my lord and master, if these people are guilty of an error and are sinning against their god, and if we find out that they have committed this offence, then we may
21 go and make war on them. But if these people have committed no wickedness, leave them alone, my lord, for fear the god they serve should protect them and we become
22 the laughing-stock of the world.' When Achior stopped speaking there were protests from all those who stood round the tent. Holophernes' officers and all the people from the coastal region and from Moab demanded that
23 Achior should be cut to pieces. 'We are not going to be afraid of the Israelites,' they said, 'a people quite incapable
24 of putting an effective army in the field. Let us go ahead, Lord Holophernes; your great army will swallow them whole.'

* 1–2. Holophernes is puzzled by the Jewish preparation for resistance. He summons the loyal vassals, who between them occupy almost all the territory round Judaea. (We had not been told that the Moabites and Ammonites had yielded like the Phoenicians and Philistines, any more than we had been told of the *pitfalls*.)

3. His questions to them about the Jews have scornful overtones. But the dramatic situation is building up in a way that the Jews loved. First, it is their sworn enemy (verse 4, cp. 1 Macc. 1: 41–50) who emphasizes their uniqueness.

5. Secondly, in answer to Holophernes there enters another favourite character of Jewish literature, the sympathetic Gentile. *Achior* is in the same tradition as Balaam the seer (Numbers 22), Rahab the Canaanite (Joshua 2–6) and the Ethiopian eunuch (Acts 8).

The account he gives of Jewish history differs in certain respects from that in the historical books of the Old Testament.

6–7. The version of the story of Abraham is the later version, more like that of Acts 7 than of Genesis 11–12. *descended from the Chaldaeans* because Abraham came from Ur of the Chaldees.

8. *the God of Heaven* is a phrase that came into use after the exile. *now* means 'from then on'. The sequence of thought would be clearer if there were brackets round the passage between the two mentions of *Mesopotamia* (i.e. Harran) in verses 7 and 8.

15. *Heshbon* is the Amorite capital.

16. The list of the tribes which *occupied* Judaea before the Jews is shorter than the usual list (e.g. in Joshua 9), but it also contains the addition of *the Shechemites*. Shechem is added here possibly out of hostility to the Samaritan community whose centre it was.

17–18. The Old Testament prophets would have been quick to reject the view that the Jews remained faithful to *the path*, i.e. the Law, until near the time of the exile.

20. The slightly odd reference to finding out about an *offence* is taken up later in the story by Judith herself (11: 17) where it plays an integral part in her plan.

21. The motif of the *laughing-stock* echoes the similar fear of the Jews (4: 12): both parties were afraid of loss of face, though the Gentiles could not understand any weapon but force of arms (verse 23). ✳

HOLOPHERNES DISMISSES ACHIOR
WHO JOINS THE JEWS

When the hubbub among the men around the council **6** had subsided, Holophernes, the Assyrian commander-in-chief, said to Achior and all the Ammonites, in the presence of the assembled foreigners: 'And who are you, 2

Achior, you and your Ammonite mercenaries, to play the prophet among us as you have done today, telling us not to make war against the people of Israel because their god will protect them? What god is there but Nebuchadnezzar? 3 He will exert his power and wipe them off the face of the earth; and their god will not rescue them. We who serve Nebuchadnezzar will strike them all down as if they were only one man. They will not be able to stand up to the 4 weight of our cavalry; we shall overwhelm them. Their mountains will be drenched with blood, and their plains filled with their dead. They cannot stand their ground against us; they will be completely wiped out. This is the decree of King Nebuchadnezzar, lord of the whole earth. He has spoken; and what he has said will be made 5 good. As for you, Achior, you Ammonite mercenary, the words you have spoken today are treason, so from today you shall not see my face again until I have taken vengeance 6 on this brood of runaways from Egypt. But when I come back, the warriors of my bodyguard will run you through 7 and add you to their victims. My men are going to take you away now to the hill-country and leave you in one 8 of the towns in the passes. You will not die until you share 9 their fate. If you are so confident that they will not fall into our hands, you need not look downcast. I have spoken; and nothing that I have said will fail to come true.'

10   Then Holophernes ordered his men, who were standing by in his tent, to seize Achior, take him off to Bethulia, 11 and hand him over to the Israelites. So they seized him and took him outside the camp to the plain, and from there into the hill-country, until they arrived at the springs 12 below Bethulia. When the men of the town saw them,

they picked up their weapons and came out of the town to the top of the hill; then all the slingers pelted the enemy with stones to prevent them from coming up. But they 13 slipped through under cover of the hill, tied Achior up and left him lying at the foot of it, and went back to their master. When the Israelites came down from the town and 14 found him there, they untied him and took him into Bethulia, where they brought him before the town magistrates then in office, Ozias son of Mica, of the tribe of 15 Simeon, and Chabris son of Gothoniel, and Charmis son of Melchiel. The magistrates summoned all the elders of 16 the town; and all the young men and women came running to the assembly. When Achior had been brought before the people, Ozias asked him what had happened. He 17 answered by telling them all that had taken place in Holophernes' council, what he himself had said in the presence of the Assyrian commanders, and how Holophernes had boasted of what he would do to Israel. Then 18 the people prostrated themselves in worship and cried out to God: 'O Lord, God of heaven, mark their arrogance; 19 pity our people in their humiliation; show favour this day to those who are thy own.' Then they reassured Achior 20 and commended him warmly. Ozias took him from the 21 assembly to his own house, and gave a feast for the elders; and all that night they invoked the help of the God of Israel.

* In reply to Achior, Holophernes resorts to his characteristic bluster, directed indiscriminately against Achior and the Jews. The plan he devises for dealing with Achior is not very plausible, nor is Achior's journey to Bethulia really necessary to the story in its present form.

6. The free N.E.B. translation *warriors of my bodyguard*

conceals a textual uncertainty: the Greek, according to the preferable text, means 'the sword of my army and the spear of my servants'.

The story of Achior's arrival in Bethulia is vividly told, especially verses 12–14 and 16–18: the author is now at last getting into his stride. We also meet now the elder Ozias, the weak and wavering Jew who serves as a foil to the faithful Gentile Achior.

In another Jewish version of the story Achior, instead of being *commended* by the people of Bethulia, was disbelieved and hung up alive. Judith was also mistrusted, both on going out and on returning, until she showed Achior the head of Holophernes and he recognized it. That more dramatic version also gave Achior a more essential role, and one could wish it had been followed here. ✳

HOLOPHERNES BESIEGES BETHULIA

7 The next day Holophernes ordered his whole army and all his allies to strike camp and march on Bethulia, seize the passes into the hill-country, and make war on the
2 Israelites. So the whole force set out that day, an army of a hundred and seventy thousand infantry and twelve thousand cavalry, not counting the baggage train of the
3 infantry, an immense host. They encamped in the valley near Bethulia, beside the spring; and their camp extended in breadth towards Dothan as far as Belbaim, and in length from Bethulia to Cyamon which faces Esdraelon.
4 When the Israelites saw their numbers they said to each other in great alarm, 'These men will strip the whole country bare; the high mountains, the valleys, and the
5 hills will never be able to bear the burden of them.' Then each man stood to arms; and they lit the beacons on the towers and remained on guard all that night.

On the following day Holophernes led out all his cavalry 6
in full view of the Israelites in Bethulia, and reconnoitred 7
the approaches to their town. He inspected the springs
and seized them; and when he had stationed detachments
of soldiers there, he returned to his army. Then all the rulers 8
of the Edomites and all the leaders of Moab and the commanders from the coastal region came to him and said,
'Listen to our advice, Lord Holophernes, and save your 9
army from a crushing defeat. These Israelites do not trust 10
in their spears but in the height of the mountains where
they live; for it is no easy task to get up to the tops of these
mountains of theirs. Now, Lord Holophernes, avoid 11
fighting a pitched battle with them, and you will not lose
a single man. Remain in your camp and keep your men in 12
their quarters; but let your servants take possession of the
spring at the foot of the hill, for that is where all the 13
townspeople of Bethulia get their water. When they are
dying of thirst they will surrender the town. Meanwhile,
we and all our people will go up to the tops of the neighbouring hills and camp there to see that not a man gets
away from the town. They and their wives and children 14
will waste away with famine; and before the sword
reaches them, their streets will be strewn with their
corpses. So you will make them pay heavily for rebelling 15
against you, instead of receiving you peaceably.' Holo- 16
phernes and all his staff approved this plan; and he gave
orders that it should be carried out. The Moabite force 17
moved forward in company with five thousand Assyrians
and encamped in the valley, where they seized the springs
which were the Israelites' water-supply. Then the Edomites 18
and Ammonites went up and encamped in the hill-country

opposite Dothan, and sent some of their number south-east[a] in the direction of Egrebel, which is near Chus on the Mochmur ravine. The rest of the Assyrian army encamped on the plain. They filled the entire country-side, their tents and baggage train forming an immense encampment, for they were a vast host.

✷ The military narrative becomes somewhat more convincing as the action moves nearer home, though there are still a few loose ends.

2. Holophernes' army had increased by 50,000 since 2: 15, presumably because of contingents from Phoenicia and Moab etc.

3. It is essential to the story that Bethulia's water supply, like that of many another place in Palestine, came from *the spring* or springs in the valley below the town; but the casual mention of it here anticipates and rather spoils the more explicit references in verses 12 and 17 (where 5,000 men are grossly excessive for the task in hand). *Belbaim* and *Cyamon* are unidentified.

13. The way in which the Edomite and Moabite forces *go up to the tops of the neighbouring hills* seems to contradict what was said in verse 10, and indeed to make nonsense of the whole military topography; but perhaps they should be regarded as lightly armed local troops, quite distinct from the heavy and fully-equipped Assyrian army which remained in the plain.

18. *Egrebel*, *Chus* and *Mochmur* have not been certainly identified. ✷

DEJECTION IN BETHULIA

19 Then the Israelites cried out to the Lord their God. Their courage failed, because all their enemies had
20 surrounded them and there was no way of escape. The

[a] *Or* south and east.

whole Assyrian army, infantry, cavalry, and chariots, kept them blockaded for thirty-four days. The citizens of Bethulia came to the end of their household supplies of water. The cisterns too were running dry; drinking-water 21 was so strictly rationed that there was never a day when their needs were satisfied. The children were lifeless, the 22 women and young men faint with thirst. They collapsed in the streets and gateways from sheer exhaustion.

Then all the people, young men, women, and children, 23 gathered round Ozias and the magistrates of the town, shouting loudly. In the presence of the elders they said: 'May God judge between us, for you have done us a great 24 wrong in not coming to terms with the Assyrians. Now 25 we have no one to help us. God has sold us into their power; they will find us dead of thirst, and the ground strewn with our corpses. Surrender to them; let Holo- 26 phernes' people and his army sack the town. It is better for 27 us to be taken prisoner; for even as slaves we shall still be alive, and shall not have to watch our babies dying before our eyes, and our wives and children at their last gasp. We call heaven and earth to witness, we call our God, 28 the Lord of our fathers, to witness against you – the God who is punishing us for our sins and for the sins of our fathers. We pray that he may not let our forebodings come true this day.' Then the whole assembly broke into 29 loud lamentation and cried to the Lord God. Ozias said to 30 them, 'Courage, my friends! Let us hold out for five more days; by that time the Lord our God may show us his mercy again. Surely he will not finally desert us. But if 31 by the end of that time no help has reached us, then I will do what you ask.' Then he dismissed the men to their 32 various posts; and they went off to the walls and towers of the town. The women and children he sent indoors. Throughout the town there was deep dejection.

✻ The Jewish reaction to the seizure of their water supply is again vividly and convincingly portrayed.

20. The figure of *thirty-four days* is variously given in the manuscripts, but precision is irrelevant.

21. *cisterns* were public water-tanks hewn out of solid rock.

27. After *prisoner* the manuscripts all continue with the words 'than to die of thirst' which are inadvertently omitted by N.E.B.

28. The N.E.B. translation of the end of this verse makes poor sense and is difficult to get out of the Greek. Fortunately there is equally good manuscript authority for a different text which when translated would run: '*We call heaven and earth to witness*... that you *should* take this step (i.e. surrender the village) *this day*.' This fits much better with Ozias' reply.

30. Ozias asks for *five days* where the elders of Jabesh-gilead, in somewhat similar circumstances, asked for seven (1 Sam. 11: 3). He is hoping not for reinforcements but for rain, as 8: 31 shows. His grey weakness and the people's black despair throw into relief the brightly burning faith of Judith. ✻

Judith kills Holophernes

JUDITH IS INTRODUCED

8 News of what was happening reached Judith, daughter of Merari, son of Ox, son of Joseph, son of Oziel, son of Helkias, son of Elias, son of Chelkias, son of Eliab, son of Nathanael, son of Salamiel, son of Sarasadae, son of 2 Israel. Her husband Manasses, who belonged to her own

tribe and clan, had died at the time of barley harvest. While 3
he was out in the fields supervising the binding of the
sheaves, he got sunstroke, took to his bed, and died in
Bethulia his native town; and they buried him beside his
ancestors in the field between Dothan and Balamon. For 4
three years and four months Judith had lived at home as
a widow; she had a shelter erected on the roof of her house; 5
she put on sackcloth and always wore mourning. After 6
she became a widow she fasted every day except sabbath
eve, the sabbath itself, the eve of the new moon, the new
moon, and the Israelite feasts and days of public rejoicing.
She was a very beautiful and attractive woman. Her hus- 7
band Manasses had left her gold and silver, male and
female slaves, livestock and land, and she lived on her
estate. No one spoke ill of her, for she was a very devout 8
woman.

✻ Now at last with the introduction of the heroine the
narrative gets into full stride, and from here on it hardly falters.

1. The only other person named Judith in the Bible is a wife
of Esau in Genesis 26: 34. Probably the author uses the name
here because of its meaning: 'Judith' means 'Jewess' and this
Judith is the Jewess par excellence (cp. Bethulia, p. 83). Her
genealogy is the longest of any woman in the Bible. It is surprising that Simeon is not mentioned in it, in view of the stress
she lays on him in the next chapter; but he is implied by the
mention of *Salamiel, son of Sarasadae*, known from Num. 1: 6
as a leading member of the tribe of Simeon.

4. Judith is portrayed as scrupulously pious. Her piety is
shown first by her married life. She married a husband from
her own tribe – a strong pious motif in Tobit – and when he
died she remained unmarried, like Anna the 'prophetess' of
Luke 2: 36f. (or Dido in Virgil's *Aeneid* 4, for on this matter

Roman and Jewish piety agreed). Secondly she followed all the prescribed rituals, especially by fasting, i.e. taking no food during the hours of daylight (cp. 12: 9). Moreover she adhered to the later custom of interrupting her fast not only on sabbaths and new-moons but also on their *eves*. The *feasts* are the three great feasts of the Passover, Pentecost and Tabernacles. Finally her devout way of life is shown by her building a shelter, or retreat for meditation, on the roof of her house – what the Old Testament elsewhere calls a 'roof-chamber'.

7. Judith is portrayed also as rich – which might indeed have been inferred from the fact that Manasses was buried in a cave (16: 23) on his own property. That Judith should be both rich and pious runs counter to the usual biblical tradition whereby 'poor' is almost a synonym for 'righteous'. Perhaps this arises from dramatic considerations: as in Greek tragedy, it would have seemed strange for a poor woman to mix on equal terms with the other *dramatis personae*. Alternatively the author may be influenced by the (less specifically Jewish) picture of the 'capable wife' in Prov. 31; cp. the reference to Judith's wisdom in 8: 29. ✻

JUDITH REJECTS SURRENDER

9 When Judith heard of the shameful attack which the people had made upon Ozias the magistrate, because they were demoralized by the shortage of water, and how he had sworn to surrender the town to the Assyrians after 10 five days, she sent her maid who had charge of all her property to ask Ozias, Chabris, and Charmis, the elders of 11 the town, to come and see her. When they arrived she said to them: 'Listen to me, magistrates of Bethulia. You had no right to speak as you did to the people today, and to bind yourselves by oath before God to surrender the town to our enemies if the Lord sends no relief within so 12 many days. Who are you to test God at a time like this,

and openly set yourselves above him? You are putting the 13
Lord Almighty to the proof. You will never understand!
You cannot plumb the depths of the human heart or under- 14
stand the way a man's mind works; how then can you
fathom man's Maker? How can you know God's mind,
and grasp his thought? No, my friends, do not rouse the
anger of the Lord our God. For even if he does not choose 15
to help us within the five days, he is free to come to our
rescue at any time he pleases, or equally to let us be destroyed by our enemies. It is not for you to impose con- 16
ditions on the Lord our God; God will not yield to threats
or be bargained with like a mere man. So we must wait 17
for him to deliver us, and in the mean time appeal to him
for help. If he sees fit he will hear us.

'There is not one of our tribes or clans, districts or towns, 18
that worships man-made gods today, or has done so
within living memory. This did happen in days gone by,
and that was why our ancestors were abandoned to their 19
enemies to be slaughtered and pillaged, and great was
their downfall. But we acknowledge no god but the Lord, 20
and so we are confident that he will not spurn us or any
of our race. For our capture will mean the loss of all 21
Judaea, and our temple will be looted; and God will hold
us responsible for its desecration. The slaughter and 22
deportation of our fellow-countrymen, and the laying
waste of the land we inherited, will bring his judgement
upon us wherever we become slaves among the Gentiles.
Our masters will regard us with disgust and contempt.
There will be no happy ending to our servitude, no return 23
to favour; the Lord our God will use it to dishonour us.

'So then, my friends, let us set an example to our fellow- 24

countrymen; for their lives depend on us, and the fate of
25 the sanctuary, the temple, and the altar rests with us. We
have every reason to give thanks to the Lord our God; he
26 is putting us to the test as he did our ancestors. Remember
how he dealt with Abraham and how he tested Isaac, and
what happened to Jacob in Syrian Mesopotamia when he
27 was working as a shepherd for his uncle Laban. He is not
subjecting us to the fiery ordeal by which he tested their
loyalty, or taking vengeance on us: it is for discipline that
the Lord scourges his worshippers.'

28   Ozias replied, 'You are quite right; everything you say
29 is true, and no one can deny it. This is not the first time that
you have given proof of your wisdom. Throughout your
life we have all recognized your good sense and the sound-
30 ness of your judgement. But the people were desperate
with thirst and compelled us to make this promise and to
31 pledge ourselves by an oath we may not break. Now, you
are a devout woman; pray for us and ask the Lord to send
rain to fill our cisterns, and then we shall no longer faint
for lack of water.'

32   'Hear what I have to say', replied Judith. 'I am going to
do a deed which will be remembered among our people
33 for all generations. Be at the gate tonight yourselves, and
I will go out with my maid. Before the day on which you
have promised to surrender the town to our enemies, the
34 Lord will deliver Israel by my hand. But do not try to
find out my plan; I will not tell you until I have accom-
35 plished what I mean to do.' Ozias and the magistrates said
to her, 'Go with our blessing, and may God be with you
36 to take vengeance on our enemies.' So they left the roof-
shelter and returned to their posts.

✳ 9. The *maid* who is now introduced is never named. Though a slave (16: 23), she *had charge of all her property*, just as Joseph had, when a slave, over Potiphar's (Gen. 39: 4). The character of a maid – especially a nurse – is a common one in Greek tragedy, where she acts as a confidante, often the only one available to a heroine. Esther, in a similar situation, took two maids with her (Rest of Esth. 15: 2), but they play a minor role compared with Judith's maid. The latter is now sent to fetch Ozias etc. so that Judith may remain in her place of retirement.

Judith's long speech shows a deep understanding of two theological problems, those of faith and suffering. These are the two themes of the book of Job, and in this passage the author of Judith can stand comparison with the author of Job.

12–17. The first section considers the nature of faith in God. Her criticism of the attempt to test God or to bargain with him (so N.E.B. rightly translates in verse 16) recalls God's answer to Job out of the whirlwind in chapters 38 and 40; but Judith is more explicit than Job in giving up the desire for detailed knowledge of God's plan and in relying instead on his goodness.

18–27. The second section considers the problem of suffering, i.e. the question why God allows his loyal servants to suffer. She agrees with Job's friends that *some* suffering is a punishment for sin: the exile was just such a punishment for idolatry. But since the return the Jews have been loyal to God. Therefore another explanation must be sought. The stories of Abraham (Gen. 12 and 22), Isaac (Gen. 24–6) and Jacob (Gen. 27–9) suggest that God sends suffering on his servants to test them; and, if that is so, their proper response is one of gratitude (verse 25), because the suffering is a mark of his attention and even of his favour. This view is mentioned briefly in Job 5: 17: 'Happy the man whom God rebukes! therefore do not reject the discipline of the Almighty.'

21. Bethulia is the key to Jerusalem and the temple.

22 f. If we do let our fellow-countrymen down, God will punish us again with a miserable and ignominious exile; there will be no 'happy ending' as there was when Sennacherib besieged Jerusalem (2 Kings 19).

27. The final verse of Judith's speech needs closer scrutiny. The N.E.B. translation contradicts verse 25: God *is* testing their loyalty, and doing so with just as fiery an ordeal as their ancestors faced. A preferable text is offered by some manuscripts and versions: 'He is subjecting us to the ordeal by which he tested their loyalty, not taking vengeance on us.'

The word translated *discipline* here and in Job 5: 17 would be better rendered 'warning': it is something which looks forward rather than backwards. The idea is like that expounded in Wisd. of Sol. 16: 6, where God is said to send suffering on people 'to remind them of the requirements of [his] law'.

28. Ozias' reply is again that of a weak man, chiefly concerned to justify himself. He cannot go back on his word (no *oath* was actually mentioned in 7: 31), so he asks Judith to help him meet it by praying for what at that time of year would be a miracle (1 Sam. 12: 17).

32. The initiative is all Judith's, as is the execution; contrast Esther (chapter 4) who has to be persuaded to act. ✻

JUDITH'S PRAYER

9 Then Judith prostrated herself, put ashes on her head, and uncovered the sackcloth she was wearing; and at the time when the evening incense was being offered in the
2 temple in Jerusalem, she cried to the Lord: 'O Lord, the God of my forefather Simeon! Thou didst put in his hand a sword to take vengeance on those foreigners who had stripped off a virgin's veil to defile her, uncovered her thighs to shame her, and polluted her womb to dishonour her. Thou didst say, "It shall not be done"; yet

they did it. So thou didst give up their rulers to be slain, 3 and their bed, which blushed for their treachery, to be stained with blood; beneath thy stroke slaves fell dead upon the bodies of princes, and princes upon their thrones. Thou didst give up their wives as booty, and their daughters 4 as captives, and all their spoils to be divided among thy beloved sons, who, aflame with zeal for thy cause and aghast at the pollution of their blood, called on thee to help them. O God, thou art my God, hear now a widow's prayer. All that happened then, and all that happened 5 before and after, thou didst accomplish. The things that are now, and are yet to be, thou hast designed; and what thou didst design has come to pass. The things thou hast 6 foreordained present themselves and say, "We are here." Thy ways are prepared beforehand: foreknowledge determines thy judgement.

'Thou seest the Assyrians assembled in their strength, 7 proud of their horses and riders, boasting of the power of their infantry, and putting their faith in shield and javelin, bow and sling. They do not know that thou art the Lord who stamps out wars; the Lord is thy name. Shatter their 8 strength by thy power and crush their might in thy anger. For they have planned to desecrate thy sanctuary, to pollute the dwelling-place of thy glorious name, and to strike down the horns of thy altar with the sword. Mark 9 their arrogance, pour thy wrath on their heads, and give to me, widow as I am, the strength to achieve my end. Use 10 the deceit upon my lips to strike them dead, the slave with the ruler, the ruler with the servant; shatter their pride by a woman's hand. For thy might lies not in numbers nor 11 thy sovereign power in strong men; but thou art the God

of the humble, the help of the poor, the support of the
weak, the protector of the desperate, the deliverer of the
12 hopeless. Hear, O hear, thou God of my forefather, God
of Israel's heritage, ruler of heaven and earth, creator of the
waters, king of all thy creation, hear thou my prayer.
13 Grant that my deceitful words may wound and bruise
them; for they have cruel designs against thy covenant,
thy sacred house, the summit of Zion, and thy children's
14 home, their own possession. Give thy whole nation and
every tribe the knowledge that thou alone art God, God
of all power and might, and that thou and thou alone art
Israel's shield.'

✽ Judith's prayer is not one of the more notable sections of the
book. Its most attractive feature is the absence of any petition
for herself, except as the agent of God's purpose; contrast
Esther's prayer in the parallel situation (Rest of Esth. 14: 3–19).
We also miss another common feature of such prayers (e.g.
Dan. 9, Baruch 1: 15ff.), namely repentance of national sins;
but this silence is in line with the theology of chapter 16. The
two distinctive features here are the stress on Simeon (verses 2–
4) and on Jerusalem and the holy places (verses 1, 8, 13).

1. Judith's preparation for prayer is ritually correct. She
uncovered the sackcloth, i.e. took off what she was wearing over
it; later (10: 3) she took it off itself in turn. *incense* is a symbol
of prayer rising to God; but even so the reference to Jerusalem
is rather forced. It is now evening on the first of the five days.

2. The reference to *Simeon* is surprising. In Genesis (34: 30
and 49: 5) Simeon is heavily criticized for killing the Gentile
Shechem and all his family in revenge for Shechem's rape of
Simeon's sister Dinah. The reason for his favourable mention
here seems to be that Judith is afraid of suffering the fate of
Dinah – indeed in an earlier version of the tale she may have
done so – and thus she sees Simeon as a defender of the right.

But there may well be more to it than that, in view of the gratuitous references to the Shechemites in 5: 16 and to Simeon in 6: 15. Perhaps they are all prompted by some political or religious incident of the time which is lost to us but which led the author to want to rehabilitate Simeon.

Where N.E.B. has *veil* all manuscripts give 'womb'. This is clearly a mistake that has arisen from later on. The word translated *veil* by the N.E.B. is similar in sound to those translated *thighs* and *womb*: the author is building up a rhetorical climax.

3. The Jerusalem Bible replaces *thrones* at the end of this verse by 'slaves'. There is no manuscript authority for this, but it is supported by the phrasing of verse 10 and is certainly in accordance with the rather crude rhetoric of the prayer.

6. The personification of *things*, i.e. events, is surprising. The nearest parallel to it is Baruch 3: 34, where the stars likewise say 'We are here!'

7–14. In the second half of her prayer Judith seeks to apply the case of her ancestor Simeon to the present predicament. As the Shechemites *polluted* Dinah, so the Assyrians *have planned...to pollute* the temple in Jerusalem. As Dinah was a *virgin*, so Judith is a *widow* – each of them weak women. But with the help of God, weakness will again overcome strength.

The theology here is simple. The Lord of Hosts is invoked with time-honoured phrases: *the Lord is thy name* is taken from Exod. 15: 3. But this all-powerful God is *the God of the humble* etc. This characteristic Old Testament note is picked up in Mary's song in Luke 1: 46–55, usually called the Magnificat, which can be seen as a kind of summary of the whole story of Judith.

10. For a man to die *by a woman's hand* was of course an especial shame to him and glory to her (cp. Abimelech's instructions to his armour-bearer: 'Draw your sword and dispatch me, or men will say of me: A woman killed him' in Judg. 9: 54).

Of all the rhetorical devices in this prayer, the most

remarkable is the use of repeated parallel phrases. There are examples with three limbs each in verses 2, 4, 8, 9, four each in verses 7 and 13, and five each in verses 11 and 12 – a gradual build-up of intensity. Such parallelism is basic to Hebrew poetry and common also in rhythmic prose. In the New Testament we find a group of three limbs in the Lord's Prayer (Matt. 6: 9f.), three successive groups of four in a sermon of Jesus (Luke 6: 20–8), and a group of six in 1 Tim. 3: 16 – all of them much more powerful and convincing than these in Judith. ✶

JUDITH GOES TO THE ASSYRIAN CAMP

10 1-2 When Judith had ended her prayer, prostrate before the God of Israel, she rose, called her maid, and went down into the house, where she was accustomed to spend her 3 sabbaths and festivals. She removed the sackcloth she was wearing and took off her widow's weeds; then she washed, and anointed herself with rich perfume. She did her hair, put on a headband, and dressed in her gayest clothes, which she used to wear when her husband Manasses was 4 alive. She put on sandals and anklets, bracelets and rings, her ear-rings and all her ornaments, and made herself very attractive, so as to catch the eye of any man who might 5 see her. She gave her maid a skin of wine and a flask of oil; then she filled a bag with roasted grain, cakes of dried figs, and the finest bread, packed everything up, and gave it all to her maid to carry.

6   They went out towards the gate of Bethulia and found Ozias standing there, with Chabris and Charmis the elders 7 of the town. When they saw Judith transformed in appearance and quite differently dressed, they were filled with admiration of her beauty, and said to her, 'The God of

our fathers grant you favour and fulfil your plans, so that
Israel may triumph and Jerusalem may be exalted!' Judith
bowed to God in worship. Then she said to them, 'Order 9
the gate to be opened for me, and I will go out to accomplish all that you say.' They ordered the young men to
open the gate as she had asked. When they had done so, 10
Judith went out, accompanied by her maid; and the men
of the town watched her until she had gone down the hill-
side and crossed the valley, and then they lost sight of her.

The women went straight across the valley and were 11
met by an Assyrian outpost; they seized Judith and ques- 12
tioned her: 'What is your nationality? Where have you
come from? Where are you going?' 'I am a Hebrew,'
she replied; 'but I am running away from my people,
because they are going to fall into your hands and be
devoured. I am on my way to Holophernes, your com- 13
mander-in-chief, with reliable information. I will show
him a route by which he can gain command of the entire
hill-country without losing a single man.'

As the men listened to her story they looked at her face 14
and were amazed at her beauty. 'You have saved your life', 15
they said, 'by coming down at once to see our master.
Go to his tent straight away. Some of us will escort you
and hand you over to him. When you are in his presence, 16
do not be afraid; just tell him what you have told us, and
he will treat you kindly.' They detailed a hundred of their 17
number to accompany her and her maid, and they brought
the two women to Holophernes' tent.

As the news of her arrival spread from tent to tent, men 18
came running from all parts of the camp. They gathered

round her as she stood outside Holophernes' tent waiting
19 until he had been told about her. Her wonderful beauty
made them think that the Israelites must be a wonderful
people. They said to each other, 'Who can despise a nation
which has such women as this? We had better not leave
a man of them alive, for if they get away they will be able
to outwit the whole world.'

20 Then Holophernes' bodyguard and all his attendants
21 came out and took her into the tent. He was resting on his
bed under a mosquito-net of purple interwoven with gold,
22 emeralds, and precious stones. When Judith was announced
he came out into the front part of the tent, with silver
23 lamps carried before him. He and his attendants were all
amazed at the beauty of her face as she stood before them.
She prostrated herself and did obeisance to him; but his
slaves raised her up.

✳ This whole tale is excellently told, with many vivid and even
humorous touches. Especially amusing is the way in which the
men successively fall victim to her charms (10: 14f., 18f.,
23f.).

3–4. Her preparations are of two kinds. First she *made
herself very attractive*, wearing *her gayest clothes*, i.e. a linen gown
(16: 8) and *all her ornaments*, doubtless of gold (8: 7). Jerome,
mistaking the frank tone of the author, adds the comment
that 'God miraculously increased her beauty because her
ornaments were designed not for pleasure but for virtue'.

5. Secondly, she takes food with her so as not to be con-
taminated by gentile food or even gentile dishes. She is more
scrupulous than Esther; indeed piety did not demand *the
finest* (the Greek means ritually pure) bread until Pharisaic
times (see note on 8: 4).

10. *the men...watched her*: the author seems to have forgot-

ten that her departure took place by night (8: 33; 11: 3).
But for the rest nothing is out of place.

19. A fine example of Jewish national humour. ✶

HOLOPHERNES BEFRIENDS JUDITH

'Take heart, madam,' said Holophernes; 'do not be **11**
afraid. I have never harmed anyone who chose to serve
Nebuchadnezzar, king of all the earth. I should never have 2
raised my spear against your people in the hill-country if
they had not insulted me; they brought it on themselves.
Now tell me why you have run away from them and 3
joined us. By coming here you have saved your life.
Take heart! You are in no danger tonight or in the future;
no one will harm you. You will enjoy the good treatment 4
which is given to the subjects of my master King
Nebuchadnezzar.'

Judith replied, 'My lord, grant your slave a hearing and 5
listen to what I have to say to you. The information I am
giving you tonight is the truth. If you follow my advice, 6
God will do some great thing through you, and my lord
will not fail to attain his ends. By the life of Nebuchad- 7
nezzar, king of all the earth, and by the living might of
him who sent you to bring order to all creatures, I swear:
not only do men serve him, thanks to you, but wild
animals also, cattle, and birds, will owe their lives to your
power as long as Nebuchadnezzar and his dynasty reign.[a]
We have heard how wise and clever you are. You are 8
known throughout the world as the man of ability

[a] not only...reign: *or* thanks to you and to your power, not only do
men serve him, but wild animals also, cattle, and birds, will live at the
disposal of Nebuchadnezzar and his household; *the text and meaning are
uncertain.*

unrivalled in the whole empire, of powerful intelligence
9 and amazing skill in the art of war. We know about the
speech that Achior made in your council, because the men
of Bethulia rescued him, and he told them what he had said
10 to you. Do not disregard what he said, my lord and master,
but give full weight to his words. They are true. No
punishment ever falls on our race and the sword does not
11 subdue them, except when they sin against their God. But
now, my lord, you are not to be thwarted and cheated of
success, for they are doomed to die. Sin has them in its
power, and when they do wrong they will arouse their
12 God's anger. Because they have run out of food and their
water-supply is low, they have decided to lay hands on
their cattle; they mean to consume everything that God
13 by his laws has prohibited as food; and they have resolved
to use up the firstfruits of the grain and the tithes of wine
and oil, although these are dedicated and reserved for
the priests who stand in attendance before our God in
Jerusalem, and no layman may so much as handle them.
14 They have sent men to Jerusalem to get permission from
the senate, because even the people there have done this.
15 As soon as ever word reaches them and they act on it, on
that very day they will be given up to you to be destroyed.
16   'So, my lord, when I learnt all this, I ran away from
them; and God has sent me to do with you things that
will be the wonder of the world, wherever men hear
17 about them. For I, your servant, am a religious woman:
day and night I worship the God of heaven. I will stay
with you now, my lord; and each night I shall go out into
the valley and pray to God, and he will tell me when they
18 have committed their sins. Then, when I return and bring

you word, you may lead out your whole army, and you
will meet with no resistance from any of them. I will 19
guide you across Judaea until you reach Jerusalem, and
I will set up your throne in the heart of the city. They will
follow you like sheep that have lost their shepherd, and
not a dog will so much as growl at you. I have been given
foreknowledge of this. It has been revealed to me, and I
have been sent to announce it to you.'

Judith's words delighted Holophernes and all his atten- 20
dants, and they were amazed at her wisdom. 'In the whole 21
wide world', they said, 'there is not a woman to compare
with her for beauty of face or shrewdness of speech.'
Holophernes said to her, 'Thank God for sending you out 22
from your people, to bring strength to us and destruction
to those who have insulted my lord! You are a beautiful 23
woman and your words are good. If you do as you have
promised, your God shall be my God, and you shall live
in King Nebuchadnezzar's palace and be renowned
throughout the world.'

✶ 5. Judith's speech to Holophernes has in its time aroused
much foolish criticism. Some critics have complained that
after saying she will tell him *the truth* she goes on to tell him
a pack of lies. Other critics reply that in doing so she is only
following the morality of the patriarchal age – and indeed of
most of the Old Testament – whereby the end justifies the
means. Her previous reference in her prayer (9: 13) to
'deceitful words' shows that she at least had no moral
qualms. But in truth the whole moral argument is mis-
conceived: if it is legitimate to kill in war, it can hardly be
wrong to lie; and, provided again that the cause is good, God's
blessing may rest upon craftiness no less than upon physical
courage.

6. The phrasing of this verse is the first of many delicious examples of dramatic irony (see 11: 16; 12: 4, 14, 18). Holophernes interprets it in one way, Judith (and the reader) in the opposite way. *my lord* could refer equally to God or to Holophernes.

7. The same critics who complain of Judith's lying complain also of her 'blasphemy' in swearing by the life of Nebuchadnezzar. But she does so just as Daniel does (Dan. 2: 38), in order to win the enemy's trust for her own ends. The text of verse 7 is uncertain, as the N.E.B. footnote says. But the main point is that the *content* of her oath is the previous verse 6; the whole of verse 7 is merely an expanded formula.

10–19. Judith now proceeds, very carefully, to lay the essential traps. For her plan to succeed, she must (i) get the confidence of Holophernes, (ii) gain time by guaranteeing him *delayed* victory: if she gives no reason for the delay he will just attack at once, (iii) contrive a situation where she can kill him. For *complete* success, she must also (iv) escape herself, and tell the Jews about his death before his own troops hear of it. The passage 11–15 deals with (ii) above. We may think the detail excessive, but dramatically it lends conviction to her speech, and in any case these ritual details obviously meant a good deal to the author.

12. The reference to their having *run out of food* is a new factor, not part of Holophernes' plan, which was confined to water (7: 12f.). The mention of *cattle* presumably refers to the prohibition on eating the fat and the blood (Lev. 3: 17); the Old Latin manuscripts here mention the blood explicitly. *prohibited* foods include bats, mice, lizards, snails (Lev. 11), such as might well be eaten in time of siege.

13. The *firstfruits* and the *tithes* were *reserved for the priests* and Levites (Num. 18), partly for sacrificial purposes and partly for their own use. The statement that laymen might not *so much as handle them* goes beyond anything recorded elsewhere, even in late rabbinic tradition. Perhaps it is a colourful embellishment, not to be taken literally.

14. We should certainly not take literally the statement that the people of Jerusalem *have done this*; but it is essential to item (ii) of her plan.

17–19. She now turns to item (iv) of her plan. She persuades Holophernes that she must be allowed out of the camp each night, so that she can advise him of the psychological moment for his assault (17f.). She hints that she possesses the gift of prophecy: she is a *religious woman* and has *been given foreknowledge*. Another Jewish version of the story goes further than that, and twice refers to Judith as a 'daughter of prophets'. What is not clear is why she needs to go out of the camp in order to get the message: perhaps it was supposed that a prophetess would be ineffective in enemy-occupied territory.

23. Holophernes is completely taken in; his last '*If*...' does not mean that he is having doubts. The phrase *your God shall be my God* need not be an offer to be converted, for most Gentiles regarded all religions as equally valid. ✳

JUDITH KILLS HOLOPHERNES AND
ESCAPES HOME

Holophernes then commanded them to bring her in **12** where his silver was set out, and he ordered a meal to be served for her from his own food and wine. But Judith 2 said, 'I will not eat any of it, in case I should be breaking our law. What I have brought with me will meet my needs.' Holophernes said to her, 'But if you use up all 3 you have with you, where can we get you a fresh supply of the same kind? There is no one of your race here among us.' Judith replied, 'As sure as you live, my 4 lord, I shall not finish what I have brought with me before the Lord accomplishes through me what he has planned.'

5 Holophernes' attendants brought her into the tent; and she slept until midnight. Shortly before the morning watch
6 she got up and sent this message to Holophernes: 'My lord, will you give orders for me to be allowed to go out and
7 pray?' Holophernes ordered his bodyguard to let her pass. She remained in the camp for three days, going out each night into the valley of Bethulia and bathing in the spring.
8 When she came up from the spring, she prayed the Lord, the God of Israel, to prosper her undertaking to restore her
9 people. Then she returned to the camp purified, and remained in the tent until she took her meal towards evening.

10 On the fourth day Holophernes gave a banquet for his personal servants only, and did not invite any of the army
11 officers. He said to Bagoas, the eunuch in charge of all his affairs: 'Go to the Hebrew woman who is in your care, and persuade her to join us and to eat and drink with us.
12 It would be a disgrace if we let such a woman go without enjoying her company. If we do not win her favours she
13 will laugh at us.' Bagoas left Holophernes' presence, and went to Judith and said, 'Now, my beauty, do not be bashful; come along to my master and give yourself the honour of his company. Drink with us and enjoy yourself, and behave today like one of the Assyrian women in
14 attendance at Nebuchadnezzar's palace.' 'Who am I to refuse my master?' said Judith. 'I am eager to do whatever pleases him; and it will be something to boast of till my
15 dying day.' She proceeded to dress herself up and put on all her feminine finery. Her maid went ahead of her, and spread on the ground in front of Holophernes the fleeces which she had received from Bagoas for her daily use, so

that she might recline on them when she ate. When 16
Judith came in and took her place, Holophernes was beside
himself with desire for her. He shook with passion and was
filled with an ardent longing to possess her; indeed he had
been looking for an opportunity to seduce her ever since
he first set eyes on her. So he said to her, 'Drink and enjoy 17
yourself with us.' 'Indeed I will, my lord,' said Judith; 18
'today is the greatest day of my whole life.' Then she took 19
what her servant had prepared, and ate and drank in his
presence. Holophernes was delighted with her, and drank 20
a great deal of wine, more, indeed, than he had ever
drunk on any single day since he was born.

When it grew late, Holophernes' servants quickly **13**
withdrew. Bagoas closed the tent from outside, shutting
out all the attendants from his master's presence, and they
went to bed; the banquet had lasted so long that they were
all worn out. Judith was left alone in the tent, with Holo- 2
phernes lying sprawled on his bed, dead drunk.

Judith had told her maid to stand outside the sleeping- 3
apartment and wait for her mistress to go out, as she did
every day; she had said that she would be going out to
pray, and had explained this to Bagoas also. When they 4
had all gone and not a soul was left, Judith stood beside
Holophernes' bed and prayed silently: 'O Lord, God of
all power, look favourably now on what I am about to
do to bring glory to Jerusalem, for now is the time to 5
help thy heritage and to give success to my plan for
crushing the enemies who have risen up against us.' She 6
went to the bed-rail beside Holophernes' head and took
down his sword, and stepping close to the bed she grasped 7
his hair. 'Now give me strength, O Lord, God of Israel',

8 she said; then she struck at his neck twice with all her
9 might, and cut off his head. She rolled the body off the
bed and took the mosquito-net from its posts; a moment
later she went out and gave Holophernes' head to the maid,
10 who put it in her food-bag. The two of them went out
together, as they had usually done for prayer. Through
the camp they went, and round that valley, and up the hill
to Bethulia till they reached the gates.

11   From a distance Judith called to the sentries at the gates:
'Open! Open the gate! God, our God, is with us, still
showing his strength in Israel and his might against our
12 enemies. He has shown it today!' When the citizens
heard her voice, they hurried down to the gate and sum-
13 moned the elders of the town. Everyone high and low
came running, hardly able to believe that Judith had returned. They opened the gate and let the two women in;
14 they lit a fire to see by, and gathered round them. Then
Judith raised her voice and cried, 'Praise God! O praise
him! Praise God, who has not withdrawn his mercy from
the house of Israel, but has crushed our enemies by my
15 hand this very night!' Then she took the head from the
bag and showed it to them. 'Look!' she said. 'The head
of Holophernes, the Assyrian commander-in-chief! And
here is the net under which he lay drunk! The Lord has
16 struck him down by the hand of a woman! And I swear
by the Lord who has brought me safely along the way
I have travelled that, though my face lured him to destruction, he committed no sin with me, and my honour is
unblemished.'

17   The people were all astounded; and bowing down in
worship to God, they said with one voice, 'Praise be to

thee, O Lord our God, who hast humiliated the enemies
of thy people this day.' And Ozias said to Judith, 'My 18
daughter, the blessing of God Most High is upon you, you
more than all other women on earth; praise be to the
Lord, the God who created heaven and earth, and guided
you when you struck off the head of the enemy commander. The sure hope which inspired you[a] will never 19
fade from men's minds while they commemorate the
power of God. May God make your deed redound to 20
your honour for ever, and shower blessings upon you!
You risked your life for our country when it was faced
with humiliation. You went boldly to meet the disaster
that threatened us, and held firmly to God's straight road.'
All the people responded: 'Amen! Amen!'

✻ 12: 5. *The tent* which Judith was given was a separate
tent in the headquarters (14: 17).

6. There is a slight loose end here: it would seem that
Holophernes had either forgotten her implicit request in
11: 17 or had failed to tell his bodyguard to let her go.

7. Why did she bathe in *the spring*? It was a post-exilic
custom to wash before prayer – especially no doubt after
contact with Gentiles. But a different explanation is suggested
by other Jewish versions of the story. In two of these Judith
is (or pretends to be) 'unclean', i.e. menstruous. This certainly
looks like part of the original folk-tale. If the Jews can hold
out for five more days, Judith can fob Holophernes off for
that period, a day at a time. During it she can claim, as an old
wives' superstition, the need to bathe in a local spring. At the
end of it, whether she yields to him or not (one Jewish version
has it that she does, and that, instead of the innocent mosquito
net, she takes his nightshirt to wrap the head in), she can
leave camp on a similar pretext. Such a sequence of events,

[a] *Or* which you inspire.

well suited to a folk-tale, would provide a much simpler method of delaying Holophernes, as required by point (ii) of the plan, than the complicated and rather unconvincing argument of 11: 11–19, which had to be introduced when the old story was bowdlerized.

The climax of the story is splendidly told.

11. For Bagoas see p. 78.

12. The psychology is entirely convincing.

15. To *recline* at meals was common, at least in circumstances of luxury.

19. Judith still keeps to the ritually pure food.

13: 9. After killing Holophernes, she takes the *mosquito-net* partly as a trophy, partly perhaps for proof, if proof were to be needed (see note on 6: 6).

11. The excitement of Judith and the people on her return is shown by the repetition of *Open* and *God*. Similarly *Praise* is repeated three times in verse 14.

18. While the people bless God, Ozias blesses Judith and God. His words to her here (together with 15: 10) are much used in the liturgy of the Roman Catholic Church on feasts of the Blessed Virgin Mary.

19. The Greek words translated *the sure hope which inspired you* mean simply 'your hope', but some good manuscripts give instead 'your praise', which is preferable. *

The triumph of Israel

THE FRUITS OF VICTORY

14 Then Judith said to them, 'Listen to me, my friends; take this head and hang it out on the battlements of your wall.

2 As soon as dawn breaks and the sun rises, take up your weapons, every able-bodied man of you, and march out of the town. You must set a commander at your head, as

if you were going down to the plain to attack the Assyrian outpost; but do not go down. The Assyrians will take up 3 their weapons and make for their camp, and rouse the commanders, who will run to Holophernes' tent but will not find him. They will all be seized with panic and will flee from you; then pursue them, you and all who live 4 within Israel's borders, and cut them down in their tracks. But first of all summon Achior the Ammonite to me, so 5 that he may see and recognize the man who treated Israel with contempt and sent him to us as if to his death.'

They summoned Achior from Ozias's house. When he 6 came and saw Holophernes' head held by one of the men in the assembly of the people, he fainted and fell down. They lifted him up, and he threw himself at Judith's feet 7 and did obeisance to her, and said, 'Your praises will be sung in every camp in Judah and among all nations. They will tremble when they hear your name. Tell me now the 8 whole story of what you have done during these days.' Then Judith, in the hearing of the people, told him everything from the day she left until that very moment. As she 9 ended her story, the people raised a great shout and made the town ring with their cheers. And when Achior realized 10 all that the God of Israel had done, he came to full belief in God, and was circumcised, and admitted as a member of the community of Israel, as his descendants still are.

When dawn came they hung Holophernes' head on the 11 wall; then they all took their weapons and went out in companies into the approaches to the town. When the 12 Assyrians saw them, they sent word to their leaders, who then went to the generals, captains, and all the other officers. They came to Holophernes' tent and said to his 13 steward: 'Wake our master. These slaves have had the audacity to offer us battle; they are asking to be utterly

14 wiped out.' Bagoas went in and knocked at the screen of the inner tent, supposing that Holophernes was sleeping

15 with Judith. When there was no reply, he drew aside the screen, went into the sleeping-apartment, and found the dead body sprawling over a footstool, and the head gone.

16 He gave a great cry, wailing and groaning aloud, and

17 tore his clothes. Then he went into the tent which Judith had occupied; and not finding her he rushed out to the

18 people shouting, 'The slaves have played us false. One Hebrew woman has brought shame on Nebuchadnezzar's kingdom. Look! Holophernes is lying on the ground, and

19 his head is gone!' His words filled the officers of the Assyrian army with dismay; they tore their clothes, and the camp rang with their shouts and cries.

15 When the news spread to the men in the camp, they

2 were thrown into consternation at what had happened. In terror and panic they all scattered at once, with no attempt to keep together, and fled by every path across the plain

3 and the hill-country. Those who were encamped in the hills round Bethulia also took to flight. Then all the

4 Israelites of military age sallied out after them. Ozias sent men to Bethomesthaim, Choba, and Chola, and the whole territory of Israel, to give news of what had happened and to tell them to sally out against the enemy and

5 destroy them. When the news reached them, every man in Israel joined the attack and cut them down, going as far as Choba. The men from Jerusalem and all the hill-country also joined in, for they had been told what had happened in the enemy camp. The men of Gilead and

Galilee outflanked the Assyrians and inflicted heavy losses
on them, continuing beyond Damascus and the district
round it. The rest of the inhabitants of Bethulia fell upon 6
the camp and made themselves rich with the spoils. When 7
the Israelites returned from the slaughter, they took
possession of what remained. The villages and hamlets in
the hill-country and in the plain got masses of booty, for
there was a huge quantity of it.

Joakim the high priest and the senate of Israel came from 8
Jerusalem to see for themselves the great things the Lord
had done for his people, and to meet Judith and wish her
well. When they arrived they praised her with one voice 9
and said, 'You are the glory of Jerusalem, the heroine of
Israel, the proud boast of our people! With your own 10
hand you have done all this, you have restored the fortunes
of Israel, and God has shown his approval. Blessings on
you from the Lord Almighty, for all time to come!' And
all the people responded, 'Amen!'

The looting of the camp went on for thirty days. They 11
gave Judith Holophernes' tent, with all his silver, and his
couches, bowls, and furniture. She took them and loaded
her mule, then got her wagons ready and piled the goods
on them. All the Israelite women came running to see 12
her; they sang her praises, and some of them performed
a dance in her honour. She took garlanded wands in her
hands and gave some also to the women who accompanied
her; and she and those who were with her crowned them- 13
selves with olive leaves. Then, at the head of all the people,
she led the women in the dance; and the men of Israel, in
full armour and with garlands on their heads, followed
them singing hymns.

✴ There are some puzzles in the narrative of what happened on Judith's return. In chapter 13 Judith praised God, then showed the head of Holophernes to the people, who in turn praised God. In chapter 14 Judith gives instructions for an attack on the Assyrian camp. Then she breaks off – '*But first of all summon Achior. . .so that he may see and recognize* [Holophernes].' Achior, having done so, says to Judith: '*Tell me now the whole story.*' Judith *in the hearing of the people told him everything* and the people again cheered.

The clearest evidence of a loose end is the phrase *but first of all* in 14: 5. Why wait to tell the story until (a) she has given orders for the next day and (b) Achior has arrived? The sequence would run much more smoothly if the events of 14: 5–9 came between those of 13: 16 and 13: 17. This would also fit the version of the story whereby Judith herself was scarcely believed until Achior identified the head (see p. 90).

As a matter of fact Jerome, in his translation, did put the equivalent of verses 5–7 between 13: 20 and 14: 1. Some scholars think he was following a manuscript now lost to us with a different text. But it seems more likely that he made the change himself in order to solve the puzzle.

2. The N.E.B. translation makes the manoeuvre somewhat obscure. What Judith meant was: *march out of the town*, with a *commander at your head, as if you were going down*, etc. The ruse was necessary so that the weaker side could keep the initiative.

10. Achior's conversion and circumcision is a matter of some interest. Deuteronomy 23: 3 laid down that 'No Ammonite or Moabite, even down to the tenth generation, shall become a member of the assembly of the LORD.' But the book of Ruth (the Moabitess) stands as evidence that the original harsh rule was at least open to exceptions.

11. The treatment of the defeated enemy's head was fairly common: see 1 Macc. 7: 47 (= 2 Macc. 15: 35) for similar treatment of the defeated Greek general Nicanor – the incident which doubtless inspired this.

15: 4. *Bethomesthaim* and *Choba* were mentioned in chapter 4, but neither they nor *Chola* are identified.

5. The military details of the Jewish pursuit are imperfect. *Jerusalem* (65 km (40 miles) to the south) and *Gilead* (32 km (20 miles) east across the Jordan) and even more *Damascus* (160 km (100 miles) north) are really too far off, but the mention of them is designed to reinforce the point that Bethulia is the key to the whole strategic situation.

12. The celebrations in honour of Judith have plenty of general parallels in biblical literature, e.g. the dance after David killed Goliath (1 Sam. 18: 6). But there are certain Greek features here, which belong to a later period. *garlanded wands* are branches intertwined with ivy and vine-leaves, much used in the worship of Bacchus. No such reference is of course intended here, but all the same the Greek word (*thyrsus*) is not found elsewhere in the Septuagint except at 2 Macc. 10: 7.

13. Likewise it was a Greek custom to crown oneself with *olive leaves* (see note on 3: 7). ✷

JUDITH'S SONG

In the presence of all Israel, Judith struck up this hymn of **16** praise and thanksgiving, in which all the people joined lustily:

'Strike up a song to my God with tambourines;   2
  sing to the Lord with cymbals;
  raise a psalm of praise[a] to him;
  honour him and invoke his name.
The Lord is a God who stamps out wars;   3
  he has brought me safe from my pursuers
  into his camp among his people.

[a] *Some witnesses read* a new psalm.

4   The Assyrian came from the mountains of the north;
    his armies came in such myriads
      that his troops choked the valleys,
    his cavalry covered the hills.

5   He threatened to set fire to my land,
    put my young men to the sword,
    dash my infants to the ground,
    take my children as booty,
    and my maidens as spoil.

6   The Lord Almighty has thwarted them by a woman's
      hand.

7   It was no young man that brought their champion low;
    no Titan struck him down,
    no tall giant set upon him;
    but Judith daughter of Merari disarmed him by the
      beauty of her face.

8   She put off her widow's weeds
    to raise up the afflicted in Israel;
    she anointed her face with perfume,
    and bound her hair with a headband,
    and put on a linen gown to beguile him.

9   Her sandal entranced his eye,
    her beauty took his heart captive;
    and the sword cut through his neck.

10 The Persians shuddered at her daring,
    the Medes were daunted by her boldness.

11 Then my oppressed people shouted in triumph, and the
      enemy were afraid;
    my weak ones shouted, and the enemy cowered in fear;
    they raised their voices, and the enemy took to flight.

12 The sons of servant girls ran them through,

wounding them like runaway slaves;
they were destroyed by the army of my Lord.

'I will sing a new hymn to my God.   13
O Lord, thou art great and glorious,
thou art marvellous in thy strength, invincible.
Let thy whole creation serve thee;   14
for thou didst speak and all things came to be;
thou didst send out thy spirit and it formed them.
No one can resist thy voice;
mountains and seas are stirred to their depths,   15
rocks melt like wax at thy presence;
but to those who revere thee
thou dost still show mercy.
For no sacrifice is sufficient to please thee with its   16
    fragrance,
and all the fat in the world is not enough for a burnt-
    offering,
but he who fears the Lord is always great.
Woe to the nations which rise up against my people!   17
The Lord Almighty will punish them on the day of
    judgement;
he will consign their bodies to fire and worms;
they will weep in pain for ever.'

When they arrived at Jerusalem they worshipped God.   18
As soon as the people were purified, they offered their
burnt-offerings, freewill offerings, and gifts. Judith dedi-   19
cated to God all Holophernes' possessions, which the people
had given to her; and the net, which she had taken for
herself from the sleeping-apartment, she presented as

20 a votive offering. For three months the people continued
their celebrations in Jerusalem in front of the sanctuary;
and Judith remained with them.

21   At the end of that time they all returned to their own
homes. Judith went back to Bethulia and lived on her
estate. In her time she was famous throughout the whole
22 country. She had many suitors; but she remained unmarried all her life after her husband Manasses died and
23 was gathered to his fathers. Her fame continued to increase;
and she lived on in her husband's house until she was a
hundred and five years old. She gave her maid her liberty.
She died in Bethulia and was buried in the same tomb as
24 her husband Manasses, and Israel observed mourning
for her for seven days. Before her death she divided her
property among all those who were most closely related
to her husband Manasses, and among her own nearest
relations.

25   No one dared to threaten the Israelites again in Judith's
lifetime, or for a long time after her death.

* Judith's song is intended to be the climax of the book –
indeed it is quite possible that the story was originally composed as a narrative introduction to the song. In thought and
style it contains many echoes of the Psalms: but it is especially
close to other songs of triumph, especially that of Deborah
and Barak after Jael had killed Sisera (Judg. 5) and that of
Moses and Miriam after the crossing of the Red Sea
(Exod. 15).

One notable feature in common between Judith's and
Deborah's songs is the way that in both of them the heroine
sometimes speaks in the first person, sometimes is spoken of
in the third. As the text of Judith's song stands, she speaks
in the first person in verses 2–5, but is spoken of in verses 6–10;

from 11–17 she again speaks in the first person. But there is another obvious difference between these three sections. Only the centre section refers specifically to Judith. The rest, except perhaps for verse 3 *b*, could fit in many contexts; indeed the *my* of verses 5 and 11 suit the mouth of a king better than of Judith.

But whether verses 6–10 are the original core of the song, or were themselves inserted into an earlier, more general, psalm, the whole is now worked up so much that it cannot convincingly be dissected. In any case, as verse 1 shows, it is possible that sections were sung alternately by Judith and the people, rather as Miriam echoed Moses in Exod. 15 (verses 1 and 21).

3. In the last line some manuscripts give a preferable reading: He has set up *his camp among his people.*

7. *no Titan* and *no. . .giant* do not refer to Greek mythology. Giants are just 'men of gigantic size' (Num. 13: 32). The Greek word *Titans* is sometimes used in the Septuagint to translate the Hebrew *Rephaim*, used sometimes of pre-Israelite inhabitants of Canaan, thought to have been giants.

10. The clear reference to *Persians* and *Medes* is surprising. If we are right in seeing these verses as the core of the whole book, then Judith's exploits in so far as they are historical belong to the Persian period (say 550–330 B.C.), even though the present book was undoubtedly composed much later.

12. The parallelism demands that the first line read 'they ran them through *like* sons of servant girls'; there is some support in the Greek manuscripts for this change, which would have required the addition of only one letter in the supposed Hebrew original.

15. The N.E.B. translation of the first line is an attempt to make sense of a Greek text which means 'mountains are shaken with waters from their foundations'. But once again it is better to suppose the loss of a single letter in the Hebrew original and emend to read '*like* water'.

16. This verse contains the only suggestion in Judith that

ritual is not enough. For the negative part of the thought
cp. Ps. 51: 16:

> Thou hast no delight in sacrifice;
> if I brought thee an offering, thou wouldst not
> accept it.

But the psalmist continues in words that go much deeper
than Judith's:

> My sacrifice, O God, is a broken spirit;
> a wounded heart, O God, thou wilt not despise.

The reference to the fear of the Lord is common in the
Wisdom literature: e.g. Ecclus. 1: 11: 'The fear of the Lord
brings honour and pride' and 1: 14: 'The essence of wisdom is
the fear of the Lord.'

17. This verse contains the only reference in the book to
what happens after death. A similar primitive note is struck
at the end of the Song of Deborah and in the last verse of
Isaiah. The latter passage (not by the prophet himself)
obviously influenced Judith here:

> they shall come out and see
> the dead bodies of those who have rebelled against me;
> their worm shall not die nor their fire be quenched.

18. The idea of going to Jerusalem had not previously been
mentioned. After the purifications, made necessary by contact
with the dead, the dedications followed the lines laid down in
Deut. 13: 16f. for booty taken from impious enemies. The
victory celebrations lasted improbably long; but cp. 1: 16.

23. Judith's exceptionally long life follows both the literary
tradition of the lives of the great heroes and the theological
tradition that the godly person is rewarded by longevity
(cp. Job 42: 16) and by a peace and prosperity which outlive
him – by forty years in the case of Jael (Judg. 5: 31 *b*).

24. Judith's will follows the prescriptions of Num. 27: 11.

The Vulgate adds a note at the end that a festival was
instituted by the Jews to commemorate her achievement.
This would have been in line with the institution of the
Feast of Purim at the end of Esther, or of Nicanor's Day to

celebrate Judas Maccabaeus' victory over Nicanor (1 Macc. 7: 49). But there is no other reference to such a feast in the case of Judith, either in the manuscripts of this book or in any other source. *

*   *   *   *   *   *   *   *   *   *   *   *   *

THE BOOKS OF JUDITH AND TOBIT
AS LITERATURE

Most of the literary features of Judith and Tobit are common to 'popular' literature everywhere, whether it is the ancient Greek novel, the tales of the Arabian Nights or Elizabethan drama outside Shakespeare. In attempting to assess Judith and Tobit we must ask how good they are *of their kind*. For the moment it is enough to say that Judith is most closely related to popular drama, Tobit to popular romance.

The first of the features common to all popular literature is a preference for incident over character. The basic ingredients of the plot are (i) love and (ii) *either* a journey (quest) *or* a conflict (military or political); the sequence of events contains (iii) at least one reversal of fortune, and it leads to (iv) a 'happy' ending. Tobit and Judith both have their happy ending – it would be hard for a biblical book not to. Judith has one large reversal of fortune, Tobit many small ones. The thread of Judith is a conflict, that of Tobit a quest. But there is no real love interest in either book, because for all biblical authors except the writer of the Song of Songs romantic love is overshadowed by covenant-love between God and his people.

Secondly, the characters in popular literature tend to be not only static but stereotyped, morally black or white, not grey. Apart from the hero, stock figures are the tyrant villain (Holophernes, also Asmodaeus) and the chaste heroine (Judith and Sarah). Now it is clear that what is missing in both

Judith and Tobit is the hero. It is also clear why: God is the absent hero of both books. Judith, it is true, represents God effectively in herself, and can in a sense be hero as well as heroine; there would certainly have been no role in the story for her husband. In Tobit it is rather Raphael who represents God, leaving an altogether humbler and unheroic role for Tobias.

A third feature of popular literature may be called pathos, which is seen in various ways. The incidents themselves are violent and appeal to the simpler emotions. The style is often rhetorical (for Judith, see p. 78). The characters themselves are given to emotional outbursts, e.g. the bombast of Holophernes or the tearfulness of Anna. Often the heightened emotion leads them from prose to verse: indeed a mixture of the two is common.

Fourthly, the popular mind is typically indifferent to accuracy about time and place, and to philosophy above the level of proverbs and wise sayings. Conversely, it welcomes the supernatural in one form or another. God, angels and demons either participate directly in the action or affect it indirectly through dreams and omens. Neither author nor reader wanted everyday realism.

Now already under this fourth heading it is clear that Judith is a more sophisticated work than Tobit. Judith dispenses entirely with the supernatural, and the story develops consecutively and logically in such a way as to hold attention and suspend disbelief. The author does seek to write convincing history, and his theological interest is philosophical in the sense of being systematic.

But it is in the character-drawing – and especially in the interweaving of character and plot – that Judith shows itself something above the level of the popular. Judith herself is shown at her subtlest in the speeches, especially in the moral indignation and intelligence of chapter 8, the cautious flatteries of chapter 11 and the exultation of 13: 14–16. Her charm and beauty are shown by the immediate capitulation of successive groups of the enemy (10: 14 and 19; 12: 16). Holophernes is the nearest to a stock character, but even he does not lack skilful touches (12: 13). Achior is 'stock' only in the sense that Jewish popular literature often contained a Gentile who shows understanding and favour towards the Jews, sometimes being converted in the end, e.g. the heathen sailors in Jonah. His own development is gradual and psychologically fitting: he had long been a reluctant admirer of the Jews, but his actual conversion is started by Holophernes and is completed by Judith. Similarly his foil Ozias moves weakly from premature confidence (6: 21) through moral indecision (7: 31) into equally pathetic hope (8: 31) and then back to his position of apparent authority (13: 18ff.).

There are in fact certain respects in which Judith has the air of a Greek tragedy. Two thirds of the second part of the book are in direct speech of one sort or another. Chapters 11 and 12 contain a good deal of the 'tragic irony' beloved of the Greeks, where the speaker utters words which mean one thing to the person addressed and another to the audience (or readers) who know the story. Judith herself could be a Greek tragic heroine with no difficulty at all: indeed her wealth and position, emphasized in chapter 8, are much more typical of Greek than of Hebrew literature – as is also the subordinate character of the maid. Finally the phrasing of 8: 29 and the antitheses of 9: 3 and 16: 7 seem to derive ultimately from Greek rhetoric.

This point must not be pressed too far. The book of Judith belongs fairly and squarely within the Jewish tradition. But, though popular, it is not unsophisticated, and its *literary* qualities do seem to owe something to that Greek culture which had been permeating Palestine for at least two centuries before it was written.

Popular romance differs from popular drama in a number of ways. The narrative thread is usually the quest rather than the conflict – the *Odyssey* rather than the *Iliad*. The dramatic hero is one in whom human strengths (and weaknesses) are raised to the highest pitch. The hero of romance is often a man of very common clay, who nevertheless moves happily from the world of domestic comedy into that of magical adventure and back again. The subordinate characters are also more or less 'stock'. They include in addition to the 'helper' – and indeed the dog – the old wise man and the mother-figure, who between them set the hero on his way and welcome him back.

The book of Tobit, then, falls clearly into the category of popular romance. In fact we know the stories which lie behind it – none of them specifically Jewish – and we can see how the author has woven them skilfully together and given them a typically Jewish pious colouring (p. 5). It remains here to consider the place of Tobit within its category.

What stands out above all is the *Jewishness* of Tobit, and that particularly in the longer text followed by N.E.B. It is typically Jewish to be more interested in the moral than the plot. The author of Genesis, before telling the story of Abraham's sacrifice of Isaac, warns his readers that 'God put Abraham to the test'. Similarly, the author of Tobit reveals the outline of his story near the start, and thus removes much of the suspense at one blow. For the same reason he shows less concern than the author of Judith to see that events follow realistically upon one another. He allows his character to remember (6: 13) or forget (4: 1) or suggest (6: 9f.) things quite innocently as the immediate story requires, without either giving a reason or arousing suspicion for not doing so.

Also typically Jewish is the domestic humour (especially 2: 11–14 and 10: 1–7). It is the humour of the weak who can laugh not only at the strong but at themselves as well. It is the humour of extended family life, such as has sustained the Jews of the Dispersion throughout their long history of deprivation and persecution. (The 'feel' of Tobit is echoed in many of the Hasidic tales of Eastern Europe collected by Gollancz in *The New Year of Grace*.) Luther was right to call Tobit a comedy.

It is also in this respect that Tobit's contrast with Judith strikes deepest. In Judith the humour is bitter and there is no forgiveness. In Tobit there is no villain worth mentioning, and all the main parties are reconciled. The contrast comes across particularly in the use which the two authors make of dramatic irony: in Judith we laugh grimly at Holophernes (11: 6 note), in the book of Tobit we smile gently at Tobit himself (5: 13 note). The two books exemplify the two Jewish reactions to misfortune: one, to counter-attack bravely but vindictively; the other, to band together for defence, equally bravely but with a forgiving humour.

To complete the picture, a word may be added about the third of the three biblical romances, the book of Esther. Esther is found in two versions, as the N.E.B. explains. The longer one, which follows Judith in the N.E.B. Apocrypha, contains some additional chapters which are preserved only in Greek manuscripts.

Esther is in many ways like Judith. The story is about a beautiful Jewish woman who uses her charms on a heathen king in order to save her people from destruction. The story is better told than the first half of Judith but less well than the second. In character it is, briefly, more sophisticated and less pious than Judith. Its greater sophistication is shown, for example, in the presence of what pretend to be historical documents (in chapters 13 and 16 – only found in the Greek additions); in the sustained irony of the king's treatment of the villain Haman (chapters 7 and 8); and in the enjoyment of the sexual aspects of the story (e.g. 7: 8, 2: 12–14). Its lesser piety is shown, for example, in the lack of conviction in prayers (e.g. 14: 18; the prayers, too, are found only in the Greek additions); in the reluctance of the heroine Esther to help her people in the hour of need (4: 11); and in the replacement of religious by nationalistic feeling – the final triumph of the Jews in chapter 9 is even more vindictive than in Judith.

*   *   *   *   *   *   *   *   *   *   *   *   *

THE REST OF THE CHAPTERS
OF THE BOOK OF

ESTHER

WHICH ARE FOUND
NEITHER IN THE HEBREW
NOR IN THE SYRIAC

✳ ✳ ✳ ✳ ✳ ✳ ✳ ✳ ✳ ✳ ✳ ✳ ✳

ESTHER IN THE CANON

The book of Esther occupies a unique place in the Old Testament canon. Among the sacred books, none was more loved by the Jewish people and rabbinic commentators; none is extant in more manuscript copies, and except for the Pentateuch (the five books, Genesis to Deuteronomy) none was more expounded or elaborated in the Jewish tradition. In official synagogue rolls it is often given a place of honour directly after the Torah, that is, following Deuteronomy.

Few portions of the Old Testament show less textual variation among the existing Hebrew manuscripts; yet few have such surprising and extensive additions. The earliest extant presentation of such additions is that in the Greek version. Originating probably around the middle of the second century B.C., possibly not long after the Hebrew original, these additions are transmitted in the Greek manuscripts of the Old Testament text, and became an integral part of the Greek canon. The material of the additions was evidently also known to Josephus, the Jewish historian, in the first century A.D.

The Greek version with additions probably arose in Palestine, like the Hebrew counterpart. Yet the additions exhibit enough differences in style and content from the parts which have parallels in Hebrew, for it to be suspected that they were added to the original Greek translation of the Hebrew by a secondary hand as part of an elaborating process taking place in the Jewish community soon after or even at the same time that the book was written. In summary therefore, the Hebrew text of Esther was composed in Palestine perhaps in the early second century B.C., after a period of oral transmission of traditions originating in Babylonia; the Greek translation took place by the middle of that century, and the additions entered soon after. For a fuller discussion of the problems in understanding the book of Esther (origin, unity, Purim, comparison with Judith, etc.), the reader is referred to the commentary in the volume on the Five Scrolls (Ruth, Esther, Ecclesiastes, Song of Songs, Lamentations) in this series.

THE STORY OF ESTHER

The Hebrew book of Esther tells the story of a beautiful Jewish girl living in the Persian Diaspora, who comes to the throne as the wife of Xerxes through the planning of her uncle and guardian, Mordecai. Soon after she becomes queen, a plot to destroy all the Jews in the kingdom is contrived by Haman, the king's principal adviser. He has been insulted and infuriated by Mordecai's refusal to bow down to him and honour him, and consequently persuades the king to send out a letter to all the provincial governors and the satraps, announcing the plans for extermination.

Mordecai manages to get the news of the plot to Esther, and persuades her to risk her life in intercession before the king. Esther then carries out a clever stratagem of revealing the consequences of Haman's plan through dinner parties with him and the king. The book artfully weaves into this segment the supplementary themes of Haman's conceit and ambition, and the dramatic and progressive collapse of his fortunes, until he is misunderstood by the king to be attempting to violate the queen herself and is then hanged on the gallows which he had prepared for Mordecai. A keynote is struck when Haman's wife, Zeresh, says: 'If Mordecai, in face of whom your fortunes begin to fall, belongs to the Jewish race, you will not get the better of him; he will see your utter downfall' (6: 13). The Jews are spared, indeed are allowed to wreak terrible vengeance upon their enemies in a fearful slaughter on the 13th of the month of Adar (13th *and* 14th in Susa, the capital city), Esther and Mordecai establish Purim as a great holiday, and Mordecai is promoted to the position vacated by the unfortunate Haman.

THE NATURE OF THE ADDITIONS

In the major apocryphal additions, the following parts are introduced: (i) the prologue, an introductory apocalyptic dream of Mardochaeus (or, Mordecai), and a short account of how Mardochaeus overhears a plot to take the king's life and denounces the traitors; (ii) the letter of Artaxerxes authorizing Haman's evil plot (inserted after *3: 13*); (iii) the prayer of Mardochaeus, the prayer of Esther as she prepares to go in to the king to intercede, and Esther's approach to the throne (after *4: 17*); (iv) the letter of Artaxerxes accusing Haman, countermanding his instructions, and establishing Adar 13 as a day of national commemoration (after *8: 12*); and (v) the epilogue, explaining the dream as it came true, establishing Purim on Adar 14 and 15, and noting the bringing of the book to, it is presumed, Alexandria. Other minor additions are scattered throughout the book, and are noted below.

The Greek additions offer embellishment chiefly in material that is documentary (letters), meditative (prayers), or structural (prologue and epilogue, dream and explanation). They differ from the sizeable elaborations in Targums, for example, in that the Targumic material is primarily narrative or explanatory additions; the only narrative accretions in the Greek are the details of Esther's approach to the throne, discovery of the plot (*12: 1–6*), and a few isolated phrases (*1: 6, 7; 2: 21; 4: 1; 6: 4; 9: 19*).

CHAPTER NUMERATION

The order of material in the original text followed the logical development of the account. Jerome, however, when he translated these additions, which have no Hebrew counterparts, placed them in a group at the end of the book, where they were later accorded chapter numbers in sequence after the other material. Therefore that which should begin the book is counted as chapter 11, for example. The chapter and verse numbers in italics show the sections which appear in the Hebrew; those in Roman type indicate the additions, beginning at chapter 11.

VIEWPOINTS AND FEATURES OF THE ADDITIONS

The Hebrew book of Esther has been subjected to a variety of interpretations; these are discussed in the commentary volume mentioned on p. 133. They range from the narrative and prophetic to the cultic and mythological (cp. the commentary on Esther). Its purpose is tied to the festival of Purim, either as offering a supposedly historical basis for the holiday or serving as the festival legend used during the celebration, or both. But its purpose must also have been to encourage and fortify the Jewish nation in times of oppression or danger, and it probably grew out of and was addressed specifically to such a situation.

The Greek additions bring several important changes of emphasis into the book, although the original story remains essentially the same. The framework of prologue and epilogue causes a subtle shift in the tone of the whole book, like the framework in Job (1–2, 42). The old story is given a new cast by being introduced as the chain of events which are predicted by a dream of Mardochaeus. For a comparison in type of literature we would have to turn to Daniel, for example. The scene with all its figures and symbols seems strangely familiar: two great dragons in battle, global war involving all nations, the cry of the righteous, at dawn a help coming as though from a great river rising out of a little spring. Like Dan. 8: 20ff., the epilogue in Rest of Esth. 10: 4–13 explicitly clarifies the images. These features are sharply reminiscent of apocalyptic thinking, with its accent upon universal struggle, dramatic deliverance of the righteous by a trustworthy power, foretelling in dreams, employment of metaphors and mysterious figures of speech, and radical opposition of good and evil. A most significant variant in form occurs in that, whereas usually in apocalyptic literature there is stress upon that which is expected or predicted for the future, in the additions to Esther one encounters a *realized apocalypse*, like that in the first portions of Dan. 11 and Dan. 8: 20ff. The realized apocalypse has as its objective the reinforcing of confidence in contemporary predictions and promises by showing how past predictions came true under the same guiding power: if God revealed to Mardochaeus that he would deliver the Jews, and he did so, surely he will bring salvation in the crises that may now threaten!

The absence of any reference to God in the Hebrew Esther has been explained as due to the fact that the book was used in the secular and rather riotous holiday of Purim, when among other things it has been said that one may drink until one cannot distinguish between 'Blessed be Mordecai' and 'Cursed be Haman'. This omission of the name of God is corrected in the major additions and at other places in the

Greek text (cp. *2: 20*; *4: 8*; *6: 13*). Mardochaeus' remark at the end, 'All this is God's doing' (10: 4), becomes a theological directive to what in the Hebrew tradition was a tale of human affairs without any specific application to theological belief, although the story was meant to be understood as developing under divine control.

In the Greek Esther one misses the familiar touch in Hebrew at 5: 11 where Haman boasts of his wealth, honours, 'and his many sons'; the Greek does not sound the note of need to 'unite' (8: 11 and 9: 2) in order for the Jews to defend themselves and overcome their enemies. Mardochaeus' motives for refusing to pay homage to Haman are attributed to fear of God rather than to arrogance (13: 12–14; cp. Dan. 3: 12, 18, and 6: 10). The absence in the Hebrew account of any reference to the events of major theological importance in the history of Israel is repaired by reference in the Greek to the patriarchs (13: 15; 14: 5) and to the exodus (13: 16). The Greek lays a noteworthy emphasis on keeping the Jewish laws (*2: 20*; 13: 4; *8: 11*) which is also not in the Hebrew text.

The names appearing in the text are Greek forms of the Hebrew counterparts – Mardochaeus and Mordecai, Astin and Vashti, Muchaeus and Memucan, Gai and Hegai – but two significant changes should be noted. Whereas the Hebrew, Ahasuerus, is usually interpreted as Xerxes, the Greek explicitly says 'Artaxerxes'. And Haman, who is everywhere in the Hebrew identified as 'the Agagite' and 'the enemy of the Jews', is identified in the Greek usually as 'the Bugaean', but four times (*9: 24* footnote; 16: 10; and 12: 6 in Luc. Sept.; see also 16: 14) as 'the Macedonian', and in one manuscript as the 'Gogite'. These are small but specific examples of development in the tradition; in the first instance, with Artaxerxes, the movement is toward historical identification, and in the second, with Haman's sub-titles, there is an attempt to add historical and/or symbolical and apocalyptic interpretation. Whereas 'Agagite' links the earlier Esther tradition to the memory of Saul's battle against Agag the king of the Amalekites (1 Sam. 15), 'Macedonian' refers to a period when the Greeks could be regarded by the Jews as the great threat and enemy, after the days of Alexander the Great of Macedon. From the period of the Seleucid influence or domination over Palestine, 312–140 B.C., only the last few decades would fit well the situation described. 'Gogite' recalls the whole symbolism of the apocalypse in Ezek. 38–9 (see notes on 12: 6 and 16: 10).

It has been observed that the additions are in contradiction with certain details in the Hebrew text. Real and insoluble contradictions are in fact not numerous, however. Mardochaeus' role in 11: 3 and 12: 1–6 appears to place him in the court, able to contact the king, whereas in 2: 21–3 he has to report through Esther the queen. In 12: 5 he receives a reward, but in 6: 3 he had received no such reward. In 8: 8 the king's order is irrevocable, but in 16: 17f. the letter of Haman is summarily disregarded.

✯ ✯ ✯ ✯ ✯ ✯ ✯ ✯ ✯ ✯ ✯ ✯ ✯

NOTE. The portions of the Book of Esther commonly included in the Apocrypha are extracts from the Greek version of the book, which differs substantially from the Hebrew text (translated in *The New English Bible: Old Testament*). In order that they may be read in their original sequence, the whole of the Greek version is here translated, those portions which are not normally printed in the Apocrypha being enclosed in square brackets, with the chapter and verse numbers in italic figures. The order followed is that of the Greek text, but the chapter and verse numbers are made to conform to those of the Authorized Version. Proper names are given in the form in which they occur in the Greek version.

PROLOGUE: THE DREAM OF MARDOCHAEUS

11 2 IN THE SECOND YEAR of the reign of Artaxerxes the Great King, on the first day of Nisan, Mardochaeus son of Jairus, son of Semeius, son of Kisaeus, of the tribe of

Benjamin, had a dream. Mardochaeus was a Jew living in 3
the city of Susa, a man of high standing, who was in the
royal service; he came of those whom Nebuchadnezzar 4
king of Babylon had taken into exile from Jerusalem
with Jechonias king of Judah. This was his dream: din and 5
tumult, peals of thunder and an earthquake, confusion
upon the earth. Then appeared two great dragons, ready 6
to grapple with each other, and the noise they made was
terrible. Every nation was roused by it to prepare for war, 7
to fight against the righteous nation. It was a day of dark- 8
ness and gloom, with distress and anguish, oppression and
great confusion upon the earth. And the whole righteous 9
nation was troubled, dreading the evils in store for them,
and they prepared for death. They cried aloud to God; and 10
in answer to their cry there came as though from a little
spring a great river brimming with water. It grew light, 11
and the sun rose; the humble were exalted and they
devoured the great. After he had had this dream and had 12
seen what God had resolved to do, Mardochaeus woke;
he kept it before his mind, seeking in every way to understand it, until nightfall.

✳ The prologue places the entire book in a certain perspective,
that of the apocalyptic dream. The whole complex of events
is foreseen, and only remains to be played out in history; in
such a world of apocalyptic vision, God's providence is certain and his deliverance absolutely determined even when
momentary circumstances seem to indicate no basis for hope.

2. The New Year's Day dream of Mardochaeus, and presumably also the incident of the discovery of the plot in the
courtyard (12: 1–6), take place in the second year of Artaxerxes,
five years before the presentation of Esther (2: 16), and the year
before the banquet described in 1: 3.

Mardochaeus' descent from Kisaeus, or Kish, the father of Saul (cp. 1 Sam. 9 :1), links him of course with Israel's first king.

4. If Mardochaeus came to Babylonia in the first exile, under Jehoiachin (Jechonias) in 597 B.C., he would be much more than one hundred years old in the days of Artaxerxes I (465–424 B.C.). Obviously the historical gap was not taken into account by the narrator who, centuries later, was not concerned about, or informed in, chronological data of that type.

6–7. *two great dragons* in battle, a situation which causes a world-wide attack on the *righteous nation*, are somewhat weakly explained in 10: 8 as being not nations but two persons, Mardochaeus and Haman. This explanation seems inconsistent with the cosmic dimensions of the vision, and serves to remind us that political comment was not the primary goal of the additions.

righteous nation is a concept found often, for example earlier in Isa. 26 and 60 and later in the Targums; it does not necessarily reflect a developing legalism or self-righteousness, but rather an awareness of the special character of this people of God (cp. Exod. 19: 6, 'holy nation').

11. *sun* may be merely poetic imagery, meaning 'daylight'; but it may also suggest, like Mal. 4: 2, a more individualized, or hypostatized, manifestation of divine help. The exaltation of the *humble* is a theme found as far back as the song of Hannah (1 Sam. 2: 1–10, which was the basis for the Magnificat, Mary's song in Luke 1: 46–55), and is a constant biblical theme; Lucian's recension of the Septuagint reads 'rivers' (*potamoi*) for 'humble' (*tapeinoi*). ✲

A PLOT FIRST DISCOVERED

12 Now when Mardochaeus was resting in the royal courtyard with Gabatha and Tharra, the two eunuchs who guarded the courtyard, he heard them deep in dis-

cussion. He listened carefully to discover what was on 2
their minds, and found that they were plotting violence
against King Artaxerxes. He denounced them to the king,
who had the two eunuchs interrogated. They confessed 3
and were led away to execution. Then the king wrote 4
an account of the affair, to have it on record; Mardochaeus
also wrote an account of it. The king gave Mardochaeus 5
an appointment at court, and rewarded him for his services.
But Haman, the son of Hamadathus, a Bugaean, who 6
enjoyed the king's favour, sought to injure Mardochaeus
and his people because of the two eunuchs.

* These verses offer an account parallel to that in *2: 21–3*,
although it is here expanded and is in some details
contradictory.

5. The reward to Mardochaeus seems to contradict the
statement in *6: 3–4* that he had not in fact been rewarded with
anything.

6. The meaning of 'Bugaean' has not been satisfactorily
explained. The word, or variations such as 'Macedonian',
'Agagite', and 'Gogite', appears in variant readings of the
text in *3: 1*; *8: 3, 5*; *16: 10, 14*; *9: 10, 24*. The confusion in the
Greek is illustrated by the fact that Lucian's recension of the
Septuagint renders 'Muchaeus' in *1: 16* as 'Bougaeus'. *

A Jewess becomes queen in Persia

[Those events happened in the days of Artaxerxes, the *1*
Artaxerxes who ruled from India to Ethiopia, a hundred
and twenty-seven provinces. At this time he sat on his 2
royal throne in the city of Susa. Then in the third year of 3

his reign he gave a banquet for the King's Friends and persons of various races, the Persian and Median nobles and
4 the leading provincial governors. And afterwards, after
displaying to them the wealth of his empire and the
splendour of his rich festivities for a hundred and eighty
5 days, when these days of feasting were over, the king gave
a banquet for all the people of various races present in the
city of Susa; it was held in the court of the king's palace and
6 lasted six days. The court was decorated with white cur-
tains of linen and cotton stretched on cords of purple, and
these were attached to blocks of gold and silver resting on
stone and marble columns. There were couches of gold
and silver set on a pavement of malachite, marble, and
mother-of-pearl. There were mats of transparent weave
elaborately embroidered with roses arranged in a circle.
7 The cups were of gold and silver, and there was displayed
a miniature cup made of carbuncle worth thirty thousand
talents. The wine was abundant and sweet, from the king's
8 own cellar. The drinking was not according to a fixed rule,
but the king had laid it down that all the stewards of his
9 palace should respect his will and that of the guests. In
addition, Queen Astin gave a banquet for the women in
the same palace where King Artaxerxes was.

10   On the seventh day, when he was in high good humour,
the king ordered Haman, Mazan, Tharra, Borazes, Zathol-
tha, Abataza, and Tharaba, the seven eunuchs who were
11 in attendance on the king's person, to bring the queen
before him, so that he might place the royal diadem on
her head and let her display her beauty to the officers and
people of various races; for she was indeed a beautiful
21 woman. But Queen Astin refused to obey him and come

with the eunuchs. This offended the king and made him angry.

Then the king said to his courtiers, 'You hear what 13 Astin said. Give your ruling and judgement in the matter.' Then the nobles of Persia and Media who were closest to 14 the king – Harkesaeus, Sarsathaeus, and Malesear, who sat next him in the chief seats – approached him and de- 15 clared what should be done according to the law to Queen Astin for disobeying the order which the king sent her by the eunuchs. Then Muchaeus said to the king and the 16 nobles: 'Queen Astin has done wrong, and not to the king alone, but to all his nobles and officers as well.' (For he had 17 repeated to them what the queen had said and how she had defied the king.) 'And just as she defied King Artaxerxes, 18 so now the nobles of Persia and Media will find that all their ladies are bold enough to treat their husbands with contempt, when they hear what she said to the king. If it 19 please your majesty, let a royal decree go out from you, and let it be inscribed among the laws of the Medes and Persians, that Astin shall not again appear before the king; this is the only course. And let the king give her place as queen to another woman who is more worthy of it than she. Let whatever law the king makes be proclaimed 20 throughout his empire, and then all women will give due honour to their husbands, rich and poor alike.' The advice 21 pleased the king and the princes, and the king did as Muchaeus had proposed. Letters were sent to all the pro- 22 vinces of the empire, to each province in its own language, in order that every man might be respected in his own house.

Later, when the anger of King Artaxerxes had died 2 down, he remembered Astin and what she had done, and

2 how he had given judgement against her. So the king's attendants said: 'Let beautiful girls of unblemished virtue

3 be sought out for your majesty. Let your majesty appoint commissioners in all the provinces of the empire to select these beautiful virgins and bring them to the city of Susa, into the women's quarters. There let them be committed to the care of the king's eunuch in charge of the women, and let them be provided with cosmetics and everything

4 else they need. Then the one who is most acceptable to the king shall become queen in place of Astin.' The advice pleased the king, and he acted on it.

5　Now there was a Jew in the city of Susa named Mardochaeus, son of Jairus, son of Semeius, son of Kisaeus, of the

6 tribe of Benjamin; he had been carried into exile from Jerusalem when it was taken by Nebuchadnezzar king of

7 Babylon. He had a foster-child named Esther, the daughter of his father's brother Aminadab. She had lost her parents, and he had brought her up to womanhood. She was a very

8 beautiful girl. When the king's edict was proclaimed, many girls were brought to Susa to be entrusted to Gai, who had charge of the women, and among them was

9 Esther. She attracted his notice and received his special favour: he readily provided her with her cosmetics and allowance of food, and also with seven maids assigned to her from the king's palace. He gave her and her maids honourable treatment in the women's quarters.

10　Esther had not disclosed her race or country, because

11 Mardochaeus had forbidden her to do so. Every day Mardochaeus passed along by the forecourt of the women's quarters to keep an eye on Esther and see what would happen to her.

The period after which a girl was to go to the king was 12
twelve months. This was for the completion of the required
treatment – six months with oil and myrrh and six months
with perfumes and cosmetics. Then the girl went to the 13
king. She was handed to the person appointed, and accompanied him from the women's quarters to the king's
palace. She entered the palace in the evening and returned 14
in the morning to Gai, the king's eunuch in charge of the
women, in another part of the women's quarters. She did
not go to the king again unless summoned by name.

When the time came for Esther, daughter of Aminadab 15
the uncle of Mardochaeus, to go to the king, she neglected
none of the instructions of Gai the king's eunuch in charge
of the women; for Esther charmed all who saw her. She 16
was taken to King Artaxerxes in the twelfth month, that
is, the month Adar, in the seventh year of his reign. The 17
king fell in love with her, finding her more acceptable
than any of the other girls, and crowned her with the
queen's diadem. Then the king gave a banquet lasting 18
seven days for all the King's Friends and the officers, to
celebrate Esther's marriage. He also granted a remission
of taxation to all subjects of his empire.

Mardochaeus was in attendance in the courtyard. But 19,20
Esther had not disclosed her country – such were the instructions of Mardochaeus; but she was to fear God and
keep his commandments just as she had done when she was
with him. So Esther made no change in her way of life.

Two of the king's eunuchs, officers of the bodyguard, 21
were offended at the advancement of Mardochaeus and
plotted to kill King Artaxerxes. This became known to 22
Mardochaeus, who told Esther, and she revealed the plot

23 to the king. The king interrogated the two eunuchs and had them hanged, and he ordered that the service Mardochaeus had rendered should be recorded in the royal archives to his honour.

✽ 2: 20. The Greek introduces here an important statement that is not found in the Hebrew: 'but she was to fear God and keep his commandments just as she had done when she was with him. So Esther made no change in her way of life.' This addition and others like it shift the accent in the story, from an uncomplicated secular and nationalistic tale to a narrative with more sober and conscious religious impulse. ✽

A plot against the Jews

3 After this King Artaxerxes promoted Haman son of Hamadathus the Bugaean, advancing him and giving him prece-
2 dence above all the King's Friends. So all who were at
court did obeisance to Haman, for so the king had com-
3 manded; but Mardochaeus did not do obeisance. Then the
king's courtiers said to him, 'Mardochaeus, why do you
4 flout the king's command?' Day by day they challenged
him, but he refused to listen to them. Then they informed
Haman that Mardochaeus was resisting the king's com-
5 mand. Mardochaeus had told them that he was a Jew. So
when Haman learnt that Mardochaeus was not doing
6 obeisance to him, he was infuriated and plotted to exterminate all the Jews under Artaxerxes' rule.

7 In the twelfth year of King Artaxerxes he arrived at
a decision by casting lots, taking the days and the months
one by one, to decide on one day for the destruction of the

whole race of Mardochaeus. The lot fell on the thirteenth[a] day of the month Adar.

Then Haman said to King Artaxerxes: 'There is a cer- 8 tain nation dispersed among the other nations of your empire. Their laws are different from those of every other nation; they do not keep your majesty's laws. It is not to your majesty's advantage to tolerate them. If it please 9 your majesty, let an order be made for their destruction; and I will contribute ten thousand talents of silver to the royal treasury.' So the king took off his signet-ring and 10 gave it to Haman to seal the decree against the Jews. 'Keep 11 the money, and deal with these people as you will', he said.

On the thirteenth day of the first month the king's secre- 12 taries were summoned, and in accordance with Haman's instructions, they wrote in the name of King Artaxerxes to his army commanders and governors in every province from India to Ethiopia. There were a hundred and twenty-seven provinces in all, and each was addressed in its own language. Instructions were dispatched by courier to all 13 the empire of Artaxerxes to exterminate the Jewish race, on a given day of the twelfth month, Adar, and to plunder their possessions.]

THE FIRST LETTER OF ARTAXERXES

This is a copy of the letter: **13**

'Artaxerxes the Great King to the governors of the one hundred and twenty-seven provinces, from India to Ethiopia, and to the subordinate officials.

[a] *So some witnesses, and compare 8: 12 (p. 160); other witnesses read* fourteenth.

147

2 'Ruler as I am over many nations and master of all the world, it is my will – not in the arrogance of power, but because my rule is mild and equitable – to ensure to my subjects a life permanently free from disturbance, to pacify my empire and make it safe for travel to its farthest limits, and to restore the peace that all men long for.

3 I asked my counsellors how this object might be achieved and received a reply from Haman. Haman is eminent among us for sound judgement, one whose worth is proved by his constant goodwill and steadfast loyalty, and who has gained the honour of the second place at our

4 court. He represented to us that scattered among all the races of the empire is a disaffected people, opposed in its laws to every nation, and continually ignoring the royal ordinances, so that our irreproachable plans for the unified administration of the empire cannot be made effective.

5 We understand that this nation stands alone in its continual opposition to all men, that it evades the laws by its strange manner of life, and in disloyalty to our government commits grievous offences, thus undermining the security

6 of our empire. We therefore order that those who are designated to you in the indictments drawn up by Haman, our vicegerent and second father, shall all, together with their wives and children, be utterly destroyed by the sword of their enemies, without mercy or pity, on the thirteenth[a] day of Adar, the twelfth month, of the

7 present year. Those persons who have long been disaffected shall meet a violent death in one day so that our government may henceforth be stable and untroubled.'

[a] Gk. fourteenth; see note on 3: 7 (p. 147).

148

☆ The translation conveys something of the formal, elegant, somewhat pretentious style of the letter.

5. The reader is struck by the familiar ring of this accusation. It reflects years of the 'Jewish experience' in living in the Diaspora, or under foreign domination, where the determined and self-conscious practice of being Jewish was regarded as offensive.

6. It is difficult to explain why the Greek reads 'fourteenth' here and in *3: 7* (where the Hebrew reads 'twelfth'). In any case, in agreement with the rest of the book, only 'thirteenth' could be meant here.

7. *violent death*, literally, 'thrown violently into Hades'. ☆

[Copies of the document were posted up in every province, **3** 14 and all nations of the empire were ordered to be ready by that day. The matter was expedited also in Susa. While 15 the king and Haman caroused together, the city of Susa was thrown into confusion.

When Mardochaeus learnt all that was being done, he tore **4** his clothes, put on sackcloth and sprinkled himself with ashes; and he rushed through the city, crying loudly: 'An innocent nation is being destroyed.' He went as far as the 2 king's gate, and there he halted, because no one was allowed to enter the courtyard clothed with sackcloth and ashes. In every province where the king's decree was 3 posted up, there was a great cry of mourning and lamentation among the Jews, and they put on sackcloth and ashes. When the queen's maids and eunuchs came and 4 told her, she was distraught at the news, and sent clothes for Mardochaeus, urging him to take off his sackcloth; but he would not consent. Then Esther summoned Hachra- 5 thaeus, the eunuch who waited upon her, and ordered him to obtain accurate information for her from Mardo-

7 chaeus.[a] So Mardochaeus told him all that had happened, and how Haman had promised to pay ten thousand talents into the royal treasury to bring about the destruc-

8 tion of the Jews. He also gave him a copy of the written decree for their destruction which had been posted up in Susa, to show to Esther; and he gave him a message for her, that she should go to the king and plead for his favour and entreat him for her people. 'Remember', he said, 'those days when you were brought up in my humble home; for Haman, who stands next to the king, has spoken against us and demanded our death. Call upon the Lord, and then speak for us to the king and save our

9 lives.' Hachrathaeus returned and told her what Mardo-
10 chaeus had said. She sent him back with this message:
11 'All nations of the empire know that if any person, man or woman, enters the king's presence in the inner court un-bidden, there is no escape for him. Only one to whom the king stretches out the golden sceptre is safe; and it is now thirty days since I myself was called to go to the king.'

12,13   When Hachrathaeus delivered her message, Mardo-chaeus told him to go back and say: 'Do not imagine, Esther, that you alone of all the Jews in the empire will

14 escape alive. For if you remain silent at such a time as this, the Jews will somewhere find relief and deliverance, but you and your father's family will perish. Who knows whether it is not for such a time as this that you have been

[a] *Some witnesses add* (6) So he went out to Mardochaeus in the street opposite the city gate.

made a queen?' Esther gave the messenger this answer to *15*
take back to Mardochaeus: 'Go and assemble all the Jews *16*
who are in Susa and fast for me; for three days take neither
food nor drink, night or day, and I and my maids will also
go without food. Then in defiance of the law I will enter
the king's presence, even if it costs me my life.' So *17*
Mardochaeus went away and did as Esther had bidden
him.]

THE PRAYER OF MARDOCHAEUS

And Mardochaeus prayed to the Lord, calling to mind all **13** 8
the works of the Lord. He said, 'O Lord, Lord and King *9*
who rulest over all, because the whole world is under thy
authority, and when it is thy will to save Israel there is no
one who can stand against thee: thou didst make heaven *10*
and earth and every wonderful thing under heaven; thou *11*
art Lord of all, and there is no one who can resist thee, the
Lord. Thou knowest all things; thou knowest, Lord, that *12*
it was not from insolence or arrogance or vainglory that
I refused to bow before proud Haman, for I could gladly *13*
have kissed the soles of his feet to save Israel; no, I did it so *14*
that I might not hold a man in greater honour than God;
I will not bow before any but thee, my Lord, and it is not
from arrogance that I refuse this homage. And now Lord, *15*
God and King, God of Abraham, spare thy people; for
our enemies are watching us to bring us to ruin, and they
have set their hearts upon the destruction of thy chosen
people, thine from the beginning. Do not disdain thy *16*
own possession which thou didst ransom for thyself out
of Egypt. Hear my prayer, and have mercy on thy *17*
heritage, and turn our mourning into feasting, that we

may live and sing of thy name, Lord; do not put to silence
18 the lips that give thee praise.' And all Israel cried aloud with
all their might, for death stared them in the face.

* At this point there begins the large middle section of additions, comprising the prayer of Mardochaeus, the prayer of
Esther, and the entrance of Esther to the king. It contains
the fine devotional material added to the book.

12. The clarification of Mardochaeus' motives in refusing
obeisance to Haman prevents what the Hebrew version
allows, namely the thought that he was too proud or petulant.
The more pious Greek version changes such possibilities,
and brings his motives into agreement with the traditional
Israelite values of fidelity in worship and confession and
humility in personal attitude.

13–14. Like Judith (cp. Judith 10: 23), he is ready to humble
himself for the sake of his people. It is only because of faithfulness to God that he refuses. *

THE PRAYER OF ESTHER

14 Then Queen Esther, caught up in this deadly conflict,[a]
2 took refuge in the Lord. She stripped off her splendid attire
and put on the garb of mourning and distress. Instead of
proud perfumes she strewed ashes and dung over her
head. She abased her body, and every part that she had
delightfully adorned she covered with her dishevelled
3 hair. And so she prayed to the Lord God of Israel:

'O my Lord, thou alone art our king; help me who am
4 alone, with no helper but thee; for I am taking my life
5 in my hands. Ever since I was born I have been taught by
my father's family and tribe that thou, O Lord, didst

[a] caught...conflict: *or* seized by mortal anxiety.

choose Israel out of all the nations, and out of all the
founders of our race didst choose our fathers for an everlasting possession, and that what thou didst promise them,
thou didst perform. But now we have sinned against thee, 6
and thou hast handed us over to our enemies because we 7
honoured their gods; thou art just, O Lord. But they are 8
not content with our bitter servitude; they have now
pledged themselves to their idols to annul thy decree and 9
to destroy thy possession, silencing those who praise thee,
extinguishing the glory of thy house, and casting down
thy altar. They would give the heathen cause to sing the 10
praises of their worthless gods, and would have a mortal
king held in everlasting honour.

'Yield not thy sceptre, O Lord, to gods that are nothing; 11
let not our enemies mock at our ruin, but turn their plot
against themselves, and make an example of the man who
planned it. Remember us, O Lord, make thy power known 12
in the time of our distress, and give me courage, O King of
gods, almighty Lord. Give me the apt word to say when 13
I enter the lion's den. Divert his hatred to our enemy, so
that there may be an end of him and his confederates.

'Save us by thy power, and help me who am alone and 14
have no helper but thee, Lord. Thou knowest all; thou 15
knowest that I hate the splendour of the heathen, I abhor
the bed of the uncircumcised or of any Gentile. Thou 16
knowest in what straits I am: I loathe that symbol of pride,
the headdress that I wear when I show myself abroad,
I loathe it as one loathes a filthy rag; in private I refuse to
wear it. I, thy servant, have not eaten at Haman's table; 17
I have not graced a banquet of the king or touched the
wine of his drink-offerings; I have not known festive joy 18

from the time that I was brought here until now except in
19 thee, Lord God of Abraham. O God who dost prevail
against all, give heed to the cry of the despairing: rescue
us from the power of wicked men, and rescue me from
what I dread.'

* This prayer is an excellent example of a synthesis of traditional themes and motifs in the faith of Israel: kingship,
election, covenant, patriarchal promise, family piety, promise
and fulfilment; sin, chastisement, penitence, and the righteousness of God; aversion and disdain for idols and other gods;
cry for help, upright life in observing the scruples of the faith,
personal asceticism. While expressing the orthodox faith in
the ancient terms, it also communicates much of the situation
in or after which it was written: a time of oppression by
wicked men, profanation of the altar, and the obstruction of
worship in the temple – indeed, the time of the Maccabees
and of Antiochus IV Epiphanes around 167 B.C.

11. *gods that are nothing*, literally, 'those not existing'.
The participle is the same as in Exod. 3: 14, in the Septuagint,
where God is said to designate his name as 'the being one'.

13. *lion's den*, literally, 'before the lion'. The reference is
a way of describing the king's court. *

ESTHER'S ENTRANCE TO THE KING

15 On the third day Esther brought her prayers to an end. She
took off the clothes she had worn while she worshipped
2 and put on all her splendour. When she was in her royal
robes and had invoked the all-seeing God, her preserver,
3 she took two maids with her; on one she leaned for sup-
4 port, as befitted a fine lady, while the other followed,
5 bearing her train. She was blushing and in the height of
her beauty; her face was as cheerful as it was lovely, but

her heart was in the grip of fear. She passed through all 6
the doors and reached the royal presence. The king was
seated on his throne, in the full array of his majesty. He
was all gold and precious stones, an awe-inspiring figure.
He looked up, his face glowing with regal dignity, and 7
glanced at her in towering anger. The queen fell, changing
colour in a faint, and swooning on the shoulder of the maid
who went before her.

Then God changed the spirit of the king to gentleness, 8
and in deep concern he leapt from his throne and took her
in his arms until she came to herself. He soothed her with
reassuring words: 'Esther, what is it? Have no fear of me, 9
your loving husband; you shall not die, for our order is 10
only for our subjects. Come to me.' And the king lifted his 11
golden sceptre and laid it upon her neck; then he kissed 12
her and said, 'You may speak to me.' She answered, 'I saw 13
you, my lord, looking like an angel of God, and I was
awestruck at your glorious appearance; your countenance 14
is so full of grace, my lord, that I look on you in wonder.'
But while she was speaking she fell down in a faint; the 15, 16
king was distressed, and all his attendants comforted her.

✳ This passage seems to have been added for the enjoyment
of the story-teller and of the listener. One of the Targums
places a long prayer on the lips of Esther at this point, and
Megillah, a tractate in the Talmud, has her quoting Ps. 22,
'My God, my God, why hast thou forsaken me?'
   The Hebrew version presents in two verses a matter-of-fact
account of her entrance, and of the king's acknowledgement
and invitation for her to approach the throne and touch the
sceptre. ✳

5 3 [Then the king said, 'What is your wish, Queen Esther?
  What is your request? Up to half my empire, it shall be
4 given you.' 'Today is a special day for me', said Esther.
  'If it please your majesty, will you come, and Haman
5 with you, to a banquet which I shall give today?' The king
  ordered Haman to be sent for in haste, so that Esther's wish
  might be fulfilled; and they both went to the banquet to
6 which Esther had invited them. Over the wine the king
  said to her, 'What is it, Queen Esther? Whatever you ask
7 for shall be yours.' Esther said, 'This is my humble request:
8 if I have won your majesty's favour, will your majesty
  and Haman come again tomorrow to the banquet which
  I shall give for you both, and tomorrow I will do as I have
  done today.'

9 So Haman went out from the royal presence in good
  spirits and well pleased with himself. But when he saw
  Mardochaeus the Jew in the king's courtyard, he was filled
10 with rage. He went home, and called for his friends and
11 his wife Zosara, and held forth to them about his wealth
  and the honours with which the king had invested him,
12 how he had made him first man in the empire. 'Queen
  Esther', he said, 'invited no one but myself to accompany
  the king to her banquet; and I am invited again for to-
13 morrow. Yet all this is no pleasure to me so long as I see that
14 Jew Mardochaeus in the courtyard.' Then his wife Zosara
  and his friends said to him: 'Have a gallows put up, seventy-
  five feet[a] high, and in the morning speak to the king and
  have Mardochaeus hanged upon it. Then you can go with
  the king to the banquet and enjoy yourself.' Haman thought
  this an excellent plan, and the gallows was made ready.

[a] *Gk.* fifty cubits.

The triumph of the Jews

That night the Lord kept sleep from the king, so he 6 ordered his private secretary to bring the court chronicle and read it to him. He found written there the record about 2 Mardochaeus, how he had given information about the two royal eunuchs who, while they were on guard, had plotted violence against King Artaxerxes. Whereupon the 3 king said, 'What honour or favour did we confer on Mardochaeus for this?' The king's courtiers who were in attendance replied, 'You have done nothing for him.' While the king was inquiring about the service that Mardo- 4 chaeus had rendered, Haman appeared in the courtyard. 'Who is that in the court?' asked the king. Now Haman had just come in to recommend to the king that Mardochaeus should be hanged on the gallows which he had prepared; so the king's servants said, 'It is Haman standing in the 5 court.' 'Call him', said the king. Then the king said to 6 Haman, 'What shall I do for the man I wish to honour?' Haman said to himself, 'Whom would the king wish to honour but me?' So he said to the king, 'For the man 7 whom the king wishes to honour, let the king's attendants 8 bring a robe of fine linen from the king's own wardrobe and a horse from the king's own stable. Let both be 9 delivered to one of the king's most honourable Friends, and let him robe the man whom the king loves and mount him on the horse, and let him proclaim through the city: "This shall be the lot of any man whom the king honours."' Then the king said to Haman, 'An excellent 10

suggestion! Do all this for Mardochaeus the Jew who
serves in the courtyard. Let nothing that you have said be
11 omitted.' So Haman took the robe and put it on Mardochaeus, and mounted him on the horse; then he went
through the city, proclaiming: 'This shall be the lot of any
man whom the king wishes to honour.'

12   Then Mardochaeus returned to the courtyard, and
Haman hurried off home with head veiled in mourning.
13 He told his wife Zosara and his friends what had happened
to him. They replied, 'If Mardochaeus is a Jew, and you
have been humiliated before him, you are a lost man. You
cannot get the better of him, because the living God is
on his side.'

14   While they were still talking with Haman, the king's
eunuchs arrived and hurried him away to the banquet
which Esther had prepared.

7   So the king and Haman went to the queen's banquet.
2 Again on that second day, over the wine, the king said,
'What is it, Queen Esther? What is your request? What
is your petition? You shall have it, up to half my empire.'
3 Queen Esther answered: 'If I have won your majesty's
favour, my request is for my life, my petition is for my
4 people. For it has come to my ears that we have been sold,
I and my people, to be destroyed, plundered, and enslaved,
we and our children, male and female. Our adversary is
5 a disgrace to the king's court.' The king said, 'Who is it
6 that has dared to do such a thing?' 'Our enemy', said
Esther, 'is this wicked Haman.' Haman stood dumb-
7 founded before the king and the queen. The king rose from
the banquet and went into the garden, and Haman began
to plead with the queen, for he saw that things were going

badly for him. When the king returned to the banqueting 8
hall from the garden, Haman in his entreaties had flung
himself across the queen's couch. The king exclaimed,
'What! You assault the queen in my own house?' At
those words Haman turned away in despair. Then 9
Bugathan, one of the eunuchs, said to the king, 'Look!
Haman has even prepared a gallows for Mardochaeus, the
man who reported the plot against the king, and there it
stands, seventy-five feet[a] high, in Haman's compound.'
'Have Haman hanged on it', said the king. So Haman was 10
hanged on the gallows that he himself had prepared for
Mardochaeus. After that the king's rage died down.

That day King Artaxerxes gave Esther all that had 8
belonged to Haman the persecutor; and Mardochaeus was
called into the king's presence, for Esther had told him how
he was related to her. Then the king took off his signet- 2
ring, which he had taken back from Haman, and gave it
to Mardochaeus. And Esther put Mardochaeus in charge
of Haman's estate.

Once again Esther spoke before the king, falling at his 3
feet and pleading with him to avert the calamity planned
by Haman and to frustrate his plot against the Jews. The 4
king stretched out the golden sceptre to Esther, and she
rose and stood before the king. 'May it please your 5
majesty,' she said; 'if I have won your favour, let an order
be issued recalling the letters which Haman sent in pur-
suance of his plan to destroy the Jews in your empire. How 6
can I bear to see the downfall of my people? How escape
myself when my country is destroyed?' Then the king 7
said to Esther: 'I have given Haman's property to you,

[a] *Gk.* fifty cubits.

and hanged him on the gallows because he threatened the
8 lives of the Jews. If you want anything further, you may
draw up an order in my name, in whatever terms you
think fit, and seal it with my signet. An order written at
the king's direction and sealed with the royal signet cannot
be contravened.'

9 And so, on the twenty-third day of the first month, Nisan,
in the same year, the king's secretaries were summoned;
and the Jews were informed in writing of the instructions
given to the administrators and chief governors in the
provinces, from India to Ethiopia, a hundred and twenty-
seven provinces, to each province in its own language.
10 The orders were written as from the king and sealed with
11 his signet, and dispatched by courier. By these documents
the king granted permission to the Jews in every city to
observe their own laws and to defend themselves, and to
deal as they would with their opponents and enemies,
12 throughout the empire of Artaxerxes, on a given day, the
thirteenth of the twelfth month, Adar.]

THE SECOND LETTER OF ARTAXERXES

16 The following is a copy of this letter:

'Artaxerxes the Great King to the governors of the one
hundred and twenty-seven provinces, from India to
Ethiopia, and to those who are of our allegiance, greeting.
2 'Many who have been honoured only too often by the
lavish generosity of their benefactors have grown arrogant
3 and not only attempt to ill-treat our subjects but, unable
to carry the favours heaped upon themselves, even plot

mischief against those who grant them. Not content with 4
destroying gratitude in men, they are carried away by the
insolence of those who are strangers to good breeding;
they even suppose that they will escape the justice of all-
seeing God, who is no friend to evil-doers. And often, 5
when the king's business has been entrusted to those he
counts his friends, they have, by their plausibility, made
those in supreme authority partners in shedding innocent
blood and involved them in irreparable misfortunes, for 6
their malevolence with its misleading sophistries has
imposed upon the sincere goodwill of their rulers. The 7
evil brought about by those who wield power unworthily
you can observe, not only in records of tradition and history but also in your familiar experience, and apply the 8
lesson to the future. Thus we shall peacefully free this
realm from disturbance for the benefit of all, making no 9
changes but always deciding matters which come under
our notice with firmness and equity. Now Haman son of 10
Hamadathus, a Macedonian, an alien in fact with no
Persian blood, a man with nothing of our kindly nature,[a]
was accepted by us and enjoyed[b] so fully the benevolence 11
with which we treat every nation that he was proclaimed
our Father, and all along received obeisance from everyone
as second only to our royal throne. But this man in his 12
unbridled arrogance planned to deprive us of our empire
and our life by using fraud and tortuous cunning to bring 13
about the destruction of Mardochaeus, our constant
benefactor who had saved our life, and of Esther, our
blameless consort, together with their whole nation. For 14
he thought that by these methods he would catch us

[a] *Or* a man fallen away greatly from our favour.   [b] *Or* won.

defenceless and would transfer to the Macedonians the
15 sovereignty now held by the Persians. But we find that
the Jews, whom this triple-dyed villain had consigned to
extinction, are no evil-doers; they order their lives by the
16 most just of laws, and are children of the living God, most
high, most mighty, who maintains the empire in most
wonderful order, for us as for our ancestors.

17 'You will therefore disregard the letters sent by Haman
18 son of Hamadathus, because he, the contriver of all this,
has been hanged aloft at the gate of Susa with his whole
household, God who is Lord of all having speedily brought
19 upon him the punishment that he deserved. Copies of this
letter are to be posted up in all public places. Permit the
20 Jews to live under their own laws, and give them every
assistance so that on the thirteenth day of Adar, the twelfth
month, on that very day, they may avenge themselves on
those who were ranged against them[a] in the time of their
21 oppression. For God, who has all things in his power, has
made this a day not of ruin, but of joy, for his chosen
22 people. Therefore you also must keep it with all good
cheer, as a notable day among your feasts of commemora-
23 tion, so that henceforth it may be a standing symbol of
deliverance to us and our loyal Persians, but a reminder
24 of destruction to those who plot against us. Any city or
country whatsoever which does not act upon these orders
shall incur our wrath and be wiped out with fire and sword.
No man shall set foot in it and even the beasts and birds
shall shun it for all time.

[a] *Or* may defend themselves against their assailants.

✻ 5. *friends* means the king's highest officials (cp. 1 Macc. 2: 18).

10–11. *Macedonian*: cp. 12: 6. The Greeks and Persians were adversaries for nearly 200 years, from the time of Darius the Great in 520 B.C. until Alexander the Great of Macedon destroyed the Persian Empire in the latter part of the fourth century. Identification of Haman as Macedonian, however, must reflect memories after Persia's great fall to Alexander, and further directs the story of Esther against the hellenistic Seleucids, Israel's specific enemies from Antioch in the days of the Maccabees.

12. The allegation of a plot against the king's life has basis in facts given previously only in the additions (12: 2, 6), not in the Hebrew.

14. Haman starts out being the enemy of the Jews, and ends as the great traitor who will betray all to the Greeks. Perhaps his treason is used as a sign against certain persons in Palestine who connived for the hellenization of Israel.

15–16. Hardly a confession that a Persian king, Zoroastrian by faith, would be expected to make, these words rather reflect the traditional Hebrew confession, as it is expressed for example in Deut. 4: 6–8. ✻

['Let copies be posted up conspicuously throughout the **8** 13 empire, so that the Jews may be prepared by that day to fight against their enemies.'

Mounted messengers set out with all speed to do what 14 the king commanded; and the decree was posted up also in Susa.

Mardochaeus left the king's presence in royal robes, 15 wearing a golden crown and a turban of fine linen dyed purple, and all in Susa rejoiced to see him. For the Jews 16 there was light and gladness in every province and every 17

city. Wherever the decree was posted up there was joy and
gladness for the Jews, feasting and merriment. And many
of the Gentiles were circumcised and professed Judaism,
because they were afraid of the Jews.

9 On the thirteenth day of the twelfth month, Adar, the
decree drawn up by the king arrived. On that very day the
2 enemies of the Jews perished. No one offered resistance,
3 because they were afraid of them. The leading provincial
governors, the princes, and the royal secretaries paid all
respect to the Jews, because fear of Mardochaeus weighed
4 upon them. For they had received the king's decree that
his name should be honoured throughout the empire.[a][b]
6 In the city itself the Jews slaughtered five hundred men,
7, 8 including Pharsanestan, Delphon, Phasga, Pharadatha,
9 Barsa, Sarbacha, Marmasima, Ruphaeus, Arsaeus, and
10 Zabuthaeus, the ten sons of Haman son of Hamadathus,
the Bugaean, the Jews' great enemy; and that day they
took plunder.

11   When the number of those killed in Susa was reported
12 to the king, he said to Esther, 'In the city of Susa the Jews
have killed five hundred men. What do you suppose they
have done in the surrounding country? Whatever further
13 request you have will be granted.' Esther answered him,
'Let the Jews be allowed to do the same tomorrow, and
14 hang up the bodies of Haman's ten sons.' The king con-
sented; he handed over the bodies of Haman's sons to the
15 Jews of the city to be hung up. The Jews in Susa assembled

[a] For they...empire: *probable reading; Gk. obscure.*
[b] *Some witnesses add from the Heb.* (5) So the Jews put their enemies to
the sword with great slaughter and destruction; they worked their will
on those who hated them.

on the fourteenth day of Adar also, and killed three
hundred, but they took no plunder.

The rest of the Jews in the empire rallied together in self-   16–17
defence, and so were quit of their enemies; for they
slaughtered fifteen thousand of them on the thirteenth of
Adar; but they took no plunder. On the fourteenth they
rested, and made that day a day of rest, with rejoicing and
merriment. The Jews in the city of Susa had assembled also   18
on the fourteenth day of the month; they did not rest on
that day, but they kept the fifteenth day with rejoicing
and merriment. That is why Jews who are dispersed over   19
the remoter parts keep the fourteenth day of Adar as a
holiday with rejoicing and merriment, sending presents of
food to one another; but those who live in the principal
cities keep the fifteenth of Adar as a holiday, sending
presents of food to one another.

Then Mardochaeus wrote down the whole story in a   20
book and sent it to all the Jews in the empire of Artaxerxes,
far and near, ordering them to establish these holidays,   21
and to keep the fourteenth and fifteenth of Adar, because   22
these were the days on which the Jews were quit of their
enemies, and to keep the whole month of Adar, in which
came the great change from sorrow to joy and from mourning to holiday, as a time for feasting and merriment, days
for sending presents of food to friends and to the poor.

So the Jews formally accepted the account which Mar-   23
dochaeus wrote: how Haman son of Hamadathus, the   24
Bugaean,[a] fought against them; how he cast lots to decide
the date of their destruction; how he came before the king   25
with a proposal to hang Mardochaeus; and how all the

[a] *Some witnesses read* the Macedonian.

evils which he had plotted against the Jews recoiled on his
26 own head, and he and his sons were hanged. This is why
these days were named 'Purim', which in the Jews'
language means 'lots'. Because of all that was recorded
in this letter – all that they had experienced, all that had
happened – Mardochaeus directed that this festival should
27 be observed, and the Jews undertook, on behalf of themselves, their descendants, and all who should join them, to
28 do so without fail. These were to be days of commemoration, duly celebrated age after age in every town, family,
and province. These days of Purim were to be kept for all
time, and the commemoration was never to cease throughout all ages.

29   Queen Esther daughter of Aminadab, and Mardochaeus
the Jew, recorded in writing all that they had done, and
30–31 confirmed the regulations for Purim. They made themselves responsible for this decision and staked their life
32 upon the plan.[a] Esther established it for all time by her
decree, and it was put on record.

10   The king made decrees for the empire by land and sea.
2 His strength and courage, his wealth and the splendour of
his empire, are recorded in the annals of the kings of the
3 Persians and Medes. Mardochaeus acted for King Artaxerxes; he was a great man in the empire and honoured by
the Jews. His way of life won him the affection of his
whole nation.]

EPILOGUE: THE MEANING OF THE DREAM

4, 5 Mardochaeus said, 'All this is God's doing. For I have been
reminded of the dream I had about these things; not one

[a] They made...plan: *possible meaning; Gk. obscure.*

of the visions I saw proved meaningless. There was the 6
little spring which became a river, and there was light and
sun and water in abundance. The river is Esther, whom the
king married and made queen; the two dragons are Haman 7
and myself; the nations are those who gathered to wipe 8
out the Jews; my nation is Israel, which cried aloud to God 9
and was delivered. The Lord has delivered his people, he
has rescued us from all these evils. God performed great
miracles and signs such as have not occurred among the
nations. He made ready two lots, one for the people of 10
God and one for all the nations; then came the hour and 11
the time for these two lots to be cast, the day of decision by
God before[a] all the nations; he remembered his people 12
and gave the verdict for his heritage.

'So they shall keep these days in the month of Adar, the 13
fourteenth and fifteenth of that month, by gathering with
joy and gladness before God from one generation of his
people to another, for ever.'

✶ Reading this section reminds one of Dan. 8: 19–26; the
difference between this epilogue and the text of Daniel lies
in the fact that Esther represents all the events as having already
taken place. Additions to Esther therefore are an example of
the realized apocalypse, bearing a special word of encouragement and support to people who were anxious and weary
under years of struggle against alien lords and who needed
reassurance of God's abiding and effective deliverance.

6. *river* and *water* were symbols of life in the Old Testament,
cp. Ezek. 47: 1ff., Isa. 12: 3, and Ps. 46: 4, 'There is a river
whose streams gladden the city of God.'

9. This passage follows the old pattern of danger (oppression), cry, and deliverance which is used, for example, in the

[a] *Or* the day of judgement by God upon...

stories of the Judges by the Deuteronomistic historians. *miracles and signs* is a characteristic term of that theology developed by the Deuteronomistic teachers; it is as much a technical term in the Greek of the Septuagint as in the Hebrew, and refers especially to the mighty deliverance in the exodus. Events described in Esther therefore become another experience typical of God's exemplary act of salvation in the exodus.

11–12. Purim is described through these verses as a type of the day of judgement, wherein God renders *the verdict* for (literally, 'declares to be righteous') his special people. *

THE SUBSCRIPTION

11 1 In the fourth year of the reign of Ptolemy and Cleopatra, Dositheus, who said that he was a levitical priest, and Ptolemaeus his son, brought the foregoing letter about Purim, which they said was authentic and had been translated by Lysimachus son of Ptolemaeus, a resident in Jerusalem.

* Esther is unusual in that it offers so much information on authorship and origin (cp. Ecclus., 'Preface'). The fourth year mentioned here probably indicates the year 114 B.C., the fourth of Ptolemy VIII (others have suggested Ptolemy XII, that is, 78–77 B.C., and Ptolemy XIV, 48 B.C.). It is likely that the *letter* referred to was the whole Greek book of Esther, and that it originated in the present form before 140 B.C., while the Jews still could feel rather friendly toward the Persians. After that date, the Persians (or, rather, now the Parthians) under Mithradates I had defeated the Seleucids and were a threat also to the Jews. *

*   *   *   *   *   *   *   *   *   *   *   *   *

BARUCH

✻ ✻ ✻ ✻ ✻ ✻ ✻ ✻ ✻ ✻ ✻ ✻ ✻

WHAT THE BOOK IS ABOUT

The book of Baruch contains no story. It consists of an introduction (1: 1-14) leading into three sections: first, a psalm of repentance (1: 15-3: 8); secondly, a hymn in praise of God's wisdom (3: 9-4: 4); and, thirdly, a song of encouragement (4: 5 to the end). Although the three sections are now linked, they were originally quite distinct. The introduction claims Baruch's authorship for the first section: even if that claim were accepted, the other two sections could not be by him.

Only the second section contains anything original, and that not a great deal. The interest of the book of Baruch lies paradoxically in its anonymity and its datelessness. The three sections represent ideas that continued not merely to exist but to *live* among the Jews for centuries. Each of them could have been written at almost any time between, say, 300 B.C. and A.D. 100.

REASONS FOR SEPARATING THE BOOK
INTO SECTIONS

At first sight the book looks reasonably unified. The joins between the sections are smoothed over; see notes on 3: 9, 3: 24 and 4: 4. But a careful reading even in English shows the second section to be quite different in tone from the other two. That section has nothing to say, as the others have, about problems of exile and return, repentance and forgiveness. It is not (except in its link-verses) calling upon the Jews to do anything: it consists not of pleas but of statements. Unlike either of the other sections, its argument unfolds logically, and its general treatment of its theme is concentrated where theirs is diffuse. In all ways it is the odd man out.

The evidence for considering the third section to be by a different hand from the first is perhaps easier to grasp. The fact that the third is in poetry while the first is in prose does not prove they are by different authors. But there are a number of discrepancies between them, of which it will suffice to mention two. The hostile attitude to Babylon in the third is the opposite of that in the first; see note on 4: 31. And God, who is known in the third section as 'The Everlasting', is nowhere called by that title in sections one or two. In the first he is usually 'the Lord our God', in the second simply 'God'.

THE LIFE AND TIMES OF BARUCH

The manuscripts claim that the whole book was written by Baruch son of Neriah, and the first section contains many references to the events of his lifetime. This Baruch was secretary to the great prophet Jeremiah and appears also as his close associate (see Jer. 32, 36, 43, 45). When Jeremiah decided in about 605 B.C. to commit to writing his prophecies about the impending fate of Jerusalem, he dictated them to Baruch and then asked him to read them aloud in the temple 'to all the people'. King Jehoiakim heard of it, had the text read to him, and then deliberately burned it. Jeremiah, who had by then gone into hiding with Baruch, not only rewrote the text but added further prophecies of personal ruin for Jehoiakim (Jer. 36).

All these prophecies proved true both for Jerusalem and for Jehoiakim. He himself died shortly after the Babylonian advance began, and his young son Jeconiah promptly surrendered Jerusalem to Nebuchadnezzar. Jeconiah (who is known as Coniah in Jer. 37: 1 and as Jehoiachin in 2 Kings 24) was taken off to Babylon, together with most of the leading Jews (see note on Baruch 1: 9); and in his place his uncle Zedekiah was appointed king by Nebuchadnezzar.

Zedekiah did not realize his own weakness and ten years later stupidly revolted as Jehoiakim had done. Again Nebuchadnezzar came with an army of invasion; again Jeremiah protested and foretold defeat and ruin; again his prophecies were disregarded but fulfilled. The Babylonians captured Jerusalem (in 587 B.C.), pulled down the walls, burned the temple and deported most of the people except the poorest (2 Kings 25: 8–12).

Jeremiah stayed in Judaea with Gedaliah, the governor appointed by the Babylonians. When Gedaliah was assassinated, he advised those who had been with him to remain in Judaea. But they chose to disregard his advice and went to Egypt, taking Jeremiah and Baruch with them (Jer. 43: 3–7). From then on both of them were regarded with some suspicion by their fellow-Jews, and there may even have been a rift between them (Jer. 45: 5). We know no more of Baruch, but nowhere in the Old Testament is there any suggestion that he went to Babylon.

AUTHORSHIP OF THE FIRST SECTION

The manuscripts claim that not only the first section but the whole book was written by Baruch in exile in Babylon about 583 B.C. We have seen why that cannot be true of the second and third sections of the book; is it true of the first? There are three good reasons for thinking that it is not.

First, the history given in the introduction is inaccurate in one obvious respect (that Belshazzar was son of Nebuchadnezzar; see note on 1: 11) and at best dubious in a number of others (see notes on verses 7, 8, 9).

Second, the introduction does not fit very well even on to the first section (see note on verse 14).

Third, the bulk of the first section is modelled on the prayer in Dan. 9 (see note on verse 18). Now the book of Daniel as a whole can be securely dated about 165 B.C. It is possible that some parts of it were written earlier, but hardly as early as the sixth century B.C.

For these and other reasons most modern scholars regard the whole book of Baruch as pseudonymous, i.e. written under a false name. The Jews often compiled books under the name of a great figure of old: see for example, apart from Daniel, the book Ecclesiastes which claims to have been written by Solomon.

ORIGIN OF THE SECOND AND THIRD SECTIONS

The second section contains no references to any datable event. It seems to have been written after Job 28 – but that cannot be dated – and probably also after Ecclesiasticus about 200 B.C. (see notes on 3: 35 and 4: 1).

The third section refers to a situation where Jerusalem has recently fallen and loyal Jews have been taken into captivity abroad; but they are expected to return 'soon'. We could in theory be looking back upon a fall of Jerusalem as early as 587 B.C. or as late as A.D. 70. Actually the former is ruled out by the quotations from Isaiah 55–6, which were written no earlier than about 550–520 B.C. The suggestion of the later date depends partly upon the close resemblance of the final verses of Baruch to a passage in the so-called Psalms of Solomon, which are usually assigned to the mid-first century B.C.; but unfortunately we cannot be sure which author borrowed from the other (see note on 5: 5).

If the third section was really written after the fall of Jerusalem in A.D. 70, it is possible that the first section belongs to the same time. In that case Nebuchadnezzar and his son Belshazzar would stand for the Roman Emperor Vespasian and his son Titus who actually captured Jerusalem.

Scholars are agreed that the second section, like the first (see note on 2: 3), was originally written in Hebrew, though no fragments of a Hebrew text survive. The third section is less Hebraic in style, and some scholars hold that it was originally composed in Greek. If so, that would fit with a late date; but it is unlikely.

THE MANUSCRIPTS OF BARUCH AND
ITS PLACE IN THE BIBLE AND THE CHURCH

If any of Baruch was written after A.D. 70 it would not be surprising that the book as a whole found no place in the canon of the Old Testament. It *would* be surprising however to find the book included, as it is, in Greek manuscripts of the Septuagint. It is not in *Sinaiticus*, which unfortunately breaks off before it gets to Baruch, but it is in B, or *Vaticanus* (for these manuscripts see pp. 11 f.). We also have manuscripts of the Old Latin translation made direct from the Greek, and of a Syriac translation which may have used a Hebrew original. Between them they provide a reliable text: the problems of Baruch arise, not from words and phrases, but from the structure of the book as a whole.

The book of Baruch was much quoted by the early Fathers of the Church, from about A.D. 150 on. But the later Church, whether Catholic or Protestant, has made little use of it.

✳ ✳ ✳ ✳ ✳ ✳ ✳ ✳ ✳ ✳ ✳ ✳ ✳

A message to a conquered people

INTRODUCTION

THIS IS THE BOOK of Baruch, son of Neriah, son of **1** Mahseiah, son of Zedekiah, son of Hasadiah, son of Hilkiah, written in Babylon, on the seventh day of the **2** month, in the fifth year after the Chaldaeans had captured and burnt Jerusalem.

Baruch read the book aloud to Jeconiah son of Jehoiakim, **3** king of Judah, and to all the people who had assembled to

4 hear it: the nobles, the princes of the royal blood, the
 elders, and the whole community, high and low – in
5 short, all who lived in Babylon, by the river Soud. Then
6 they prayed to the Lord with tears and fasting; and each
7 of them collected as much money as he could, and they
 sent it to Jerusalem, to Jehoiakim the high priest, son of
 Hilkiah, son of Shallum, and to the priests and all the
8 people who were with him. This was the time when he
 took the vessels belonging to the house of the Lord which
 had been looted from the temple, and returned them to the
 land of Judah, on the tenth of the month Sivan. These were
 the silver vessels made by Zedekiah son of Josiah, king of
9 Judah, after Nebuchadnezzar king of Babylon had deported
 Jeconiah, the rulers, the captives, the nobles, and the common people from Jerusalem and taken them to Babylon.
10   They said: We are sending you money to buy whole-
 offerings, sin-offerings, and incense; provide a grain-
 offering, and offer them all upon the altar of the Lord our
11 God; and pray for Nebuchadnezzar king of Babylon,
 and for his son Belshazzar, that their life on earth may
12 last as long as the heavens. So the Lord will give us strength,
 and light to walk by, and we shall live under the protection
 of Nebuchadnezzar king of Babylon, and of Belshazzar
 his son; we shall give them long service and gain their
13 favour. Pray also for us to the Lord our God, because we
 have sinned against him, and to this day the Lord's anger
 and wrath have not been averted from us.

* For the details, and also the difficulties, of the historical
background which the author claims for his work, see
pp. 169–71.

1. We must suppose that *Baruch* had gone voluntarily to *Babylon* to join the Jews in exile there. For the question of which chapters and verses make up *the book*, see note on verse 14.

2. The number of the month has fallen out of the Greek manuscripts here, but the Old Latin manuscripts give it as the fifth. Since Jerusalem was burnt, according to the account in 2 Kings 25: 8, *on the seventh day of the* fifth *month*, it seems probable that the events of Baruch 1: 1-9 are meant to have taken place on the fifth anniversary of the capture of Jerusalem, i.e. in 582 B.C.

3. *Baruch read the book aloud*: cp. Jer. 36: 10: 'Baruch read Jeremiah's words...out of the book in the hearing of all the people.' *Jeconiah* was regarded by the Jews in exile as their rightful *king*. As a royal prisoner he was kept at public expense (2 Kings 25: 30, confirmed by Babylonian tablets of the time), and he was eventually released in 562 B.C.

4. *the river Soud* is unknown.

7. *Jehoiakim the high priest*: at the time of the capture of Jerusalem, the Babylonians had killed the high priest Seraiah together with his deputy (Jer. 52: 24-7) and had deported his son (1 Chron. 6: 15). We must presume that Jehoiakim was acting in the office, for he is not mentioned in any lists of high priests. *Hilkiah* and *Shallum* had both been high priests, being grandfather and great-grandfather respectively of Seraiah; so Jehoiakim would have been Seraiah's uncle.

8. *Sivan* is the third month so, if the assumption made in verse 2 is correct, ten months elapsed between Baruch's reading of 'the book' and his taking the money and the vessels *to the land of Judah. the silver vessels* had presumably been *made by Zedekiah* to replace the gold ones taken in the first captivity (2 Kings 24: 13); they were then looted in 587 B.C., but we must suppose that the Jews in Babylon had somehow got hold of them to return them. But a more likely sequence of events is given by Ezra 1: 7-11: that Nebuchadnezzar had on his return dedicated them, gold as well as silver, 'in the

temple of his God', and then Cyrus gave them to the Jews to take home when they returned forty years later.

9. The word *captives* is strange in this list. In fact this list is obviously modelled on the lists in Jer. 24: 1 and 29: 2 (cp. 2 Kings 24: 14); the Greek version gives 'captives' there too, but the Hebrew has 'craftsmen', which is obviously the right text, both there and here. *the common people* were in fact not deported even in the second captivity (2 Kings 24: 14).

10. *They said*: what follows, from here to verse 14, is a covering letter taken by Baruch with 'the book', which begins at verse 15. *whole-offerings* etc.: the list is found in Jer. 17: 26, except for *sin-offerings*, for which see Lev. 4: 3ff. We know from Jer. 41: 5 that the offerings continued to be made in the burnt temple after the fall of Jerusalem in 586 B.C.

11. *pray for Nebuchadnezzar*: at first sight this is strange. However, the Jews are not offering sacrifices for a heathen king but prayers for the civil power. Jeremiah himself had stressed this point: 'Seek the welfare of any city to which I have carried you off, and pray to the LORD for it; on its welfare your welfare will depend' (29: 7).

his son Belshazzar is a mistake. Belshazzar was a son of Nabonidus (558–538 B.C.), the last king of Babylon, who succeeded Nebuchadnezzar but was not related to him. The book of Daniel (5: 22) makes the same mistake. ✵

A PSALM OF REPENTANCE (Part I)

14 You are to read this book that we are sending you, and make your confession in the house of the Lord on the feast
15 day and during the festal season, and say: The Lord our God is in the right; but on us the shame rests to this very
16 day – on the men of Judah, the citizens of Jerusalem, on our kings and rulers, on our priests and prophets, and on

our fathers. We have sinned against the Lord and disobeyed   17, 18
him; we did not listen to the Lord our God or follow the
precepts he gave us. From the day when the Lord brought   19
our fathers out of Egypt until now, we have been disobe-
dient to the Lord our God and have heedlessly disregarded
his voice. So here we are today in the grip of adversity,   20
suffering under the curse which the Lord commanded his
servant Moses to pronounce, when he led our fathers out
of Egypt to give us a land flowing with milk and honey.
Moreover we refused to hear the Lord our God speaking   21
in all the words of the prophets he sent us; we went our   22
own way, each following the promptings of his own
wicked heart, serving other gods, doing what was evil
in the sight of the Lord our God.

So the Lord made good the warning he had given to us,   **2**
to our magistrates in Israel, our kings and our rulers, and
the men of Israel and Judah. Nowhere under heaven have   2
such deeds been done as were done in Jerusalem, thus
fulfilling what was foretold in the law of Moses, that we   3
should eat the flesh of our children, one his own son and
another his own daughter. The Lord made our nation   4
subject to all the kingdoms round us, our land a waste,
our name a byword to all the nations among whom he had
scattered our people. Instead of rising to the top, they   5
sank to the bottom, because we sinned against the Lord
our God and did not listen to his voice. The Lord our God   6
is in the right; but on us and our fathers the shame rests
to this very day. All these evils of which the Lord warned   7
us have come about. Yet we did not entreat the Lord that   8
we might all turn away from the thoughts of our wicked
hearts. The Lord kept strict watch and brought these   9

evils on our heads, because he is just; he laid all these com-
10 mandments upon us, but we did not listen to his voice or
follow the precepts which he gave us.

* 14. What is *this book*? Probably it is the first section 1: 15–
3: 8, all of which makes up a long psalm of national repentance. But there is a difficulty. Most of this section – certainly
from 2: 11–3: 8 – is clearly written for Jews in exile (see
especially 2: 13f. and 3: 7f.); but in that case what is the point
of having it *read* in the temple in Jerusalem *on the feast day*
(like Jer. 36: 6)? The difficulty is not eased by the fact that
the first part of the section is written for Jews in Jerusalem
(see especially 1: 15 and 2: 1; also 2: 4, where however the
N.E.B.'s translation obscures the point). For this reason some
scholars have thought that *this book* refers to one of the two
later sections in our book of Baruch or even to the *whole* of
our book except the introduction 1: 1–13. But on balance it is
better to take the words to refer to this first section 1: 15–3: 8,
and to see it as falling into two parts. It starts from the standpoint of the two groups of Jews in turn, beginning with those
who are actively invited to read it aloud, and then seeks to
bind them together in a single psalm.

the festal season is probably the octave of a great feast, i.e.
the eight days it officially lasted.

15. The N.E.B. gets the sense right but misses the parallelism of the refrain, which says that 'right is on God's side, but
shame on ours'. The phrase comes from Dan. 9: 7, and is
repeated at 2: 6.

18. This verse comes from Dan. 9: 10, and is repeated at
2: 10. It can be seen therefore that 1: 15–18 are echoed, as
a refrain, by 2: 6–10, and they mark the beginning and end of
the first part of this psalm of repentance.

In fact the whole movement of thought down to 2: 28 is
modelled on the prayer in Dan. 9: 4–19. Into it the author
has inserted phrases from Lev. 26, Deut. 28 and various

178

chapters of Jeremiah; and he has scarcely a phrase which is not found in one or other of these four sources. As well as the additions, the author has made some changes. The most important of these are the references to exile in 2: 4, 13 and 14. Paradoxically Daniel's prayer, though dramatically located in exile, refers exclusively to Jerusalem.

20. *the curse* is set out at length in Lev. 26: 14–39 and Deut. 28: 15–68.

21. *the prophets* are here, as in Dan. 9: 6, referred to favourably as those who tried to warn the Jews. Contrast verse 16 where they are included, as in Jer. 13: 13, among those who went astray. In truth there had been prophets in both groups.

2: 1–2. The paragraph starts with an almost exact quotation of Dan. 9: 12f. That passage shows more clearly that the *deeds* are not the sins but the punishment.

3. Cannibalism is not mentioned in Daniel, but it is threatened in Lev. 26: 29, and it is said to have happened during the siege of 587 B.C. (Lam. 4: 10).

One of the Syriac translations here has the note that '*one* and *another* are not found in the Hebrew'; which shows that there *was* a Hebrew text of at least the first section of Baruch, even though none of it survives.

5. The idea of *top* and *bottom* comes from Deut. 28: 13 and 44.

9. *kept strict watch*, literally 'kept awake'. The idea and the word come from Dan. 9: 14 ('The LORD has been biding his time'). *

A PSALM OF REPENTANCE (Part II)

And now, Lord God of Israel, who didst bring thy 11 people out of Egypt with a mighty hand, with signs and portents, with great power and arm uplifted, winning for thyself a renown that lives on to this day: by our sin, our 12 godlessness, and our injustice we have broken all thy commandments, O Lord our God. Be angry with us no 13

longer, for we are left a mere handful among the heathen
14 where thou hast scattered us. Listen, O Lord, to our
prayer and our entreaty, deliver us for thy own sake, and
grant us favour with those who have taken us into exile, so
15 that the whole earth may know that thou art the Lord our
God, who hast named Israel and his posterity as thy own.
16   O Lord, look down from thy holy dwelling and think
17 of us. Turn thy ear to us, Lord, and hear us; open thine eyes
and see. The dead are in their graves, the breath is gone
from their bodies; it is not they who can sing the Lord's
18 praises or applaud his justice; it is living men, mourning
their fall from greatness, walking the earth bent and feeble,
blind and famished – it is these who will sing thy praises,
O Lord, and applaud thy justice.

19   Not for any just deeds of our fathers and our kings do
we lay before thee our plea for pity, O Lord our God.
20 Thou hast vented upon us that wrath and anger of which
thou didst warn us through thy servants the prophets who
21 said: 'These are the words of the Lord: Bow your
shoulders and serve the king of Babylon and you shall
22 remain in the land that I gave to your fathers; but if you
do not listen to the Lord and serve the king of Babylon,
23 then I will banish from Jerusalem and the cities of Judah
all sounds of joy and merriment, the voice of bride and
bridegroom; the whole land shall lie waste and un-
24 inhabited.' But we did not obey thy command to serve
the king of Babylon. And so thou didst make good the
warning given through thy servants the prophets: the
bones of our kings and of our fathers have been taken from
25 their resting-place; and there they lie, exposed to the heat
by day and the frost by night. They died a painful death

by famine, sword, and disease.[a] And because of the 26 wickedness of Israel and Judah the house that was named as thine has become what it is today.

Yet thou hast shown us, O Lord our God, all thy wonted 27 forbearance and great mercy. For this is what thou didst 28 promise through thy servant Moses, on the day thou didst command him to write thy law in the presence of the Israelites: 'If you will not listen to my voice, this great 29 swarming multitude will be reduced to a tiny remnant among the heathen where I will scatter them. I know they 30 will not hear me, this stubborn people, but in the land of their exile they will come to their senses and know that 31 I am the Lord their God. I will give them a mind to understand and ears to hear. Then they will praise me in the land 32 of their exile and will turn their thoughts to me; they will 33 repent of their stubbornness and their wicked deeds, for they will recall how their fathers sinned against the Lord. Then I will restore them to the land that I swore to give 34 to their forefathers, Abraham, Isaac, and Jacob, and they shall rule over it. And I will increase their number: they shall never dwindle away. I will enter into an eternal 35 covenant with them, that I will become their God and they shall become my people. Never again will I remove my people Israel from the land that I have given them.'

O Lord Almighty, God of Israel, the soul in anguish 3 and the fainting spirit cry out to thee. Listen, Lord, and 2 have mercy, for we have sinned against thee. Thou art 3 enthroned for ever; we are for ever passing away. Now, 4 Almighty Lord, God of Israel, hear the prayer of Israel's dead and of the sons of those who sinned against thee.

[a] disease: *probable meaning (compare Jeremiah 32: 36); Gk. obscure.*

They did not heed the voice of their God, and so we are
5 in the grip of adversity. Do not recall the misdeeds of our
6 fathers, but remember now thy power and thy name, for
thou art the Lord our God, and we will praise thee, O Lord.
7 It is for this that thou hast put the fear of thee in our hearts,
to make us call upon thy name. And we will praise thee in
our exile, for we have put away from us all the wrongdoing
8 of our fathers who sinned against thee. Today we are in
exile; thou hast scattered us and made us a byword and
a curse, to be punished for all the sins of our fathers, who
rebelled against the Lord our God.

✳ 2: 11. This verse too comes almost word for word from
Dan. 9: 15. The words *And now* mark a transition. Hitherto
the speaker has looked backwards in a mood of penitence;
now he looks forward in a mood of hope for mercy. It was
common in all ancient prayers, both Hebrew and Greek, as it
is also in our Collects, to begin by reminding God of his past
mercies; and to the Jews the prototype of all mercies was the
exodus from Egypt. The reference to God's own *renown* is also
common in such passages.

12. *by our sin, our godlessness, and our injustice*: the Greek is
more forceful: it says, in three words, 'we have sinned, we
have done wrong, we have acted unjustly'; exactly the same
threefold repetition is found in Ps. 106: 6 and 1 Kings 8: 47.
But in Daniel there are only two limbs: 'we have sinned, we
have done wrong.'

13. The idea that the Jews would, as part of their punishment, be reduced to a *mere handful* comes from the prophecy
in Deut. 28: 62. If anything, their population is more likely
to have increased than decreased in exile, but the idea that its
size depended on their loyalty became an accepted part of their
interpretation of history. See also verses 29 and 34 below.

14. *for thy own sake* is explained, tactfully, in verse 15; see

Dan. 9: 19. It is remarkable that the speakers' only specific request is for favour with their masters in exile. There is no suggestion here of a return home; that comes only in verse 34 – and there it is rather hinted at than prayed for.

16. *holy dwelling* here means God's throne in heaven; cp. Deut. 26: 15.

17. Verse 17 seems to be using the argument of Ps. 30: 9 in support of the appeal for mercy:

'What profit in my death if I go down into the pit?
Can the dust confess thee or proclaim thy truth?'

18. Verse 18 is based on Deut. 28: 65f., where part of the punishment for disobedience is to be that the Jews, scattered abroad, will have 'an unquiet mind, dim eyes, and failing appetite'. If the phrase *mourning their fall from greatness* is right, it would be a note of originality in Baruch; but it is very difficult to get that or any other satisfactory translation out of the Greek.

19. The parallel passage in Dan. 9: 18 says 'it is not by virtue of our own saving acts'. There seems to be no particular reason why Baruch has changed it to refer to *our fathers and our kings*. Both ideas make good sense, however, and the latter is familiar to us from John the Baptist's words: 'do not presume to say to yourselves, "We have Abraham for our father"' (Matt. 3: 8f.).

21–5. Cp. Jer. 27: 11f.; 7: 34ff.; 36: 30.

25. Jer. 32: 36 says that Jerusalem 'is being given over to the king of Babylon, with sword, famine, and pestilence'. The Greek word used in the Septuagint there for 'pestilence' is the same as that here; so the N.E.B. translation *disease* can be regarded as certain.

27. That all these punishments could be regarded as signs of God's *forbearance and great mercy* is remarkable: the idea is that God has stopped short of total destruction in the hope that these lesser punishments will bring his people to their senses.

28. The passages in the books of *Moses* are Lev. 26: 32–45 and Deut. 28: 62–4; 30: 1–10.

35. The idea of an *eternal covenant* was common among the prophets; see Isa. 55: 3 and Jer. 32: 40. But to add the promise that the Jews will *never again* be punished with exile is to over-simplify the message of the great prophets. They had seen that the sequence covenant–sin–punishment–repentance–restoration was not something which happens once: it is rather a recurrent cycle of events. Baruch did not see this fully. But he did appreciate the lesser idea, that there is a pattern in history and that events do not follow one another capriciously.

3: 1–8. This final paragraph is a sort of summary of the psalm.

3. *we are for ever passing away*: the N.E.B. translation reads well but is hard to get out of the Greek.

4. *hear the prayer of Israel's dead* is difficult. It cannot, so soon after 2: 17, be taken literally. Possibly it can be taken meta-phorically, to refer to the Jews in exile (cp. verse 10 below and Isa. 59: 10). More likely, there was a misreading of the Hebrew text, for *mēthim*, 'dead', and *mᵉthim*, 'men', look the same before the vowels are added. This confusion is quite common in manuscripts of the Bible. ✻

A HYMN IN PRAISE OF GOD'S WISDOM (Part I)

9 Listen, Israel, to the commandments of life; hear, and learn
10 wisdom. Why is it, Israel, that you are in your enemies' country, that you have grown old in an alien land? Why
11 have you shared the defilement of the dead and been
12 numbered with those that lie in the grave? It is because you
13 have forsaken the fountain of wisdom. If you had walked in the way of God, you would have lived in peace for ever.
14 Where is understanding, where is strength, where is in-telligence? Learn that, and then you will know where to
15 find life and light to walk by, long life and peace. Has any man discovered the dwelling-place of wisdom or entered

her storehouse? Where are the rulers of the nations now? 16
Where are those who have hunted wild beasts or the birds 17
of the air for sport? Where are those who have hoarded
the silver and gold men trust in, never satisfied with their
gains? Where are the silversmiths with their patient skill 18
and the secrets of their craft? They have all vanished and 19
gone down to the grave, and others have risen to take their
place. A younger generation saw the light of day and dwelt 20
in the land. But they did not learn the way of knowledge,
or discover its paths; they did not lay hold of it; their sons 21
went far astray. Wisdom was not heard of in Canaan, nor 22
seen in Teman. The sons of Hagar who sought for under- 23
standing on earth, the merchants of Merran and Teman,
the myth-makers, the seekers after knowledge, none of
them discovered the way of wisdom, or remembered her
paths.

✻ This is the second of the three sections of the Book of
Baruch. For its relation to the other two, see p. 169.

3: 9–11. These verses link the section to what precedes, just
as 4: 4 links it to what follows. The fact that they have *grown
old in an alien land*, when added to the description of exile in
Deut. 28: 65f. (quoted in note on 2: 18), leads to the idea
that they are as good as corpses; cp. Ps. 88: 4: 'I am numbered
with those who go down to the abyss.' The further notion
that they have *shared the defilement of the dead*, if the text is
correct, shows how a good idea can be pushed to tasteless
extremes.

12. *fountain of wisdom = way of God* (verse 13) = Law of
Moses (4: 1). The recurrent refrain of God's wisdom in this
section shows that it falls into the class of so-called Wisdom
literature. This body of literature includes the books of Job,
Proverbs and Ecclesiastes in the Old Testament, together

with Ecclesiasticus and the Wisdom of Solomon in the Apocrypha. The concept of Wisdom in these books contains three separate ingredients, each of which is found here: (i) general human prudence, which brings wealth and happiness; (ii) the plan of creation known only to God (3: 29–35); (iii) specifically, the Law of Moses (3: 36–4: 4). One of the chief influences which affected the later Wisdom literature was the contact and contrast between Jewish and Greek ways of life. Consequently there is often some tension between the first and third ingredients above. Some Wisdom writers welcomed the contribution which Greek ideas could make. Others, like Baruch, take the narrower view that the Jews have nothing to learn from foreigners (verses 16–23 and 26–8).

Christianity, largely through the person of Paul, was able to reconcile the two sets of ideas more successfully than the Jews had ever done. But from time to time the tension breaks out again, and the disputes between religion and science in the period A.D. 1850–1950 could be seen as a modern version of it.

14. *Where is understanding?* Questions of this kind are common in the Wisdom literature; cp. Job 28: 12: 'But where can wisdom be found?' Often also they are rhetorical, i.e. they expect an obvious answer, as in verses 15–18 below and Job chapters 38 and 39.

16f. The description of the *rulers of the nations* is built on that of Nebuchadnezzar in Dan. 2: 37f.

18. If the N.E.B. translation is right, the movement of thought is from powerful kings through rich men to skilled craftsmen. So when Vergil came to describe the respective glories of Greece and Rome in *Aeneid* VI 847ff., he allowed the Greeks a superiority not only in science and philosophy but also in the arts and crafts. The Jewish attitude to this sort of glory is seen again in Ecclus. 38 where the craftsman is compared unfavourably to the scribe who has true wisdom available.

19. The mortality of human power, wealth and skill, as

well as strength (3: 28), is contrasted with the 'life' (4: 1) of
wisdom and goodness. But the author is thinking of the dis-
appearance or survival of nations, not of individuals – nor
indeed of generations, though verses 19–21 might seem to
suggest that.

22. *Canaan* refers especially to the wealthy commercial
cities of Phoenicia. So Ezek. 28: 3f. addresses Tyre: 'are you
wiser than Danel?...Clever and shrewd as you are, you have
amassed wealth for yourself.'

23. *Hagar* was Abraham's second wife, from whom were
supposed to be descended the Arabs, known as a nation of
traders. *Merran* is unknown. *Teman* was a region in Edom,
known also for its commercial skills. Jer. 49: 7 asks: 'Is
wisdom no longer to be found in Teman?' *myth-makers*:
the Greek word which the N.E.B. has translated so is not
found elsewhere in the Septuagint, so its meaning is uncertain.
Perhaps it refers to a skill whose possession was usually
described in the Bible in such phrases as 'reading riddles'
(Ps. 49: 4; Ecclus. 39: 3; see also the story of Ahikar the Wise
on pp. 3 f.).

HYMN IN PRAISE OF GOD'S WISDOM (Part II)

How great, O Israel, is God's dwelling-place, how vast 24
the extent of his domain! Great it is, and boundless, lofty, 25
and immeasurable. There in ancient time the giants were 26
born, a famous race, great in stature, skilled in war. But 27
these men were not chosen by God, nor shown the way of
knowledge. So their race died out because they had no 28
understanding; they lacked the wit to survive. Has any 29
man gone up to heaven to gain wisdom and brought her
down from the clouds? Has any man crossed the sea to 30
find her or bought her for fine gold? No one can know the 31
path or conceive the way that will lead to her. Only the 32

One who knows all things knows her: his understanding
discovered her. He who established the earth for all time
33 filled it with four-footed beasts. He sends forth the light,
and it goes on its way; he called it, it feared him and
34 obeyed. The stars shone at their appointed stations and
rejoiced; he called them and they answered, 'We are here!'
35 Joyfully they shone for their Maker. This is our God;
36 there is none to compare with him. The whole way of
knowledge he found out and gave to Jacob his servant,
37 and to Israel, whom he loved. Thereupon wisdom
4 appeared on earth and lived among men. She is the book
of the commandments of God, the law that stands for
ever. All who hold fast to her shall live, but those who
2 forsake her shall die. Return, Jacob, and lay hold of her;
set your course towards her radiance, and face her beacon
3 light. Do not give up your glory to another or your
4 privileges to an alien people. Happy are we, Israel, because
we know what is pleasing to God!

✲ 24–5. Reference to *Israel* at this point is odd. It looks like
an attempt to bind this second section (3: 9–4: 4) to the rest
of the book. The rest of the verse interrupts the sequence of
thought here, and would fit better just before verse 29. *God's
dwelling-place* must refer to the world, or even the universe;
but *there* (verse 26) is strange in either case, and confirms the
view that verses 24–5 are an insertion.

26. *the giants* just represent brute strength (see note on
Judith 16: 7).

28. *the wit* – rather, here, wisdom. According to Ecclus. 16: 7,
'There was no pardon for the giants of old, who revolted in
all their strength.'

The mention of the giants concludes the author's analysis
of the achievements of the Gentiles, which he contrasts with

the wisdom of the Jews. He allows them power, wealth, craftsmanship, commercial skills and, lastly, physical strength. But like Ecclesiasticus he nowhere mentions Greek philosophy and science (see notes on 3: 12 and 18).

29. A new paragraph begins at this verse (possibly with verses 24 and 25 added) and continues to verse 35. Wisdom is here treated as God's plan in creation. This paragraph is much influenced by chapter 28 of Job, especially the passage beginning with verse 12:

> But where can wisdom be found?
> And where is the source of understanding?

There is an echo also of Prov. 30: 3–4:

> I have not learnt wisdom...
> Who has ever gone up to heaven and come down again?

30. So in Job 28: 14 'the sea says, "It (i.e. wisdom) is not with me."' There is a second echo here, of Deut. 30: 11–13, where God says that his commandment is not too difficult or too remote: 'It is not in heaven, that you should say, "Who will go up to heaven for us to fetch it...?" Nor is it beyond the sea, that you should say, "Who will cross the sea for us to fetch it?".' Later on, when all these passages came to be seen by the early Church as looking forward to Christ, Paul adapted that passage of Deuteronomy in a characteristically Jewish way: 'Do not say to yourself "Who can go up to heaven?" (that is to bring Christ down) or "Who can go down into the abyss?" (that is to bring Christ up from the dead)' (Rom. 10: 6).

34. So in Ecclus. 43: 10 the stars at God's command 'stand in their appointed place; they never default at their post', i.e. as sentinels. And in Job 38: 35 the lightning says to God, 'I am ready.'

35. Here begins the final paragraph, in which wisdom is equated with the Law of Moses. This paragraph is influenced

by Ecclus. 24, where God says to Wisdom (verse 8): 'Make your home in Jacob; find your heritage in Israel', and Wisdom says (verse 12): 'I took root among the people whom the Lord had honoured.'

37. This is the most famous verse in the book of Baruch. Wisdom had been personified before, e.g. in Prov. 8: 22–31 where Wisdom herself speaks and says:

'The LORD created me the beginning of his works...
When he set the heavens in their place I was there...
Then I was at his side each day...
playing in his presence continually,
playing on the earth, when he had finished it,
while my delight was in mankind.'

But Baruch goes further in suggesting that Wisdom *lived among men*, and it may well be that not only the idea but the phrasing influenced the author of the fourth Gospel in his description of Jesus. In his prologue (1: 1–18) he describes Jesus as the Word of God, who 'was with God at the beginning' but now 'became flesh' and 'came to dwell among us'.

The translation of this verse is a little tricky, and some modern scholars have suspected it of being a Christian interpolation. But the passage of Ecclesiasticus quoted in the note on verse 35 shows that there is no reason why it should not be Jewish.

4: 1. Wisdom is further identified with *the book of the commandments of God*, exactly as in Ecclus. 24: 23.

2. *beacon*: cp. Ps. 119: 105: 'Thy word is a lamp to guide my feet.'

3. *Do not give up your glory to another*: the phrase is adapted from Second Isaiah, where God says 'I will not give my glory to another god' (42: 8; see also 48: 11).

4. The address to *Israel*, picking up 3: 9 and 3: 24, binds this central section together, and the whole verse links it to the third section which follows. *

A SONG OF ENCOURAGEMENT (Part I)

Take heart, my people, you who keep Israel's name alive. 5
You were sold to the heathen, but not to be destroyed; it 6
was because you roused God's anger that you were handed
over to your enemies. You provoked your Maker by sacri- 7
ficing to demons and to that which is not God. You forgot
the Everlasting God who nurtured you, and you grieved 8
Jerusalem who fostered you; for she saw how God's 9
anger had come upon you, and she said: Listen, you
neighbours of Zion, God has brought great grief upon
me. I have seen the captivity of my sons and daughters 10
which the Everlasting has inflicted upon them; I nursed
them in delight, but with tears and mourning I saw them 11
go. Let no one exult over me in my widowhood, 12
bereaved of so many. I have been left desolate through
the sins of my children, through their turning away from
the law of God. They would not learn his statutes, or fol- 13
low his commandments, or let God guide and train them
in his righteousness.

Come then, neighbours of Zion, remember the captivity 14
of my sons and daughters which the Everlasting has
inflicted upon them. For he brought down on them a 15
nation from far away, a ruthless nation speaking a strange
language and without reverence for age or pity for children.
They carried off the widow's beloved sons, and left her 16
in loneliness, deprived of her daughters. But I, how can 17
I help you? Only the One who brought these evils upon 18
you can deliver you from your enemies. Go your way, 19
my children, go, for I am left desolate. I have put off 20
the robes of peaceful days, and put on the sackcloth

of a suppliant. I will cry out to the Everlasting as long as I live.

21 Take heart, my children! Cry out to God, and he will rescue you from tyranny and from the power of your 22 enemies. For I have set my hope of your deliverance on the Everlasting; the Holy One, your everlasting saviour, has filled me with joy over the mercy soon to be granted 23 you. I saw you go with mourning and tears, but God will 24 give you back to me with joy and gladness for ever. For as the neighbours of Zion have now seen your captivity, so they will soon see your deliverance coming upon you from your God with the great glory and splendour of the 25 Everlasting. My children, endure in patience the wrath God has brought upon you; your enemy has hunted you down, but soon you will see him destroyed, and will put 26 your foot upon his neck. My pampered children have trodden rough paths; they have been carried off like a flock seized by raiders.

27 Take heart, my children! Cry out to God, for he who 28 afflicted you will not forget you. You once resolved to go astray from God; now with tenfold zeal you must turn 29 about and seek him. He who brought these calamities upon you will bring you everlasting joy when he delivers you.

✴ The structure of this third section of Baruch is no easier than that of the other two. The last four paragraphs are addressed to Jerusalem and thus form a clear unity. But the first four are more difficult. The passage from verses 9 b–29 is spoken by Jerusalem herself and is addressed first to the 'neighbours of Zion' (down to verse 16) and then to her own 'children' (see e.g. verse 23). The introductory verses 5–9 a are best taken also as spoken by Jerusalem to her 'children', in spite of the fact that Jerusalem must then refer to herself in the third person in verses 8 and 9 *a*.

Modern scholars have tried, reasonably enough, to break the song up into stanzas, but have not been able to agree on the distribution of the verses.

5. The *people* addressed here are now in exile (verse 23 is certain, even if the earlier verses are not). Although in the past, i.e. before their exile, they *roused God's anger...by sacrificing to demons*, now it is they *who keep Israel's name alive*, i.e. they are regarded as, if anything, more faithful than the Jews left behind in Jerusalem. *demons* here just means heathen gods; contrast verse 35.

8. *the Everlasting* is used five times as the title of God in this third section of Baruch, but it is not found in either of the other sections. It comes from Isa. 40: 28.

9. Jerusalem's lament has many echoes from the book of Lamentations. In particular, Lamentations also complains of the mockery of the neighbours (1: 21).

12. The idea of *widowhood* comes in the first verse of Lamentations.

14. *remember*: rather 'ponder', looking forward to verse 24.

15. Almost a word-for-word fulfilment of the prophecy in Deut. 28: 49.

17. Jerusalem is still speaking, because the *I* is still feminine, as the Greek shows. But *you* is now again her 'children'. This sudden switch of addressee is quite common in Hebrew.

23. *I saw you go with mourning* makes a pleasant echo of verse 11.

24. *soon*: if we were to take this literally, it could give us a date for the composition of this third section of the book. But in this sort of writing (as in love poetry) 'soon' is an expression of eagerness, not of time.

26. This verse seems misplaced: it would fit better e.g. after verse 13. ✳

A SONG OF ENCOURAGEMENT (Part II)

30 Take heart, Jerusalem! He who called you by name will
31 comfort you. Wretched shall they be who despoiled you
32 and gloated over your fall; wretched the cities where your
children were slaves; wretched the city that received
33 your sons! The same city that rejoiced at your downfall
and made merry over your ruin shall grieve over her own
34 desolation. I will strip her of the multitudes that were her
35 boast, and turn her pride to mourning. Fire from the Everlasting shall be her doom for many a day, and long shall
she be a haunt of demons.

36   Jerusalem, look eastwards and see the joy that is coming
37 to you from God. They come, the sons from whom you
parted, they come, gathered together at the word of the
Holy One from east to west, rejoicing in the glory of God.
5   Jerusalem, strip off the garment of your sorrow and
affliction, and put on for ever the glorious majesty that is
2 the gift of God. Wrap about you his robe of righteousness;
set on your head for diadem the splendour of the Ever-
3 lasting; for God will show your radiance to every land
4 under heaven. You shall receive from God for ever the
name Righteous Peace, Godly Splendour.

5   Jerusalem, arise and stand upon the height; look eastwards and see from west to east your children gathered
together at the word of the Holy One, rejoicing that God
6 has remembered them. They went away from you on
foot, led off by their enemies, but God is bringing them
home to you borne aloft in glory, like a king on his throne.
7 For God has commanded every high mountain and the
everlasting hills to be made low, and the valleys to be filled

and levelled, so that Israel may walk safely in the glory of
God. And woods and every fragrant tree shall give Israel 8
shade by God's command. For God shall lead Israel with 9
joy in the light of his glory, granting them his mercy and
his righteousness.

* This second part of the song is all addressed to Jerusalem,
presumably by the prophet on behalf of God (see 'I' in verse
34). It is however not to be regarded as an answer to the first
part, which was spoken by Jerusalem to loyal Jews. In a sense,
all participants can be regarded as standing for the same cause.

30. *He who called you by name*: cp. 2: 15 and 26, and Isa. 43:1:
'I have called you by name and you are my own.'

31–5. The hostile attitude to Babylon here is very different
from that of the first section of Baruch (1: 11 and 2: 24).

35. *shall she be a haunt of demons* because she will be a desert
(see note on Tobit 8: 3).

36f. These two verses have very much the feel of Isa. 40–
55, which is the chief influence upon this third section of
Baruch.

5: 4. Honorific names for Jerusalem are found quite often
in the other prophets; see especially Isa. 62: 4; indeed that
whole chapter has influenced this little paragraph.

5. The first half of this verse is almost identical with a verse
in one of the so-called Psalms of Solomon (11: 3): 'Rise up,
Jerusalem, arise and stand upon the height, and see your
children gathered together from East to West.' Indeed there
are other similarities between Baruch 4: 36–5: 8 and
Ps. Sol. 11 which show beyond doubt that one author
borrowed from the other. The Psalms of Solomon were
probably written in mid-first century B.C. If therefore we
could show that Baruch was the later of the two, that would
make it likely that this section referred to the fall of Jerusalem
in A.D. 70. But in fact it is not clear which author borrowed
from which.

6. The phrase *borne aloft in glory* comes from Isa. 49: 22, where it is said that 'the peoples...shall...carry your daughters on their shoulders'. But the elaboration *like a king on his throne* is the author's, and is not entirely happy.

7f. The ideas come from Isa. 40: 4 and 41: 19. ✱

✱   ✱   ✱   ✱   ✱   ✱   ✱   ✱   ✱   ✱   ✱   ✱   ✱

A LETTER OF
JEREMIAH

✻ ✻ ✻ ✻ ✻ ✻ ✻ ✻ ✻ ✻ ✻ ✻ ✻

THE PLACE OF THE LETTER OF
JEREMIAH IN THE BIBLE

In the English Bible, as in the Latin Bible, the Letter of Jeremiah follows immediately on the end of the book of Baruch. In the manuscripts of the Greek Bible the book of Lamentations comes between Baruch and this Letter. But whatever their position these three works belong together as three appendages to the book of Jeremiah proper. And in the case of the Letter it is even clearer than in the case of the other two that it was not written by the prophet himself. Quite apart from internal evidence, we have the authority of Jerome (in his preface to his commentary on Jeremiah) that the early Church already recognized it as a 'pseudepigraph', i.e. a work written later under the name of a hero of old.

The form of this Letter comes from Jer. 29: 1–23, an authentic letter written by the prophet to the Jews who had been taken off to exile in Babylon in 597 B.C. Jeremiah there urged them to settle contentedly in Babylon and he added that in seventy years' time God would bring them back home. The author of this apocryphal Letter has Jeremiah writing to them *before* they had left for Babylon and warning them against idolatry. He adds that they will have to stay there *up to seven generations* (verse 3). Unfortunately this change does not help us to tell when the Letter was composed; nor is there any other definite evidence. All that can be said with fair certainty is that it was originally written in Hebrew (see note on verse 72). Its probable date falls in the period 300–100 B.C.

Being a sermon against idolatry, it was clearly designed for Jews of the Dispersion, i.e. Jews living outside Palestine. It is not quite so clear what part of the Dispersion the author had in mind. Many of the idolatrous practices he mentions were common to Greek and Egyptian as well as to Babylonian and other Semitic religions. Nevertheless the general weight of the references certainly fits Babylonian religion, especially the worship of Bel and Tammuz: Bel is mentioned in verse 41 and the rites of Tammuz referred to in verses 31–2 and 43. Conversely there is no reference to specifically Greek or Egyptian rituals.

Jewish literature contains a large number of sermons against idolatry, both inside and outside the Bible, and many of them adopt the same satirical tone as this Letter. The earliest, and perhaps the best, of such satires is by Second Isaiah (44: 9–20, about 540 B.C.). A later one is in the book of Jeremiah (10: 1–16, probably not by Jeremiah himself). The latter passage contains many of the ideas of our Letter in much smaller compass (see especially note on verse 71).

That Jeremiah passage, like many of these sermons, runs together two theological ideas which are strictly separate. Of the ten commandments, the first said 'You shall have no other god to set against me', the second 'You shall not make a carved image for yourself' (Exod. 20: 3–4). This second commandment certainly included the command not to make any images of Yahweh, but that aspect of it plays no part in our Letter, any more than the first commandment does. Our author is concerned solely to pour scorn on the worship of idols, i.e. images of *heathen* gods.

The author's treatment of his theme, like the theme itself, is typically Jewish. The structure of his sermon is simple. After the introduction (verses 1–7) it is broken up into paragraphs, each of which ends with a refrain repeated (in one form or another) nine times. A secondary link is provided by a descriptive phrase repeated (in one form or another) ten times: 'of wood, plated with silver and gold'.

Within this framework there is no progression of argument such as we would expect from a sermon. There is not even any sorting out of the arguments: for example, the point that the idols 'cannot set up or depose a king' is made in verse 35 and repeated in verse 53; the ignominious fate of the idols at the hands of temple-robbers is described in verses 18 and 57, their incapacity in time of war in verses 15 and 48–9.

But it does not follow that the Letter is haphazard in composition. There is visible in most of it a continuous thread, but it is a thread of images, not of arguments. Thus half-way through verse 27 there begins a description of the worship the idols receive. From the irreverence of their priests we pass to the similar behaviour of the priests' wives. That leads on (verse 29) to the special case of women who are ritually unclean. After the refrain, we pick up (verse 30) the idea that in Jewish religion women are not allowed to minister in the temple at all. This leads to the mention (verse 31) of other respects in which gentile priests do things which Jewish priests may not do, and that in turn (verse 32) to the thought that heathen worship is like mourning. Only after verse 32 does there seem to be a break in this sequence of images (see also note on verses 70–1).

In our eyes this kind of composition is inappropriate to an argument. But this Letter is not so much an argument as a satire, and satire has always relied less on logical structure than on vivid reporting. In that respect some of the touches in this Letter are distinctly effective, particularly where the author descends from his rhetorical style to paint the homely details (see note on verse 59).

✻ ✻ ✻ ✻ ✻ ✻ ✻ ✻ ✻ ✻ ✻ ✻ ✻

The folly of idolatry

6[a]   A COPY OF A LETTER sent by Jeremiah to the captives who were to be taken to Babylon by the king of Babylon, conveying a message entrusted to him by God.

2   The sins you have committed in the sight of God are the cause of your being led away captive to Babylon by

3   Nebuchadnezzar king of Babylon. Once you are in Babylon, your stay there will be long; it will last for many years, up to seven generations; but afterwards I will lead you out in peace and prosperity.

4   Now in Babylon you will see carried on men's shoulders gods made of silver, gold, and wood, which fill the heathen

5   with awe. Be careful, then, never to imitate these Gentiles; do not be overawed by their gods when you see them in

6   the midst of a procession of worshippers. But say in your

7   hearts, 'To thee alone, Lord, is worship due.' For my angel is with you; your lives are in his care.

8   The idols are plated with gold and silver, they have tongues fashioned by a craftsman, but they are a fraud and

9   cannot speak. And the people take gold and make crowns for the heads of their gods, as one might for a girl fond of

10 finery. Sometimes also the priests filch gold and silver

11 from their gods and spend it on themselves; they will even give some of it to the prostitutes in the inner chamber. They dress up the idols in clothes like human beings, these

12 gods of silver, gold, and wood. But the gods, decked in

[a] *The chapter and verse numbering is that of the Authorized Version, in which this forms chapter 6 of Baruch.*

purple though they are, cannot protect themselves against
rust and moth. The dust in the temple, too, lies thick upon 13
them, so that their faces have to be wiped clean. Like a human 14
judge the god holds a sceptre, yet he cannot put to death
anyone who offends him. In his right hand he has a dagger 15
and an axe, yet he cannot deliver himself from war and pill-
age. This shows they are not gods, so have no fear of them. 16

Their gods are no more use than a broken tool, sitting 17
there in their temples. Their eyes get filled with dust from
the feet of those who come in. And just as the palace- 18
court is barricaded to secure a traitor awaiting execution,
so the priests secure their temples with doors and bolts
and bars to guard against plundering by robbers. They 19
light lamps, more than they need for themselves – yet
the idols can see none of them. They are like one of the 20-21
beams of the temple; their hearts are eaten out, as the saying is, for creatures crawl out of the ground and devour
them and their clothing. When their faces are blackened
by the smoke of the temple they are quite unaware of it.
Bats and swallows and birds of all kinds perch on their 22
heads and bodies, and cats do the same. From all this you 23
may be sure that they are not gods, so have no fear of them.

Though plated with gold for ornament, the idols will 24
not shine, unless someone rubs off the tarnish. Even when
they were being cast they did not feel it. They were bought 25
at great cost, but there is no breath in them. As they have 26
no real feet they are carried on men's shoulders, which
shows how worthless they are. Even those who serve them 27
are ashamed, because if ever an idol falls on the ground,
it does not get up by itself; nor, if anyone sets it up again,
can it move by its own effort, and if it is tilted it cannot

straighten itself. To set offerings before them is like setting
28 them before the dead. The sacrifices made to gods are
sold by the priests, who spend the proceeds on themselves.
Their wives are no better; they take portions of these
sacrifices and cure the meat, and give no share to the poor
29 or helpless. Their offerings are touched by women who are
menstruating or by mothers fresh from childbed. Be assured
by all this that they are not gods, and have no fear of them.

30 Why should they be called gods? These gods of silver,
31 gold, and wood have food served to them by women. In
their temples the priests sit shaven and shorn, with their
32 clothes rent, and their heads uncovered. They shout and
howl before these gods of theirs, like mourners at a funeral
33 feast. The priests strip vestments from the gods to clothe
34 their own wives and children. Should anyone do these
gods either injury or service they will not be able to repay it.
35 They cannot set up or depose a king. So also they are
incapable of bestowing wealth or money; if someone
makes a vow to them and does not honour it, they will
36 never exact payment. They will never save any man from
37 death, never rescue the weak from the strong. They cannot restore the blind man's sight or give relief to the
38 needy. They do not pity the widow or befriend the
39 orphan. They are like blocks from the quarry, these
wooden things plated with gold and silver, and their
40 worshippers will be humiliated. How then can anyone
suppose them to be gods or call them so?

Besides, even the Chaldaeans themselves bring these
41 idols of theirs into disrepute; for, when they see a dumb
man without the power of articulate speech, they bring
him into the temple and make him call upon Bel, as if Bel

could understand him. They cannot see the folly of it and 42
abandon the idols, because they themselves have no understanding. The women too sit in the street with cords round 43
them, burning bran for incense. And when a passer-by has
pulled one of them to him and she has lain with him, she
taunts her neighbour, because she has not been thought as
attractive as herself and her cord has not been broken.
Everything to do with these idols is fraud and delusion. How 44
then can anyone suppose them to be gods or call them so?

They are things manufactured by carpenters and gold- 45
smiths; they can be nothing but what the craftsmen wish
them to be. Even their makers' lives cannot be prolonged; 46
what, then, can the things they make expect? It is simply 47
a scandalous fraud that they have bequeathed to posterity.
When war and disasters befall the gods, it is the priests 48
who discuss amongst themselves where they and their gods
can hide. How then can men fail to see that these are not 49
gods, when they cannot save themselves from war and
disaster? Since they are nothing but wood plated with 50
gold and silver, they will in time be recognized for the
frauds they are. All the heathen and their kings will plainly 51
see that they are not gods but the work of men's hands,
with no divine power in them at all. Can there still be 52
anyone who does not realize that they are not gods?

They cannot set up a king over a country, and they can- 53
not give men rain. They cannot decide a case or redress 54
a wrong.[a] They are as helpless as crows tossed about in
mid air. When fire breaks out in a temple belonging to 55
those wooden gods all gilded and silvered, their priests

[a] *Some witnesses read* cannot judge in their own cause, or redress
a wrong done them.

will run away to safety, but the gods will be burnt up in
56 the flames like timbers. They cannot resist king or enemy.
How then can anyone allow or believe that they are gods?
57   They cannot save themselves from thieves and robbers,
58 these wooden gods, plated with silver and gold. Anyone
who can will strip away their gold and silver and make off
with the clothing they wear, and the gods can do nothing
59 to help themselves. It is better to be a king who proves
his courage than such a sham god, better a household
vessel that serves its owner's purpose, better even the
door of a house that keeps the contents safe, or a wooden
60 pillar in a palace. Sun and moon and the stars that shine so
61 brightly are sent to serve a purpose, and they obey. So too,
when the lightning flashes, it is seen far and wide. It is the
62 same with the wind; it blows in every land. And when
God orders the clouds to travel over all the world they
63 carry out their task, and so does fire when it is sent down
from above to consume mountains and forests. But idols
are not to be compared with any of these, in appearance or
64 in power. It follows that they are not to be considered gods
or called by that name, seeing that they are incapable of
pronouncing judgement or of conferring benefits on man-
65 kind. Recognize, therefore, that they are not gods, and
have no fear of them.

66   They wield no power over kings, either to curse them
67 or to bless them; and they cannot provide heavenly signs
for the nations, either by shining like the sun or by giving
68 light like the moon. They are more helpless than wild
beasts, which can at least save themselves by taking cover.
69 There is no evidence at all that they are gods, so have no
fear of them.

These wooden gods of theirs, plated with gold and silver, 70
give no better protection than a scarecrow in a plot of
cucumbers. They are like a thorn-bush in a garden, 71
a perch for every bird, like a corpse cast out in the dark.
Such are their wooden gods, with their plating of gold
and silver. The purple and fine linen[a] rotting on them 72
proves that they are not gods; in the end they will themselves be eaten away, held in contempt throughout the
land.

Better, then, is an upright man who has no idols; he 73
will be in no danger of contempt.

* 1–3. The opening is modelled on the letter in Jer. 29: 1,
but this Letter purports to be written before the Jewish
prisoners had been carried off to exile in Babylon (see p. 197).

3. *seven generations* is an intentionally vague phrase. Seven
is always a 'round' number in the Bible, nor was there any
agreement among the Jews as to how many years made
a generation.

4. *carried on men's shoulders*: i.e. by the priests in procession
(cp. verse 26), a custom which we can see depicted in
Assyrian sculptures.

7. *my angel*: cp. Exod. 23: 23–4: 'My angel will go before
you and bring you to the Amorites...You are not to bow
down to their gods...'

8. Cp. Ps. 115: 4–5:

> Their idols are silver and gold,
>   made by the hands of men.
> They have mouths that cannot speak.

11. *prostitutes*: these would be temple-prostitutes. Such
ritual prostitution was a feature of Babylonian religion which
extended also to other religions as far as Greece. Women were

[a] fine linen: *probable meaning; Gk.* marble.

attached to certain temples as prostitutes and offered themselves to men as part of their service to a god – or more often
to a mother goddess – of fertility. There are many references
to this practice in the Bible. Deuteronomy expressly lays
down that 'no Israelite woman shall become a temple-prosti-
tute' (23: 17). The prophets protested vehemently against the
practice, and it is possible that Hosea actually married such
a woman in order to redeem her. See further on verse 43.

clothes: the custom of dressing an idol in clothes, also mentioned in verse 72, was an especial feature of the worship of
Tammuz, who was son and consort of the mother-goddess
Ishtar. A Babylonian hymn in his honour runs: 'Wash
Tammuz with pure water, anoint him with good oil,
clothe him with red sparkling raiment.' See further on
verse 31.

14. *sceptre*, *dagger* and *axe* are all symbols of authority and
power. Sculptures and seal-engravings represent Babylonian
gods as wielding sceptres, swords and axes, among other
weapons. Greek gods were represented on coins with sceptre,
spear, trident, etc., and the British coin-type of Britannia
on the old pennies, with her shield and trident, is a lineal
descendant of theirs.

20. *their hearts are eaten out*: the interpretation of the Greek
is uncertain, but the N.E.B. translation probably gives the
right impression, *viz.* that the wooden idols are like wooden
beams of the temple in being rotten, not to mention blackened
and (verse 55) liable to be burnt up.

22. *cats* are not mentioned elsewhere in the Old Testament.

24. The *gold* must have been of very poor quality, to be
liable to tarnish. *cast* in the next sentence refers to bronze
statues: the author has moved from one type of construction
to another, making derogatory remarks about each.

26. *they are carried on men's shoulders*: Isa. 46: 1–7 skilfully
contrasts the images of Babylonian gods, which have to be
carried by men, with the true God who 'will carry you and
bring you to safety'.

worthless: the Greek word for *worth* is the same as that for *cost* in verse 25.

29. *women* in these situations were regarded by Jews as unclean (Lev. 12: 2).

30. *women*: in Jewish religion only a man could be a priest and serve God.

31. *the priests sit shaven and shorn*, etc.: Jewish priests were not allowed to do any of these things, which were common signs of mourning.

32. *mourners at a funeral feast*: another reference to the god Tammuz, who was believed to die and rise again like the vegetation, and whose worship therefore included ritual mourning and a funeral feast. The prophet Ezekiel (8: 14), when in exile in Babylon, had a vision of various abominations being practised in the temple in Jerusalem, including 'women sitting and wailing for Tammuz'.

35. *makes a vow*: this was a practice common to all ancient religion: a man in dire trouble would vow that, if the god to whom he prayed did as he asked, he would repay the god in such and such a way; see, e.g., the terrible story of Jephthah's daughter in Judg. 11: 29–40. To *honour* a vow in these circumstances was an obligation of the highest importance, cp. Eccles. 5: 4: 'When you make a vow to God, do not be slow to pay it, for he has no use for fools.'

41. *Bel*, like the name Baal, is strictly a title meaning 'Lord'. It was given to two different Babylonian gods of whom the one intended here is probably Marduk, the protector god of Babylon itself.

43. *The women too sit in the street*, etc.: obviously the author is again referring to ritual prostitution; see note on verse 11. It so happens that we possess a description of this practice in Babylonia from the pen of the Greek historian, Herodotus, who wrote about 430 B.C. Relevant extracts from his description are as follows: 'There is one custom among these people that is wholly shameful. Every woman who is a native of the country must once in her life go and sit in the temple of

Aphrodite' (a Greek equivalent of the Babylonian goddess, Ishtar) 'and there give herself to a strange man...Most women sit in the precinct of the temple with a band of plaited string round their heads...Tall handsome women soon manage to get home again, but the ugly ones stay a long time before they can fulfil the condition which the custom demands.'

Herodotus says nothing about *burning bran*, but another Greek author, the poet Theocritus, writing about 270 B.C., has a poem in which a woman, wanting to win a lover by magic, says: 'Now I will burn the bran: you, Artemis' (another Greek equivalent for Ishtar), 'can move even the gates of hell.' The idea behind the burning is to stoke the fires of passion.

45. Perhaps the nearest modern analogy to an idol is a computer. Some people have an almost superstitious fear of computers: if computers can think, might they one day 'take over' from men? But, like idols, *They are things manufactured*: *they can* do *nothing but what* they are programmed to do.

48. So Amenophis, king of Egypt, urged his priests to hide the images of the gods safely when his country was invaded (Josephus, *Against Apion* 1: 244, quoting Manetho, a historian who wrote about 280 B.C.).

53. *they cannot give men rain*: in hot and dry countries fertility depends entirely on rain. The Jews often praised God for sending rain and mocked heathen gods for being unable to do the same, e.g. Jer. 14: 22: 'Can any of the false gods of the nations give rain?'

54. *crows*: the author seems to be thinking of flying crows unable to keep their course in a high wind.

59. *better a household vessel*, etc.: these homely touches are far more effective than the more dramatic scenes envisaged in most of this Letter. See verses 17 (the dust) and 22 (the cats) for similar touches.

60. *they obey*: cp. Baruch 3: 34. It is of course God whom they obey. The idols are neither gods nor even the instruments of gods.

61. *seen far and wide* and *in every land*: the author has inadvertently moved on to a new point, that heathen idols are localized, unlike natural phenomena such as lightning, wind and clouds, which are international instruments of God. He takes up the same point again, after an interval, in verse 67.

70–1. So Jeremiah 10: 5 says of heathen idols: 'They can no more speak *than a scarecrow in a plot of cucumbers.*' A scarecrow is a wooden pole, doubtless with a moving part. It is mocked when the birds, which it is meant to scare away, perch on it. The idea of birds perching leads to the image of birds of prey on a dead body. A similar thread of ideas can be seen in verses 24–5; see p. 199.

72. *purple and fine linen*: the Greek manuscripts give 'purple and marble', which is obviously wrong, because marble does not rot. But the Hebrew word for marble, *shēsh*, also means fine linen, which is obviously right. So the rich man in the parable of Dives and Lazarus 'dressed in purple and the finest linen' (Luke 16: 19).

73. This verse is rightly set apart by the N.E.B. translators. It does not follow logically from verse 72, though one can see the link idea (*contempt*) in the author's mind. But it harks back to verse 5 and serves to remind the reader of the object of the Letter as a whole. The writer is out to provide not a theoretical analysis of 'the folly of idolatry' but a practical warning against it. ✶

✶   ✶   ✶   ✶   ✶   ✶   ✶   ✶   ✶   ✶   ✶   ✶   ✶

THE APOCRYPHAL ADDITIONS
TO DANIEL

✳   ✳   ✳   ✳   ✳   ✳   ✳   ✳   ✳   ✳   ✳   ✳   ✳

WHAT THEY ARE

The 'Song of the Three', 'Daniel and Susanna' and 'Daniel, Bel, and the Snake' are linked together only because 'the Three' and 'Daniel' are characters belonging to the book of Daniel. They are preserved in two separate Greek versions, but are absent from the canonical book of Daniel, part of which is preserved in Hebrew and part in Aramaic. The 'Song of the Three' is a genuine addition, as it follows Dan. 3: 23 in the Greek translations of the book. 'Daniel and Susanna' is placed before Dan. 1 in the Greek and Old Latin translations of Daniel, but becomes chapter 13 of Daniel in the Vulgate (the Latin translation of the Bible made by Jerome at the request of Pope Damasus in about A.D. 382). 'Daniel, Bel, and the Snake' is linked in the Greek translations with the prophecy of Habakkuk, but is placed at the end of the canonical book of Daniel. Whereas the 'Song of the Three' has close links with the Psalms and some of the post-exilic literature of the Old Testament, the other writings savour more of the romantic and the legendary. 'Daniel and Susanna' introduces the contrast, commonly made, between virtue and iniquity, whilst 'Daniel, Bel, and the Snake' point to the astuteness of Daniel and the unswerving character of his devotion to God. The two both emphasize the wisdom which God bestows, whilst 'Daniel, Bel, and the Snake' also belongs to what we may call 'detective literature', inasmuch as Daniel is shown as demonstrating the means whereby the priests of Bel were able to deceive the people into believing in the statue's miraculous powers.

✳   ✳   ✳   ✳   ✳   ✳   ✳   ✳   ✳   ✳   ✳   ✳   ✳

THE SONG

OF THE THREE

✳ ✳ ✳ ✳ ✳ ✳ ✳ ✳ ✳ ✳ ✳ ✳ ✳

CONTENTS

The title given to this addition to Daniel is really derived from
only one section (verses 28–68), and the addition should be
more properly divided into four parts: (i) An introduction
(verses 1–2) which links the material with the narrative in Dan.
3: 23, where the three Hebrews, Shadrach, Meshach and
Abed-nego, are in the fire; (ii) a prayer, ascribed to Azariah
(called Abed-nego by the Babylonian captors in the story in
Dan. 1: 7), which is a confession of Israel's sin and a call for
deliverance (verses 3–22); (iii) a further narrative link which
tells of the further heating of the furnace, and of the descent
of the angel of the Lord into the flames (verses 23–7); (iv) the
Song of the Three (verses 28–68) which expands the thanksgiving theme of Psalm 148 and provides a commentary on
the story of Creation. The first portion (verses 29–34) is used
as a canticle called 'Benedictus es' after the opening words of
the Latin version, whilst the major section (verses 35–66 a) is
also used as a canticle which receives its name (the 'Bene-
dicite') from the constant appeal to '*bless* the Lord'.

ORIGIN OF THE MATERIAL

It is likely that the addition has been translated from a Semitic
original, and most would favour Hebrew rather than Aramaic
for the songs and prayer, as Hebrew was the sacred language
of prayer and praise. The prose sections could have been in
Aramaic to harmonize with the language of the rest of Dan. 3.

It is unlikely that the poems originally belonged to the context in which they are found. Just as the book of Jonah incorporates a psalm as its second chapter, which purports to have been delivered 'from the belly of the fish' (Jonah 2: 1), although the psalm is not wholly suited to the context, so the book of Daniel contains these two songs which do not easily fit the occasion and were probably not composed for this present context. They seem to have been selected for their sentiments of benediction and praise, as the deliverance of the Three from the flames was felt to evoke such feelings. As in the case of the psalm in Jonah, so here the songs *anticipate* the deliverance which has not yet been fully effected.

The prayer is ascribed to Azariah, and, because of the context, it is assumed that this is the Azariah named among the trio. In the Hebrew text of chapter 1 of the book of Daniel, Azariah is named third in the list, and the same is true in the Aramaic of the third chapter, where he appears under the name 'Abed-nego'. In 'The Song of the Three', however, he appears as the second of the trio. It is possible that the prayer of Azariah did not originally belong to the story of the Three in the fire, but relates to the sin of Israel in more general terms. One may parallel the prayer of Daniel, where he is described as having 'turned to the Lord God in earnest prayer and supplication with fasting and sackcloth and ashes' (Dan. 9: 3). There, too, the element of confession is pronounced.

Of the prose sections it has been suggested that verses 23–7 originally belonged to the story of the furnace and that they should follow Dan. 3: 23, providing an explanation why 'King Nebuchadnezzar was amazed and sprang to his feet in great trepidation' (Dan. 3: 24) – an explanation which is lacking in the Aramaic text of the canonical book of Daniel.

THE OBJECT OF THE ADDITIONS

If we are right in assuming that the additions in the Greek text were not originally part of the text of Daniel, their later insertion can be explained as the desire to show that the Babylonian king was not the first to acknowledge and bless the God of Israel (as he does in Dan. 3: 28–9). Azariah anticipates the submission of Nebuchadnezzar, confessing Israel's sin and supplicating God's mercy. The prayer also refers to God's 'marvellous deliverance' (verse 20) and so suggests that God's deliverance of the Three was in response to prayer. The addition of a song on the praises of creation was felt to be appropriate to the occasion and the traditional song was rendered contemporary by the addition of the stanza:

'Bless the Lord, Hananiah, Azariah, and Mishael'
and the reference to the deliverance 'from the furnace of burning flame...from the heart of the fire' (verse 66).

THE THEOLOGY OF THE SONG OF THE THREE

The verses illustrate features of later Jewish theology. There is an overwhelming emphasis on the uniqueness of God, seen not only in his power, but also in his mercy and righteousness. He is unique, but he is still the God of the covenant, ready to champion his people, Israel, against the attacks of her enemies. The misfortunes of Israel are seen as the result of sin: 'But now, Lord, we have been made the smallest of all nations; for our sins we are today the most abject in the world' (verse 14), but penitence is seen as an acceptable sacrifice – 'because we come with contrite heart and humbled spirit, accept us' (verse 16); it is the equivalent of 'burnt-offerings of rams and bullocks and...thousands of fat lambs' (verse 17).

God is to be praised for his justice, even though it has meant calamity for the Jews (verse 5). Despite the despair at lacking ruler, prophet and leader (verse 15) the prayer expresses confidence in God's mercy, which involves deliverance.

The main psalm (verses 35–66a) summons, first of all, the entire creation to bless God (verse 35), then the heavens and all that belongs to them (verses 36–51). God is next seen as the object of the earth's praise and devotion (verse 52), whether things inanimate (verses 53–6) or animate (verses 57–9). Man, as the crown of creation, joins the hymn of praise (verse 60), and then the covenant-people (verses 61–5). Finally the theme is particularized and the Three themselves acknowledge God (verse 66), for he is the focal point of the worship of all the faithful (verses 67–8).

✻ ✻ ✻ ✻ ✻ ✻ ✻ ✻ ✻ ✻ ✻ ✻ ✻

THE PRAYER OF AZARIAH

1 THEY WALKED in the heart of the fire, praising God
2 and blessing the Lord. Azariah stood still among the
3 flames and began to pray aloud: 'Blessed art thou, O Lord, the God of our fathers, thy name is worthy of praise
4 and glorious for ever: thou art just in all thy deeds and true in all thy works; straight are thy paths, and all thy judge-
5 ments just. Just sentence hast thou passed in all that thou hast brought upon us and upon Jerusalem the holy city of our fathers: yes, just sentence thou hast passed upon our
6 sins. For indeed we sinned and broke thy law in rebellion
7 against thee, in all we did we sinned; we did not heed thy commandments, we did not keep them, we did not
8 do what thou hadst commanded us for our good. In all the punishments thou hast sent upon us thy judgements
9 have been just. Thou hast handed us over to our bitterest enemies, rebels against thy law, and to a wicked king, the

vilest in the world. And so now we are speechless for shame: 10
contempt has fallen on thy servants and thy worshippers.
For thy honour's sake do not abandon us for ever; do not 11
annul thy covenant. Do not withdraw thy mercy from 12
us, for the sake of Abraham, thy beloved, for the sake of
Isaac, thy servant, and Israel, thy holy one. Thou 13
didst promise to multiply their descendants as the stars
in the sky and the sand on the sea-shore. But now, Lord, 14
we have been made the smallest of all nations; for our sins
we are today the most abject in the world. We have no 15
ruler, no prophet, no leader now; there is no burnt-
offering, no sacrifice, no oblation, no incense, no place to
make an offering before thee and find mercy. But because 16
we come with contrite heart and humbled spirit, accept us.
As though we came with burnt-offerings of rams and 17
bullocks and with thousands of fat lambs, so let our sacrifice
be made before thee this day. Accept our pledge of loyalty
to thee,*a* for no shame shall come to those who put their
trust in thee. Now we will follow thee with our whole 18
heart and fear thee. We seek thy presence; do not put us 19
to shame, but deal with us in thy forbearance and in the
greatness of thy mercy. Grant us again thy marvellous 20
deliverance, and win glory for thy name, O Lord. Let
all who do thy servants harm be humbled; may they 21
be put to shame and stripped of all their power, and
may their strength be crushed; let them know that thou 22
alone art the Lord God, and glorious over all the world.'

The servants of the king who threw them in kept on 23
feeding the furnace with naphtha, pitch, tow, and faggots,
and the flames poured out above it to a height of seventy- 24

[a] Accept our...thee: *possible meaning; Gk. obscure.*

25 five feet.[a] They spread out and burnt those Chaldaeans
26 who were caught near the furnace. But the angel of the
Lord came down into the furnace to join Azariah and his
27 companions; he scattered the flames out of the furnace and
made the heart of it as if a moist wind were whistling
through. The fire did not touch them at all and neither
hurt nor distressed them.

✻ 1. *praising God and blessing the Lord*: the parallelism suggests that the word 'Lord' stands for Yahweh (normally LORD
in N.E.B.).

4. *thou art just in all thy deeds and true in all thy works*: the
prayer reflects the sentiment of the prayer in Nehemiah: 'In
all that has befallen us thou hast been just, thou hast kept
faith' (Neh. 9: 33). Deuteronomy also declares that his 'work
is perfect, and all his ways are just', that he is 'a faithful god...
righteous and true' (Deut. 32: 4). The word *true* expresses
faithfulness on the part of God.

9. *rebels against thy law*: the Greek uses the word for an
'apostate', but the word *rebels* recalls the words of Joshua
and Caleb to an unbelieving Israel: 'you must not rebel against
the LORD' (Num. 14: 9). The suggestion is that renegade Jews
could be even worse enemies to the pious Jew than non-Jews.
This was particularly so in the second century B.C., when Greek
influence was strong and some 'removed their marks of
circumcision and repudiated the holy covenant' (1 Macc. 1: 15).

12. *Abraham, thy beloved...Isaac, thy servant...Israel, thy
holy one*: the patriarchs Abraham and Israel are not so described elsewhere. The three are called 'servants': 'Remember
thy servants, Abraham, Isaac and Jacob, and overlook the
stubbornness of this people, their wickedness and their sin'
(Deut. 9: 27); Israel, as a nation and not as the individual
patriarch, is often called 'holy'.

[a] *Gk.* forty-nine cubits.

14. *But now, Lord*: the Greek does not here use the word 'Kurios' but 'despotes' which means 'master'. The word expresses the authority which a master could wield over his slave, and is often used in the Apocrypha.

15. *We have no ruler, no prophet, no leader now...*: this sentiment does not suit the early part of Nebuchadnezzar's reign, when Jeremiah and Ezekiel were still alive. Some would say that the language of this verse need not be taken literally, but simply reflects the general feeling of dereliction. If the verse is taken literally, it could belong to a later period in the exile, but it no doubt reflects the time after Antiochus Epiphanes had desecrated the temple in 168 B.C. and before the Maccabees had risen as the leaders of revolt. The lack of a prophet would mean that there was no clear divine word available.

16. *we come with contrite heart*: compare Ps. 51:17; Isa. 57:15.

17. *our pledge of loyalty*: the N.E.B. indicates here that the meaning of the Greek is obscure, but the Greek seems to reflect a Hebrew original which provides perfectly good sense – 'that we may follow you wholeheartedly'. A similar construction is found in Numbers: 'he followed me with his whole heart' (Num. 14:24).

23. *The servants...who threw them in*: this contradicts the Aramaic of Dan. 3:22, where it is asserted that those who had thrown the three into the furnace perished then with the heat. ✷

The praises of creation

Then the three with one voice praised and glorified and 28 blessed God in the furnace:

'Blessed art thou, O Lord, the God of our fathers;   29
    worthy of praise, highly exalted for ever.

30 Blessed is thy holy and glorious name;
    highly to be praised, highly exalted for ever.

31 Blessed art thou in thy holy and glorious temple;
    most worthy to be hymned and glorified for ever.

32 Blessed art thou who dost behold the depths from thy
        seat upon the cherubim;
    worthy of praise, highly exalted for ever.

33 Blessed art thou on thy royal throne;
    most worthy to be hymned, highly exalted for
        ever.

34 Blessed art thou in the dome of heaven;
    worthy to be hymned and glorified for ever.

35 'Let the whole creation bless the Lord,
    sing his praise and exalt him for ever.

36 Bless the Lord, you heavens;
    sing his praise and exalt him for ever.

37 Bless the Lord, you angels of the Lord;
    sing his praise and exalt him for ever.

38 Bless the Lord, all you waters above the heavens;
    sing his praise and exalt him for ever.

39 Bless the Lord, all you his hosts;
    sing his praise and exalt him for ever.

40 Bless the Lord, sun and moon;
    sing his praise and exalt him for ever.

41 Bless the Lord, stars of heaven;
    sing his praise and exalt him for ever.

42 Bless the Lord, all rain and dew;
    sing his praise and exalt him for ever.

43 Bless the Lord, all winds that blow;
    sing his praise and exalt him for ever.

Bless the Lord, fire and heat; 44
  sing his praise and exalt him for ever.
Bless the Lord, scorching blast and bitter 45
    cold;
  sing his praise and exalt him for ever.
Bless the Lord, dews and falling snow; 46
  sing his praise and exalt him for ever.
Bless the Lord, nights and days; 47
  sing his praise and exalt him for ever.
Bless the Lord, light and darkness; 48
  sing his praise and exalt him for ever.
Bless the Lord, frost and cold; 49
  sing his praise and exalt him for ever.
Bless the Lord, rime and snow; 50
  sing his praise and exalt him for ever.
Bless the Lord, lightnings and clouds; 51
  sing his praise and exalt him for ever.

'O earth, bless the Lord; 52
  sing his praise and exalt him for ever.
Bless the Lord, mountains and hills; 53
  sing his praise and exalt him for ever.
Bless the Lord, all that grows in the ground; 54
  sing his praise and exalt him for ever.
Bless the Lord, seas and rivers; 56
  sing his praise and exalt him for ever.
Bless the Lord, you springs; 55
  sing his praise and exalt him for ever.
Bless the Lord, you whales and all that swim in 57
    the waters;
  sing his praise and exalt him for ever.

58   Bless the Lord, all birds of the air;
       sing his praise and exalt him for ever.

59   Bless the Lord, you cattle and wild beasts;
       sing his praise and exalt him for ever.

60   'All men on earth, bless the Lord;
       sing his praise and exalt him for ever.

61   Bless the Lord, O Israel;
       sing his praise and exalt him for ever.

62   Bless the Lord, you priests of the Lord;
       sing his praise and exalt him for ever.

63   Bless the Lord, you servants of the Lord;
       sing his praise and exalt him for ever.

64   Bless the Lord, all men of upright spirit;
       sing his praise and exalt him for ever.

65   Bless the Lord, you that are holy and humble in heart;
       sing his praise and exalt him for ever.

66   Bless the Lord, Hananiah, Azariah, and Mishael;
       sing his praise and exalt him for ever.
       For he has rescued us from the grave and from the power
         of death:
         he has saved us from the furnace of burning flame;
         he has rescued us from the heart of the fire.

67   Give thanks to the Lord, for he is good;
       for his mercy endures for ever.

68   All who worship the Lord, bless the God of gods;
       sing his praise and give him thanks,
       for his mercy endures for ever.'

✱ 31. *Blessed art thou in thy holy and glorious temple*: it is uncertain whether the reference is to the Jerusalem or the heavenly temple. In contrast with verse 15, which speaks of the cessation of sacrifice and oblation, verse 62 suggests that the priests are still involved in the temple ritual. The original reference in verse 31 would then be to the Jerusalem temple.

32. *thy seat upon the cherubim*: the original reference was to the ark in the Holy of Holies of the temple. The cherubim stood on either side of the ark of the covenant (see 2 Sam. 6: 2), but the reference here may be to God enthroned in glory, as in the Psalms:

> He rode on a cherub, he flew through the air;
> he swooped on the wings of the wind.
> He made darkness around him his hiding-place
> and dense vapour his canopy.
>
> (Ps. 18: 10–11)

Verse 34 speaks of God 'in the dome of heaven' and seems to support this latter interpretation.

35–68. In verse 35 the summons to praise is addressed to the whole creation and in verses 36–66 to separate parts of it. They are addressed in the order in which the author believes they were created, following Genesis in the main but as he and others in these later times interpreted and expanded it.

36. *Bless the Lord, you heavens*: the language recalls the praise of the LORD in Ps. 148: 1. Similarly verse 37 echoes Ps. 148: 2 and verse 38 echoes Ps. 148: 4. In Ps. 148, however, we lack the refrain. A similar refrain occurs in Ps. 136.

The mention of angels at this point reflects the notion (found for example in the book of Jubilees, written towards the end of the second century B.C., but not in Genesis) that angels were created along with heaven and earth on the first day.

39. *hosts* is expressed in Greek by the word 'powers' (*dunameis*). In Hebrew 'hosts' could indicate Israelite armies, the angelic hosts or the heavenly bodies. We often have the

title 'Yahweh of Hosts' in the Old Testament, and the 'hosts' may have any one of these meanings. Sometimes Yahweh is thought of as the leader of the Israelite forces; at other times he is the Creator, enthroned in the heavens and so the Lord of their hosts. The reference here is probably to the heavenly bodies, which are mentioned separately in the succeeding two verses. They probably correspond to the 'lights' of Gen. 1: 14 interpreted to include all the heavenly bodies, and not only sun and moon.

40f. *sun and moon* and *stars of heaven* (see Gen. 1: 16) are probably therefore an expansion of *hosts* in verse 39.

42–6. All the phenomena in these verses are regarded as belonging to the sphere of the heavens (verse 36) just as much as the heavenly bodies. The same is true of those in verses 49–51.

47f. *nights and days* along with *light and darkness* recall Gen. 1: 14–18. By the time this Song was written the alternating day and night, light and darkness, have become associated with the rising and setting of sun and moon. The sun is recognized as the main source of light, in contrast with the earlier notion that light has a separate origin. This earlier belief is reflected in Gen. 1: 3 and is perhaps due to man's experience of dawn bringing light before sunrise.

52–4 are addressed to the *earth* and the creatures which live on it. Thus the earth is brought in before the water and its creatures, in contrast to the order in Genesis (Gen. 1: 10, 24, earth; 1: 20ff. water and its creatures).

55–9. *seas and rivers...whales* and sea creatures, *birds, cattle,* and *wild beasts* follow the Genesis order (Gen. 1: 20, 21, 22b, 24), sea creatures leading to birds in a manner interestingly anticipating evolutionary theory. N.E.B. adopts the order of some manuscripts, 56, 55. If 55 should follow 54, the springs (no parallel in Genesis) belong to the earth rather than to the *seas and rivers*, an intelligible idea for people accustomed to isolated springs and wells. *whales* stands for sea-monsters and huge fish generally.

59. *cattle and wild beasts*: the Septuagint version has 'quadrupeds and beasts of the earth', following the text of Gen. 1: 24. Here the N.E.B. inverts the order of Theodotion's Greek version (for which see *Footnotes to the N.E.B. Text*, p. ix of this commentary) which has 'wild beasts and cattle'.

60. *All men on earth* are the climax of creation as in Gen. 1: 26.

63. *servants of the Lord*: in the context the *servants* would refer to the Levites and others who were subordinate to the priests in the temple cultus.

64. *all men of upright spirit*: the Greek has 'spirits and souls of righteous men' – 'spirit' expressing the divine element in men and 'soul' the 'principle of life'. The reference is to the living rather than to the departed, as some would suggest.

65. *you that are holy*: the *holy* are the *hasidim*, those loyal to their covenant obligations. In Ps. 119 they are described as those 'whose life is blameless' (Ps. 119: 1) and as those who 'hold a steady course' (Ps. 119: 5).

66–8. It is probable that these verses are a later addition, fitting the hymn to the context. The transition to the first person – *he has rescued us* (verse 66) – is unexpected.

66. *he has saved us from the furnace of burning flame*: the first book of the Maccabees refers to the fact that 'Hananiah, Azariah, and Mishael had faith, and they were saved from the blazing furnace' (1 Macc. 2: 59).

67. This verse echoes the words:

> It is good to give thanks to the LORD,
> for his love endures for ever.
>
> (Ps. 136: 1)

68. The word *mercy* (*eleos* in Greek) undoubtedly stands for the Hebrew *ḥesed*, God's covenant-love for his people. ✻

✻   ✻   ✻   ✻   ✻   ✻   ✻   ✻   ✻   ✻   ✻   ✻   ✻

DANIEL AND
SUSANNA

✻ ✻ ✻ ✻ ✻ ✻ ✻ ✻ ✻ ✻ ✻ ✻ ✻

THE CHARACTER OF THE BOOK

The N.E.B., in adding the sub-title 'Innocence vindicated', suggests that the book has a didactic purpose, and that its chief function is to contrast the virtuous young wife Susanna who 'trusted in the Lord' (verse 35) and refused 'to sin against the Lord' (verse 23) with the elders who have given 'unjust decisions' and condemned the 'innocent' (verse 53). Susanna is depicted as looking 'up to heaven through her tears' (verse 35), whilst the elders 'no longer prayed to God, but let their thoughts stray from him' (verse 9). The book also seems to contrast the *pious* youth with the aged *scoundrels*, and the Septuagint version of the story not only emphasizes the *youth* of Daniel, but also represents the *young* rather than Daniel himself as the heroes in the tale. Daniel (whose name signifies 'God is my judge') is almost an angelic figure, the representative (as his name suggests) of God's own justice. As the clever young judge, he is able to bring divine judgement to bear upon a seemingly desperate situation.

It is probable that we have, therefore, a folk-tale, in which references to Daniel and Babylon may well be later intrusions. Once Daniel was linked with the story as the one endowed with superhuman wisdom, it would have been natural to locate the story in Babylon (verse 1). To regard Daniel and Susanna as a folk-tale obviously involves a rejection of its historicity, but the story as such points to historical improbabilities: (i) Daniel is represented as a 'young man' (verse 45), and, if we follow the traditions in Dan. 1: 1, this would place the events of the story early in the days of the Jewish exile in Babylon. A Jew in exile at that time would hardly have been 'very rich' with a house which 'had a fine garden adjoining it' (verse 4), nor would the Jews have had the right to pass the death-penalty (verse 41). (ii) The reasons given for Susanna's condemnation are extremely flimsy, whilst the behaviour of Daniel, as described, is extremely odd. Before bringing any proof of the guilt of the elders, Daniel is shown as condemning them as culprits (verses 49, 52–3, 55–7). Some scholars are inclined to see the story as a Pharisaic tract directed against the Sadducee theory of justice in the reign of Alexander Jannaeus (103–76 B.C.). The usual interpretation of the law of 'an eye for an eye, a tooth for a tooth' was that false witnesses could only be punished if their crime was discovered *after* the penalty had been inflicted on an innocent victim. About 100 B.C. Simeon ben Shetach, one of the leading Pharisees of the day, not only advocated a stricter cross-examination of witnesses, saying, 'Examine the witnesses diligently and be cautious in thy words lest from thee they learn to swear falsely', but also sought to suppress perjury by insisting that one who had sworn falsely should, if detected, be punished with the same penalty he had *sought* to inflict on another, even though the penalty had not yet been inflicted. Simeon ben Shetach also served as adviser to Alexander Jannaeus who became high priest and took the title of 'king' at the age of twenty-three, and the suggestion is made that the emphasis on youth has reference to him. Whilst it is possible that the tale was used by the Pharisees in their anti-Sadducee polemic, it is unlikely that the tale was originally composed for this purpose.

THE LANGUAGE OF THE BOOK

Although the book is not included in the Hebrew canon of the Old Testament, and the ancient Syriac and later translations were made from the Greek, many would hold that it is based upon an Hebrew or Aramaic original. Jerome indicates that the original language of the book was a subject of controversy in his time. By then the Greek translation of the Old Testament was felt to belong to the Christian Church, whilst to be part of the Hebrew Canon was regarded as an indication of genuineness and antiquity. In the preface to his commentary on Daniel he writes: 'I heard a certain Jewish teacher, when working at the History of Susanna and saying that it was the fiction of some Greek or other, raise the same objection which Africanus brought against Origen – that these etymologies of *schisei* from *schinos* and *prisei* from *prinos* [see commentary on verses 54ff.] are to be traced to the Greek.' The suggestion was being made that the pun on words was valid in the Greek and not in Hebrew, and the fact that the punning was an integral part of the story pointed to a Greek origin for the story. It seems that Origen (the third-century Alexandrian scholar) accepted the position that the objection to a Hebrew original was valid, if no pun was possible in the Hebrew, but, although he could not himself trace any such Hebrew pun, he was convinced that there must have been a similar jingle of sounds in the Hebrew. As the Syriac translation of the story incorporates a pun, it has been suggested that Aramaic (a kindred dialect to the Syriac) rather than Hebrew may have been the original language.

THE THEOLOGY OF THE BOOK

There is little that is new in the religious standpoint of the story. It is accepted that 'the law of Moses' (verse 3) is the expression of the divine will, and that divine justice demands that the 'innocent and guiltless' (verse 53) should not be put to death. Death is preferable to transgressing the law (verse 23). The experience of Susanna shows that the troubled can turn to God in time of distress (verse 42), as God knows 'all secrets' and foresees 'all things' (verse 43). God is not only omniscient: he rescues those who put their trust in him (verse 44). Accordingly Daniel is represented as inspired by God (verse 45) to save Susanna and the sentence is 'from God' transmitted through an angel (verse 55). By contrast, injustice is seen as a form of practical atheism, as it involves the rejection of God's will. The neglect of prayer is accompanied by a forgetfulness of 'the claims of morality' (verse 9). Whereas God is seen to be near at hand to rescue the innocent, 'the saviour of those who trust in him' (verse 60), he is also seen as the avenger who brings inevitable punishment to bear upon the wicked (verses 55, 59, 62).

✻   ✻   ✻   ✻   ✻   ✻   ✻   ✻   ✻   ✻   ✻   ✻   ✻

Innocence vindicated

THERE ONCE LIVED in Babylon a man named Joakim. 1 He married Susanna daughter of Hilkiah, a very beau- 2 tiful and devout woman. Her parents, religious people, had 3 brought up their daughter according to the law of Moses. Joakim was very rich and his house had a fine garden 4 adjoining it, which was a regular meeting-place for the Jews, because he was the man of greatest distinction among them.

Now two elders of the community were appointed 5 that year as judges. It was of them that the Lord had said, 'Wickedness came forth from Babylon from elders who were judges and were supposed to govern my people.' These men were constantly at Joakim's house, and everyone 6 who had a case to be tried came to them there.

When the people went away at noon, Susanna used to 7 go and walk in her husband's garden. Every day the two 8 elders saw her entering the garden and taking her walk, and they were obsessed with lust for her. They no longer 9

prayed to God, but let their thoughts stray from him and
10 forgot the claims of morality. They were both infatuated
with her; but they did not tell each other what pangs they
11 suffered, because they were ashamed to confess that they
12 wanted to seduce her. Day after day they watched eagerly
to see her.

13   One day they said, 'Let us go home; it is time for lunch.'
14 So they went off in different directions, but soon retraced
their steps and found themselves face to face. When they
questioned one another, each confessed his passion. Then
they agreed on a time when they might find her alone.

15   And while they were watching for an opportune day,
she went into the garden as usual with only her two maids;
16 it was very hot, and she wished to bathe there. No one else
was in the garden except the two elders, who had hidden
17 and were spying on her. She said to her maids, 'Bring me
soap and olive oil, and shut the garden doors so that I can
18 bathe.' They did as she told them: they closed the garden
doors and went out by the side door to fetch the things
they had been ordered to bring; they did not see the
19 elders because they were hiding. As soon as the maids had
20 gone, the two elders started up and ran to Susanna. 'Look!'
they said, 'the garden doors are shut, and no one can see us.
We are burning with desire for you, so consent and yield
21 to us. If you refuse, we shall give evidence against you that
there was a young man with you and that was why you
22 sent your maids away.' Susanna groaned and said: 'I see
no way out. If I do this thing, the penalty is death; if I do
23 not, you will have me at your mercy. My choice is made:
I will not do it. It is better to be at your mercy than to sin
against the Lord.'

With that Susanna gave a loud shout, but the two elders 24
shouted her down. One of them ran and opened the garden 25
door. The household, hearing the uproar in the garden, 26
rushed in through the side door to see what had happened
to her. And when the elders had told their story, the 27
servants were deeply shocked, for no such allegation had
ever been made against Susanna.

Next day, when the people gathered at her husband 28
Joakim's house, the two elders came, full of their criminal
design to put Susanna to death. In the presence of the 29
people they said, 'Send for Susanna daughter of Hilkiah,
Joakim's wife.' So they sent for her, and she came with her 30
parents and children and all her relatives. Now Susanna was 31
a woman of great beauty and delicate feeling. She was 32
closely veiled, but those scoundrels ordered her to be
unveiled so that they might feast their eyes on her beauty.
Her family and all who saw her were in tears. Then the 33,34
two elders stood up before the people and put their hands
on her head. She looked up to heaven through her tears, 35
for she trusted in the Lord. The elders said: 'As we were 36
walking alone in the garden, this woman came in with
two maids. She shut the garden doors and dismissed her
maids. Then a young man, who had been in hiding, came 37
and lay down with her. We were in a corner of the garden, 38
and when we saw this wickedness we ran up to them.
Though we saw them in the act, we could not hold the 39
man; he was too strong for us, and he opened the door and
forced his way out. We seized the woman and asked who 40
the young man was, but she would not tell us. That is our
evidence.'

As they were elders of the people and judges, the 41

42 assembly believed them and condemned her to death. Then
Susanna cried out loudly: 'Eternal God, who dost know
43 all secrets and foresee all things, thou knowest that their
evidence against me was false. And now I am to die,
guiltless though I am of all the wicked things these men
have said against me.'

44, 45   The Lord heard her cry. Just as she was being led off to
execution, God inspired a devout young man named
46 Daniel to protest, and he shouted out, 'I will not have
47 this woman's blood on my head.' All the people turned
48 and asked him, 'What do you mean by that?' He came
forward and said: 'Are you such fools, you Israelites,
as to condemn a woman of Israel, without making careful
49 inquiry and finding out the truth? Re-open the trial; the
evidence these men have brought against her is false.'

50   So the people all hurried back, and the rest of the elders
said to him, 'Come, take your place among us and state
your case, for God has given you the standing of an
51 elder.' Daniel said to them, 'Separate these men and keep
them at a distance from each other, and I will examine
52 them.' When they had been separated Daniel summoned
one of them. 'You hardened sinner,' he said, 'the sins of
53 your past have now come home to you. You gave unjust
decisions, condemning the innocent, and acquitting the
guilty, although the Lord has said, "You shall not put to
54 death an innocent and guiltless man." Now then, if you
saw this woman, tell us, under what tree did you see them
55 together?' He answered, 'Under a clove-tree.'[a] Then
Daniel retorted, 'Very good: this lie has cost you your life,
for already God's angel has received your sentence from

[a] clove: *literally* mastic.

God, and he will cleave[a] you in two.' And he told him to 56
stand aside, and ordered them to bring in the other.

He said to him: 'Spawn of Canaan, no son of Judah,
beauty has been your undoing, and lust has corrupted
your heart! Now we know how you have been treating 57
the women of Israel, frightening them into consorting
with you; but here is a woman of Judah who would not
submit to your villainy. Now then, tell me, under what 58
tree did you surprise them together?' 'Under a yew-tree',[b]
he replied. Daniel said to him, 'Very good: this lie has cost 59
you your life, for the angel of God is waiting with his
sword to hew[c] you down and destroy you both.'

Then the whole assembly gave a great shout and praised 60
God, the saviour of those who trust in him. They turned 61
on the two elders, for out of their own mouths Daniel had
convicted them of giving false evidence; they dealt with 62
them according to the law of Moses, and put them to
death, as they in their wickedness had tried to do to their
neighbour. And so an innocent life was saved that day.
Then Hilkiah and his wife gave praise for their daughter 63
Susanna, because she was found innocent of a shameful
deed, and so did her husband Joakim and all her relatives.
And from that day forward Daniel was a great man among 64
his people.

* 4. *his house had a fine garden adjoining it*: at the time of the
first exile from Jerusalem, Jeremiah wrote: 'These are the
words of the LORD of Hosts the God of Israel: To all the exiles
whom I have carried off from Jerusalem to Babylon: Build

[a] clove...cleave: *there is a play on words in the Gk.*
[b] yew: *literally* oak.
[c] yew...hew: *there is a play on words in the Gk.*

houses and live in them; plant gardens, and eat their produce'
(Jer. 29: 4–5). Here Joakim is represented as fulfilling the
prophet's command.

5. *that year*: this may refer *either* to a context which has
now been lost *or* to the year in which the subsequent events
are regarded as having taken place. '*Wickedness came forth
from Babylon from elders who were judges and were supposed to
govern my people*': it is not possible to identify this quotation
with any Old Testament passage, although some would link
it with Jer. 23: 15 which refers to 'a godless spirit' that 'has
spread over all the land from the prophets of Jerusalem'.
Some would see a link with the allusion to Ahab and Zedekiah, two false prophets who 'committed adultery with other
men's wives, and without my authority prophesied in my
name' (Jer. 29: 21–3). According to Jewish legend these two
false prophets had tried to seduce a daughter or wife of King
Nebuchadnezzar, and some see in this tale a background to
Daniel and Susanna.

9. *They no longer prayed to God*: the Greek has *heaven* in
place of *God*. As we know from the usage in the gospel of
Matthew, where 'kingdom of heaven' is the equivalent of
'kingdom of God' in Mark and Luke, 'heaven' was used
reverentially instead of 'God' in later Judaism.

22. *If I do this thing, the penalty is death*: the death penalty
for adultery is found in Lev. 20: 10 ('If a man commits
adultery with his neighbour's wife, both adulterer and
adulteress shall be put to death') and Deut. 22: 22 ('When
a man is discovered lying with a married woman, they shall
both die, the woman as well as the man who lay with her').

24. *Susanna gave a loud shout*: Susanna is acting in accordance with the suggestions in Deut. 22: 23–7, where a girl who
is raped is acquitted because, 'though the girl cried for help,
there was no one to rescue her' (Deut. 22: 27). Here, however,
the presence of two assailants means that their mutually corro-
borating evidence can destroy her defence.

28. *the people gathered at her husband Joakim's house*: it seems

that the house was used as a synagogue (see verse 4) and so the appropriate place for a trial. *criminal design*: the Greek adjective *anomos* (lawless) expresses the thought that they had no concern for the Law.

32. *those scoundrels*: the Greek word expresses the idea of going contrary to the Law. They were 'law-breakers', whereas Susanna is one 'brought up...according to the law of Moses' (verse 3). At this point the two were not technically breaking the Law, for a woman caught in the act of adultery was supposed to be brought to trial (compare the story in John 7: 53 – 8: 11, printed at the end of the gospel in the N.E.B.). Their false witness, however, involved a contravening of the commandments of the Law.

34. *put their hands on her head*: this appears to have been the judicial custom for witnesses. Leviticus refers to the trial of a man for blasphemy and says 'Everyone who heard him shall put a hand on his head, and then all the community shall stone him to death' (Lev. 24: 14). Here the elders are the witnesses, and the verdict lies with the entire assembly (see verse 41).

45. *God inspired a devout young man*: the Septuagint version tones down the picture of God's *direct* action, and introduces 'an angel of the Lord' as the one who 'inspires'.

46. *blood on my head*: this language represents dissent from the general verdict. Compare the story of Pilate's hand-washing in Matt. 27: 24.

48. *a woman of Israel*: Israel here stands for the whole Jewish nation, whereas verse 57 contrasts 'women of Israel', members of the northern kingdom, with 'a woman of Judah', a member of the southern kingdom.

51. *I will examine them*: the Septuagint version adds the phrase 'according to what comes into my mind', suggesting that his interpretation of the situation is the result of prophetic inspiration. This would explain the vehemence of his attack on the two elders who are upbraided for false witness *before* the falsity is proved.

53. The quotation is from the Greek version of Exod. 23: 7.

54–5, 58–9. '*Under a clove-tree*'...'*he will cleave you in two*'...'*Under a yew-tree*'...'*God is waiting with his sword to hew you down*': the N.E.B. provides a double pun (*clove...cleave*; *yew...hew*), an equivalent for one which occurs in the Greek between the *names* of the trees and the *verbs* which denote the fate of the two elders. The mastic tree is *schinos* in Greek and '*will cleave*' is represented by *schisei*; similarly, the holm-oak is *prinos* and '*will hew*' is *prisei* in the Greek.

62. *they dealt with them according to the law of Moses*: the reference is to Deut. 19: 16–19 ('you shall treat him as he intended to treat his fellow'). As the penalty for adultery was death (Deut. 22: 22), it followed that the false evidence which was intended to bring about that penalty itself led to the death penalty.

63. *shameful deed*: the phrase is derived from Deut. 24: 1.

64. *And from that day forward Daniel was a great man among his people*: the conclusion of the story provides us with the reason for the association of the story of Susanna with the story of legends about Daniel. As in the canonical book of Daniel his wisdom, itself God-given, is the means of bringing praise to God and of establishing God's righteousness. ✻

✻   ✻   ✻   ✻   ✻   ✻   ✻   ✻   ✻   ✻   ✻   ✻

DANIEL, BEL,
AND THE SNAKE

* * * * * * * * * * * * *

THE CONTENTS OF THE STORIES

This addition to the canonical book of Daniel consists of two distinct tales, the first involving the Babylonian god Bel, in which Daniel is portrayed as the worshipper of God, whereas the king, Cyrus, is represented as a worshipper of Bel, and the second telling of an enormous snake which had aroused fear and superstitious awe. As in the stories of the Three and their refusal to worship Nebuchadnezzar's statue (Dan. 3) and of Daniel's refusal to refrain from worshipping God, although it meant being thrown into the lions' pit (Dan. 6), so here Daniel appears as the great non-conformist. In the first story a simple piece of detective work shows that Bel is not really alive, and that the food and drink offerings are consumed by the priests of Bel and not by the god himself, whilst, in the second, the snake, though alive, is not immune to Daniel's stratagem, but meets with destruction. The destruction of the image of Bel and the snake leads to the demand for Daniel's death, and the story ends with Daniel's deliverance from the lions' pit and the acknowledgement of God's glory on the part of the king.

THE ORIGIN AND PURPOSE OF THE STORIES

Both stories bear the mark of legend, but they are used to indicate the folly of worshipping *either* the creature of man's hands *or* what belongs to God's created order. The 'living God' is contrasted with both the statue and the snake. The close link with the stories in chapters 3 and 6 of Daniel suggests a dependence on the canonical book of Daniel, and it is likely that the attack is not simply upon the heathen worship of the gentile world, but also upon the apostasy of Jews, whether in Babylon and other areas of Asiatic Jewish Dispersion or in the cosmopolitan atmosphere of Alexandria. The question of the origin of the stories is also linked up with the question of language. If Greek was the original language of the stories, one would look to Alexandria for their source. If, however, as is likely, they were first circulated in Hebrew or Aramaic, the Dispersion in Babylon would be a more appropriate place of origin.

The destruction of Bel

1 WHEN KING ASTYAGES was gathered to his fathers he was succeeded on the throne by Cyrus the 2 Persian. Daniel was a confidant of the king, the most honoured of all the King's Friends.

3 Now the Babylonians had an idol called Bel, for which they provided every day twelve bushels of fine flour, 4 forty sheep, and fifty gallons of wine. The king held it to be divine and went daily to worship it, but Daniel worshipped his God. So the king said to him, 'Why do you 5 not worship Bel?' He replied, 'Because I do not believe in man-made idols, but in the living God who created 6 heaven and earth and is sovereign over all mankind.' The king said, 'Do you think that Bel is not a living god? Do you not see how much he eats and drinks each day?' 7 Daniel laughed and said, 'Do not be deceived, your majesty; this Bel of yours is only clay inside and bronze outside, and has never eaten anything.'

Then the king was angry, and summoned the priests 8
of Bel and said to them, 'If you cannot tell me who it is
that eats up all these provisions, you shall die; but if you 9
can show that it is Bel that eats them, then Daniel shall die
for blasphemy against Bel.' Daniel said to the king, 'Let
it be as you command.' (There were seventy priests of Bel, 10
not counting their wives and children.) Then the king
went with Daniel into the temple of Bel. The priests said, 11
'We are now going outside; set out the food yourself, your
majesty, and mix the wine; then shut the door and seal it
with your signet. When you come back in the morning, 12
if you do not find that Bel has eaten it all, let us be put to
death; but if Daniel's charges against us turn out to be
false, then he shall die.' They treated the whole affair with 13
contempt, because they had made a hidden entrance
under the table, and they regularly went in by it and ate
everything up.

So when the priests had gone, the king set out the food 14
for Bel; and Daniel ordered his servants to bring ashes and
sift them over the whole temple in the presence of the king
alone. Then they left the temple, closed the door, sealed
it with the king's signet, and went away. During the night 15
the priests, with their wives and children, came as usual
and ate and drank everything. Early in the morning the 16
king came, and Daniel with him. The king said, 'Are the 17
seals intact, Daniel?' He answered, 'They are intact, your
majesty.' As soon as he opened the door, the king looked 18
at the table and cried aloud, 'Great art thou, O Bel! In
thee there is no deceit at all.' But Daniel laughed and held 19
back the king from going in. 'Just look at the floor,' he
said, 'and judge whose footprints these are.' The king 20

said, 'I see the footprints of men, women, and children.'
21 In a rage he put the priests under arrest, with their wives
and children. Then they showed him the secret doors
through which they used to go in and consume what was
22 on the table. So the king put them to death, and handed
Bel over to Daniel, who destroyed the idol and its temple.

✳ 1. *Astyages* occurs for the only time here. He was the
king of Media, and the Babylonian document which we know
as the Nabonidus Chronicle speaks of a mutiny among the
Medes against his rule and their delivery of him to Cyrus the
Persian. This event took place in 549 B.C. about ten years before
Cyrus captured Babylon.

3. *Bel* is the Babylonian equivalent of the Old Testament
word Ba'al, meaning 'Lord', and was a title for the gods
rather than a name for a particular god. Marduk (sometimes
spelt Merodach) was the principal god of the Babylonians
and so was Bel (*Lord*) in chief. It is likely that Marduk is
meant here. *forty sheep*: the Septuagint version of the story
has 'four' in place of the forty, and is possibly the more likely.
The text, however, emphasizes the enormous amount of food
and drink supposedly consumed by the idol.

4. *The king held it to be divine*: the story fits what we know
of Cyrus. He was concerned to be accepted by the subject-
peoples of his empire, and so identified himself with the local
religion. Nabonidus, the last Babylonian king, is said to have
offended the priests of Babylon by neglecting the daily
sacrifices and the worship of Marduk. By contrast, Cyrus (in
the Cyrus Cylinder) speaks of Merodach (i.e. Marduk)
'raising him up as a deliverer'.

7. *Daniel laughed*: as in verse 19, the story pours ridicule
on heathen worship. The idols are regarded as nonentities.

8. The Greek historian Herodotus (Book I, chapter 181)
refers to his visit to the temple of Bel in Babylon, but his
reference is to the temple of Nebo, which lay on the opposite

bank of the river from the temple of Marduk. He also refers
to the 'table' of Bel, where food was offered to the god.
He parallels the offering of a honey-cake every full moon in
the temple of Athena at Athens.

22. *Daniel...destroyed the idol and its temple*: the alternative
version of the story refers only to the destruction of the idol.
This would fit the actual history better, as the temple of
Marduk survived till the time of Xerxes who was king of
Persia from 485 B.C. to 464 B.C. The story is here concerned
to demonstrate the complete folly of Bel worship. *

The destruction of the snake

Now there was a huge snake, which the Babylonians held 23
to be divine. The king said to Daniel, 'You cannot say 24
that this is not a living god; so worship him.' Daniel 25
answered, 'I will worship the Lord my God, for he is the
living God. But give me authority, your majesty, and 26
without sword or staff I will kill the snake.' 'I give it you',
said the king. So Daniel took pitch and fat and hair, 27
boiled them together, and made them into cakes, which
he put into the mouth of the snake. When the snake ate
them, it burst. Then Daniel said, 'See what things you
worship!' When the Babylonians heard of this they 28
gathered in an angry crowd to oppose the king. 'The king
has turned Jew!' they cried. 'He has pulled down Bel,
killed the snake, and put the priests to the sword.' So they 29
went to the king and said, 'Hand Daniel over to us, or else
we will kill you and your family.' The king, finding 30
himself hard pressed, was compelled to give Daniel up to
them. They threw him into the lion-pit, and he was there 31

32 for six days. There were seven lions in the pit, and every day two men and two sheep were fed to them; but now they were given nothing, to make sure that they would devour Daniel.

33 Now the prophet Habakkuk was in Judaea; he had made a stew and crumbled bread into the bowl, and he was on the way to his field, carrying it to the reapers,
34 when an angel of the Lord said, 'Habakkuk, carry the meal you have with you to Babylon, for Daniel, who is
35 in the lion-pit.' Habakkuk said, 'My lord, I have never been to Babylon. I do not know where the lion-pit is.'
36 Then the angel took the prophet by the crown of his head, and carrying him by his hair, he swept him to Babylon with the blast of his breath and put him down above the
37 pit. Habakkuk called out, 'Daniel, Daniel, take the meal
38 that God has sent you!' Daniel said, 'O God, thou dost indeed remember me; thou dost never forsake those who
39 love thee.' Then he got up and ate; and God's angel re-
40 turned Habakkuk at once to his home. On the seventh day the king went to mourn for Daniel, but when he
41 arrived at the pit and looked in, there sat Daniel! Then the king cried aloud, 'Great art thou, O Lord, the God of
42 Daniel, and there is no God but thou alone.' So the king drew Daniel up; and the men who had planned to destroy him he flung into the pit, and then and there they were eaten up before his eyes.

* 23. *Now there was a huge snake, which the Babylonians held to be divine*: we have no evidence that the Babylonians worshipped live snakes. Some accordingly try to rationalize the story by supposing that the 'snake' refers to the mythical Tiamat, the monster of the deep, which represented the primeval chaos overthrown by Marduk, so that the order of creation could replace the chaotic deep. It is preferable to take the story as it is – another example of faith in the true God contrasted with the worship of a no-god.

25. *he is the living God*: the language recalls that of Dan. 6: 26 –

> for he is the living God, the everlasting,
>   whose kingly power shall not be weakened;
>   whose sovereignty shall have no end.

The *living God* is contrasted with the 'things you worship' (verse 27).

31. *the lion-pit*: this part of the story seems to be an elaboration of the account in Dan. 6: 16ff.

33. *Now the prophet Habakkuk was in Judaea*: this incident (verses 33–9) has no close connexion with the main story and may be a later addition. Nowhere else is Daniel associated with Habakkuk. The reference, however, provides an example of the growth of legends about the prophets.

42. *the men who had planned to destroy him he flung into the pit*: the execution of Daniel's accusers recalls the story in Dan. 6: 24. The Latin Vulgate translation adds a royal decree at this point, based upon Dan. 6: 26–8, where the king is represented as testifying to the unique character of the God of Daniel. Whether this addition is genuine or not, the story as a whole contrasts the deliverance which God effects for those who worship him with the destruction which comes to them who trust in other gods and seek to destroy the worshippers of the true God.

In conclusion, we may say that these two tales have been written up by an author who wished to bring out the ridiculous nature of heathen worship as contrasted with the *oneness* and *absoluteness* of the God of the Jews. ✷

✷   ✷   ✷   ✷   ✷   ✷   ✷   ✷   ✷   ✷   ✷   ✷   ✷

THE PRAYER OF
MANASSEH

✳   ✳   ✳   ✳   ✳   ✳   ✳   ✳   ✳   ✳   ✳   ✳   ✳

THE PLACE OF THE PRAYER OF
MANASSEH IN THE BIBLE

The background of this prayer is given in 2 Chron. 33.
Manasseh became king of Judah in 696 B.C. His father Heze-
kiah had abolished idolatry but Manasseh restored it and
persecuted the prophets whom God sent to warn him. His
wickedness was finally brought to an end by an Assyrian
invasion. The narrative in 2 Chronicles describes the sequel
(33: 11 *b*–13): 'they captured Manasseh with spiked weapons,
and bound him with fetters, and brought him to Babylon.
In his distress he prayed to the LORD his God and sought to
placate him, and made his humble submission before the God
of his fathers. He prayed, and God accepted his petition and
heard his supplication. He brought him back to Jerusalem and
restored him to the throne; and thus Manasseh learnt that the
LORD was God.'

The Chronicler goes on to tell how Manasseh reigned many
years, during which he did his best to make up for his former
wickedness. The section ends with a reference to the sources
used (verses 18 and 19): 'The rest of the acts of Manasseh,
his prayer to his God, and the discourses of the seers who
spoke to him in the name of the LORD the God of Israel, are
recorded in the chronicles of the kings of Israel. His prayer
and the answer he received to it, and all his sin and unfaithful-
ness...before he submitted, are recorded in the chronicles of
the seers.'

For 500 years after the Chronicler wrote (probably in the

fourth century B.C.), the Jews went on debating the rights and wrongs of Manasseh. Rabbinic literature preserves details of his enormities, legends about his escape from Babylon, and a delightful, if fanciful, description of how the angels tried to prevent God from forgiving him, but were overruled. But none of these many Jewish sources quote any text of his prayer.

The text as we have it is first found in an early Christian work of the second or third centuries A.D. known as the *Didascalia* or *Lessons*. In the course of teaching about God's mercy to sinners the author cites among others the case of Manasseh. He quotes parts of 2 Chron. 33, but intersperses them with other material as follows: 'and he prayed to the Lord saying "O Lord Almighty...(then follows the Prayer itself)...for ever and ever. Amen." The Lord heard his voice and had mercy on him. A flame of fire surrounded him, melting his chains. The Lord saved Manasseh from his torture, and brought him back to his throne in Jerusalem.'

In spite of various echoes of Luke, the Prayer contains no Christian material, and there seems no doubt that it comes, like the legendary matter in the narrative, from Jewish sources. It is impossible to tell when it was written or even in what language. Its historical references are few and general, its theology does not betray any period or any 'school'. The Greek in which our text is written is stylish, but could have been translated from a Hebrew original.

Once discovered, however, the Prayer spread widely among the early Church, and was included in a collection of prayers and hymns preserved in the fifth-century manuscript Codex Alexandrinus.

The Prayer of Manasseh lacks the deepest insight of the repentant sinner, the idea that his sin has separated him from the presence of God, and that what he wants above all is to be restored to it again. But it does convey finely his contrition for his past sins and his faith in God's boundless mercy.

✳   ✳   ✳   ✳   ✳   ✳   ✳   ✳   ✳   ✳   ✳   ✳   ✳

Repentance

1 L ORD ALMIGHTY,
    God of our fathers,
       of Abraham, Isaac, and Jacob,
       and of their righteous offspring;

2 who hast made heaven and earth in their manifold
       array;

3 who hast confined the ocean by thy word of command,
    who hast shut up the abyss and sealed it with thy fearful
       and glorious name;

4 all things tremble and quake in the face of thy power.

5 For the majesty of thy glory is more than man can bear,
    and none can endure thy menacing wrath against sinners;

6 the mercy in thy promise is beyond measure: none can
       fathom it.

7 For thou art Lord Most High,
    compassionate, patient, and of great mercy,
    relenting when men suffer for their sins.
    For out of thy great goodness thou, O God,
    hast promised repentance and remission to those who sin
       against thee,
    and in thy boundless mercy thou hast appointed re-
       pentance for sinners as the way to salvation.[a]

8 So thou, Lord God of the righteous,
    didst not appoint repentance for Abraham, Isaac, and
       Jacob,
    who were righteous and did not sin against thee,

[a] *Some witnesses omit* For out of...salvation.

244

but for me, a sinner,

whose sins are more in number than the sands of the 9
    sea.

My transgressions abound, O Lord, my transgressions
    abound,

and I am not worthy to look up and gaze at the height of
    heaven

because of the number of my wrongdoings.

Bowed down with a heavy chain of iron,   10

I grieve over my sins and find no relief,

because I have provoked thy anger

and done what is evil in thine eyes,

setting up idols and so piling sin on sin.

Now I humble my heart, imploring thy great goodness.   11

I have sinned, O Lord, I have sinned,   12

and I acknowledge my transgressions.

I pray and beseech thee,   13

spare me, O Lord, spare me,

destroy me not with my transgressions on my head,

do not be angry with me for ever, nor store up evil for
    me.

Do not condemn me to the grave,

for thou, Lord, art the God of the penitent.

Thou wilt show thy goodness towards me,   14

for unworthy as I am thou wilt save me in thy great
    mercy;

and so I shall praise thee continually all the days of my 15
    life.

For all the host of heaven sings thy praise,

and thy glory is for ever and ever. Amen.

* The Prayer can be summarized as follows: 'O God, infinite in power (1–5) but also in mercy (6–8), my sins are innumerable and I am justly punished (9–10). I repent (11–12). Spare and save me now (13–14) and I will glorify you for ever (15).'

3. *who hast confined the ocean* etc.: cp. Job 38: 8, 10, 11:
Who watched over the birth of the sea...
when I established its bounds,
fixing its doors and bars in place,
and said, 'Thus far shall you come and no farther'?

the abyss means the deep waters which the Jews believed lay beneath the earth.

5–6. The N.E.B. translation rather obscures the power of the Greek, which derives from a series of weighty adjectives:
unbearable is the majesty of thy glory,
unendurable thy menacing wrath against sinners,
immeasurable and unfathomable the mercy in thy promise.

7. *relenting when men suffer for their sins*: if the translation is right, what is being said here is different from what is said in other places in the Old Testament, where God is said to *relent* before men actually suffer for their sins, e.g. Jonah 3: 10: 'God saw...how they abandoned their wicked ways, and he repented and did not bring upon them the disaster he had threatened.' The Greek word used in this verse of God's relenting is the same as is used of the sinners' repentance throughout the prayer. *For out of thy great goodness* etc.: this second half of the verse has good manuscript authority, and is needed to explain the meaning of the phrase 'thy promise' in verse 6. *repentance and remission*, literally 'remission arising from repentance'. Luke 3: 3 has the phrase the other way round, literally 'repentance leading to remission of sins'. *thou hast appointed repentance*: it is a common Jewish idea that repentance is granted or withheld by God: cp. Acts 11: 18: 'This means that God has granted life-giving repentance to the

Gentiles also.' *repentance...as the way to salvation*: this sounds at first like a Christian phrase, but in fact a parallel to it is found in a Jewish work of about 100 B.C., the *Testament of the Twelve Patriarchs*: 'true repentance, made according to God's will, leads to salvation' (Testament of Gad 5: 7).

8. *Lord God of the righteous* is a phrase not elsewhere found in the Bible, but it was already implied in verse 1 'God of our fathers...and of their righteous offspring'. The idea is that God is especially the God of the righteous Jews, sometimes known as the Remnant. *Abraham, Isaac, and Jacob, who were righteous*: in the Old Testament the patriarchs were definitely not treated as perfect: the tradition that they were is of later origin. The idea that the *righteous* do not need repentance is echoed in Luke's Gospel where Jesus says, 'I have not come to invite virtuous people, but to call sinners to repentance' (5: 32) and refers to 'righteous people who do not need to repent' (15: 7). *for me, a sinner*: cp. Luke 18: 13: 'O God, have mercy on me, sinner that I am' (Authorized Version, 'God be merciful to me a sinner').

9. *I am not worthy*: cp. Luke 15: 19: 'I am no longer fit (Authorized Version, 'I am no more worthy') to be called your son.'

10. *I grieve over my sins*: the exact meaning of the Greek is uncertain, but the general drift is sure.

11. *I humble my heart*: literally, 'I bow the knee of my heart.'

13. *spare me, O Lord, spare me* echoes verse 12 'I have sinned, O Lord, I have sinned'. *condemn me to the grave*: the translation of the Greek is again uncertain. *God of the penitent* is another title that does not occur elsewhere in the Bible. In the strictest logic, it is incompatible with the previous phrase 'God of the righteous'; and in so far as that is so, the emphasis in this prayer is definitely upon 'God of the penitent', just as it is upon the penitent brother, not the righteous one, in the parable of the Prodigal Son.

15. *all the host of heaven*: i.e. the angels; cp. Luke 2: 13 'a great company of the heavenly host'.

The cumulative evidence of the parallels with Luke's Gospel (and Acts) is quite striking. Luke made much use of Jewish psalms and prayers, and he was also particularly interested in the theme of repentance and forgiveness. But none of the rare adjectives found in verses 5 and 6 above is found in Luke's writings, so we need not suppose that he actually used this passage. ✷

✷   ✷   ✷   ✷   ✷   ✷   ✷   ✷   ✷   ✷   ✷   ✷

A NOTE ON FURTHER READING

There are two good general accounts of the period from which most of the apocryphal literature springs. They are both by D. S. Russell: *Between the Testaments* (SCM Press, 1960) and *The Jews from Alexander to Herod* (New Clarendon, OUP, 1967). For individual books treated in this volume, there is nothing between the various one-volume Bible Commentaries, which give a more cursory treatment, and full scholarly editions which go into much greater detail. For the formation of the text of the apocryphal books see also *The Making of the Old Testament* (ed. Enid B. Mellor) in this same series.

INDEX

INDEX